Fiesta
Seafood Cookbook
A TASTE OF PENSACOLA

Fiesta Seafood Cookbook
A TASTE OF PENSACOLA

Published by Energy Services of Pensacola

ISBN: 978-0-615-23218-8

Edited, Designed, and Produced by
CommunityClassics™
An imprint of
FRP.INC
a wholly owned subsidiary of Southwestern/Great American, Inc.
P. O. Box 305142
Nashville, Tennessee 37230
800-358-0560

Manufactured in the United States of America
First Printing: 2009
5,000 copies

Dedication

Fiesta Seafood Cookbook is dedicated to Pensacola, its 450 years of history, and to those who live it and celebrate it. Imagine the wonderment and delight of Don Tristan de Luna de Arellano as he sailed the Gulf of Mexico on August 14, 1559, and into the great natural port of what would become Pensacola Bay.

Throughout the four-and-a-half centuries since de Luna and his followers first laid eyes on Pensacola, the city has maintained its heritage in American history and earned its designation as the City of Five Flags: Spanish, French, British, Confederate South, and United States occupations.

Today Pensacola is known as the Cradle of Naval Aviation and is home to the Blue Angels, the U.S. Navy's precision flying team. Also home to the whitest beaches in the world, our emerald waters are host to boating and fishing enthusiasts, and our southern hospitality brings visitors back again and again. Mayor Emeritus Vince Whibbs coined this phrase when greeting visitors to Pensacola, "Welcome to the western gate to the Sunshine State, where thousands live the way millions wish they could."

Celebrate with us this unique community and its people. Join us in honoring and recognizing more than four centuries of a steady march into the future.

Pensacola—it is with pride we celebrate your lasting legacy, rich history, and unique culinary style!

Table of Contents

Preface
page 5

Acknowledgments
page 6

 Fish
page 7

 Clams, Oysters & Scallops
page 69

 Crab, Crawfish, Lobster & Shrimp
page 85

 Mixed Seafood
page 137

Index
page 186

Order information
page 192

Preface

ESP proudly presents *Fiesta Seafood Cookbook!*

Since 1995, the Fiesta Seafood Grille, sponsored by ESP (Energy Services of Pensacola, the city's natural gas provider), has been a highlight of the Pensacola Seafood Festival, an annual celebration of Northwest Florida's seafood industry and a showcase of local seafood offerings. Attracting thousands of visitors from throughout the Southeast, the Festival is held in historic Seville Square and organized by the Fiesta of Five Flags. Top area chefs use the ever-popular Seafood Grille series to prepare their special seafood dishes on an outdoor gas grill while sharing the flavorful results, cooking tips, and techniques with the public.

After hundreds of requests over the years, ESP has compiled these outstanding recipes, offering anyone from the cooking novice to the experienced gourmet an opportunity to re-create these tasteful sensations in their own kitchen and explore the variety of ways to prepare the plentiful seafood bounty found in our local waters.

Abundant, fresh seafood is a hallmark of Pensacola's culture and cuisine. From upscale restaurants to small neighborhood diners, seafood—fried, broiled, blackened, grilled, boiled, poached, sautéed—is a mainstay of local menus. This collection of recipes represents the best of the culinary arts—a unique combination of ingredients and chef creativity. The result is a true taste of Pensacola, something we hope you enjoy!

Carmela Campbell
Consumer Education Specialist
Energy Services of Pensacola

Acknowledgments

Energy Services of Pensacola extends a special thanks to the chefs and restaurants featured in this cookbook for sharing their culinary talents and special seafood dishes with us through the years; to EW Bullock Associates for creative services; and to the Florida Department of Agriculture and Consumer Services-Bureau of Seafood and Aquaculture, Tallahassee, Florida, for seafood tips, facts, and information.

All proceeds from the sale of this cookbook will go to Project EUAP. The Escambia Utility Assistance Program (EUAP) is designed to provide emergency assistance to the elderly, the disabled, and families in Escambia County, Florida, who are experiencing financial difficulty and unable to pay the cost of utility service. Funds are administered by local social service agencies.

The recipes featured in this cookbook were prepared using natural gas. Adjustments may need to be made when cooking on electric appliances. Recipes were prepared with fresh seafood, unless otherwise specified. The following submitted recipes have not been retested—feel free to change them to make them your own!

Fish

Saltwater • Freshwater • Cobia • Trigger • Red Snapper • Wahoo • Bass • Flounder • Speckled Trout • Grouper • Amberjack • Red Fish • Tuna • Scamp • Sheepshead • Mullet • Black Drum

In Pensacola-area waters the variety of "finny" food is almost beyond number.

Mahi Mahi • Bream • Mingo Snapper • Spanish and King Mackerel

Such bounty has given our cooks all they need to create an array of fish-based seafood dishes to rival the finest anywhere.

With our labyrinth of bays, bayous, creeks, rivers, sounds, and sea providing such bounty of glorious, fresh fish no matter the season, our cooks have found ways to prepare dishes which bring together all the best our region has to offer—for example, pairing various fish with fresh, homegrown vegetables or local stone-ground grits. Whether it's a more traditional dish, a blackened grouper fillet matched with a cream-rich sauce, or a local delicacy like deep-fried fresh mullet, the chefs of the Pensacola area put their very own stamp on a variety of dishes fit for every occasion.

These recipes were developed in local restaurants where chefs, attune to the richness of our waters, fill their menus daily with the freshest of the fresh catch. Some chefs buy directly off the boats or from local seafood purveyors such as Joe Patti's or Maria's. Whether informed by sophisticated culinary techniques or derived from recipes that chefs learned at their grandmothers' (and grandfathers') knees and passed from generation to generation, these recipes remain wedded to our waters.

It is local bounty never taken for granted, but always prized by locals and visitors alike.

Hoisin-Marinated Sesame Amberjack with Onion and Pineapple Salsa

Amberjack
1 (6-ounce) jar hoisin sauce
2 tablespoons teriyaki sauce
4 (4-ounce) amberjack fillets
2 tablespoons sesame seeds
Salt and pepper to taste

Onion and Pineapple Salsa
1 small Vidalia onion, chopped
1 cup fresh pineapple tidbits
1/4 cup packed brown sugar substitute
2 tablespoons cider vinegar
2 tablespoons fresh lime juice
1 tablespoon minced fresh ginger
2 teaspoons Creole mustard
1 teaspoon lime zest
1 garlic clove, minced
Paprika to taste

For the amberjack, mix the hoison sauce and teriyaki sauce in a shallow dish. Add the fillets and turn to coat. Marinate, covered, in the refrigerator for 12 hours, turning occasionally; drain. Coat the fillets with the sesame seeds and season with salt and pepper. Grill on a gas grill for 5 to 8 minutes per side or until the fillets flake easily.

For the salsa, combine the onion, pineapple, brown sugar substitute, vinegar, lime juice, ginger, Creole mustard, lime zest and garlic in a medium skillet and mix well. Bring to a boil over high gas heat. Reduce the heat and simmer for 10 minutes or until thickened, stirring occasionally. Stir in the paprika. Arrange each of the fillets on a serving plate and serve with the salsa and sautéed sugar snap peas.—Serves 4—**Scott Wilson, Radley's Deli After Dark, 1996**

 When shopping, purchase seafood last and keep it cold. Ask your grocer to pack your seafood on ice for the trip home. Take a cooler if necessary to keep seafood cold.

Tarragon-Crusted Striped Bass

Lime Pistachio Butter
1/4 cup pistachios
1 cup (2 sticks) unsalted butter, softened
Grated zest and juice of 1 lime
Kosher salt and pepper to taste

Striped Bass
1/4 cup fresh tarragon, finely sliced or chopped
4 cups panko (Japanese bread crumbs)
2 teaspoons kosher salt
1 teaspoon cracked pepper
4 (8-ounce) striped bass fillets
3 cups buttermilk
Canola oil for sautéing

For the butter, spread the pistachios in a single layer on a baking sheet. Roast at 350 degrees in a gas oven for 10 minutes, stirring occasionally. Remove to a plate to cool. Pulse the pistachios in a food processor until finely chopped.

Combine the pistachios, butter, lime zest, lime juice, salt and pepper in a bowl and mix well. Shape the butter mixture into a cylinder on a sheet of baking parchment and roll to enclose. Chill until firm.

For the bass, mix the tarragon, bread crumbs, salt and pepper in a shallow dish. Dip the fillets in the buttermilk and then coat with the bread crumb mixture. Sauté the fillets in canola oil in a sauté pan over medium gas heat for 3 minutes per side or until the coating is golden brown. Arrange the fillets on individual serving plates and top each with a thick slice of the butter.— Serves 4—**Irv Miller, Jackson's, 2003**

TIP Thin fillets and steaks will thaw within eight to twelve hours in the refrigerator. Cook immediately after thawing.

Grilled Blackened Catfish with Creamy Scallion Sauce

1 cup buttermilk salad dressing
1 bunch scallions, chopped
1 (8-ounce) catfish fillet
1 teaspoon blackening seasoning
1 tablespoon butter, melted

Combine the buttermilk and scallions in a bowl and mix well. Coat the fillet with the blackening seasoning and then brush with the melted butter. Grill on a gas grill until the fillet flakes easily. Arrange the fillet on a serving plate and drizzle with the desired amount of the sauce.—Serves 1—
Gustavus Myers IV, Country Club Café, 1996

Panéed Catfish

2 (5- to 7-ounce) catfish fillets
1 cup seasoned corn flour
1/2 cup (4 ounces) clarified butter
1 tablespoon finely chopped tasso
1/4 cup shrimp stock
2 tablespoons cream
1 teaspoon chopped garlic
1 teaspoon seafood seasoning
Salt and pepper to taste
Hot cooked yellow rice
1 teaspoon chopped parsley
1 teaspoon chopped green onion

Coat the fillets with the corn flour, shaking off any excess. Heat the clarified butter in a sauté pan and add the fillets. Sauté for 3 minutes per side or until crisp. Remove the fillets to a platter and cover to keep warm, discarding the pan drippings.

Add the tasso to the sauté pan and deglaze the pan with the stock. Stir in the cream, garlic, seafood seasoning, salt and pepper. Reduce the heat and cook until the sauce coats the back of a spoon, stirring frequently. Arrange the fillets over hot cooked rice on serving plates and drizzle with the tasso sauce. Sprinkle with the parsley and green onion.—Serves 2—
Rodger Brown, Bayside Grill, 1998

Chargrilled Grouper Plaki

1 (8-ounce) grouper fillet
Salt and pepper to taste
Olive oil for coating
6 tablespoons extra-virgin olive oil
2 teaspoons chopped parsley

1 teaspoon minced garlic
2 tablespoons lemon juice
3 slices yellow onion
3 slices tomato

Season the fillet with salt and pepper and drizzle with olive oil to coat. Grill on a gas grill for 5 to 6 minutes per side or until the fillet flakes easily. Remove to a serving plate and cover to keep warm. Whisk 6 tablespoons olive oil, the parsley and garlic in a bowl. Add the lemon juice gradually, whisking constantly until combined.

Season the onion slices and tomato slices with salt and pepper and drizzle with some of the olive oil mixture. Grill the onion slices on a gas grill for 2 to 3 minutes and the tomato slices for 1 to 2 minutes. Drizzle 1 tablespoon of the remaining olive oil mixture over the fillet. Top with the tomato slices and onion slices and then drizzle with 1 tablespoon of the remaining olive oil mixture. Garnish with sprigs of parsley.—Serves 1—**Gus Silivos, Skopelos on the Bay, 1999**

Chargrilled Grouper with Red Onion Confit

12 ounces red onions, minced
4 garlic cloves, chopped
2 shallots, minced
2 tablespoons olive oil
1/2 cup vinegar
1/4 cup honey
Zest and juice of 4 oranges
Zest and juice of 2 limes

2 ounces red bell pepper, minced
1 (3-ounce) tomato, peeled, seeded
    and chopped
2 ounces currants, chopped
2 ounces raisins, chopped
4 grouper fillets
Melted butter
Salt and pepper to taste

Sauté the onions, garlic and shallots in the olive oil in a skillet. Stir in the vinegar and honey and simmer until the mixture is reduced and golden brown in color. Add the orange zest, orange juice, lime zest and lime juice and cook until reduced by half. Add the bell pepper, tomato, currants and raisins and mix well. Cook until the mixture is reduced to a syrupy consistency. Remove from the heat and cover to keep warm.

Coat the fillets with melted butter and season with salt and pepper. Grill on a gas grill for 7 to 10 minutes or until the fillets flake easily. Serve the fillets with the confit.—Serves 4—**Gus Silivos, Skopelos on the Bay, 1996**

Chargrilled Grouper with Wild Mushroom Ragout

1 (8-ounce) grouper fillet
Olive oil for coating
Salt and pepper to taste
1/4 cup olive oil
1/4 small yellow onion, sliced
4 strips red bell pepper
4 strips green bell pepper

1 cup shredded green cabbage
1/4 portobello mushroom, stemmed
    and sliced
4 to 6 shiitake mushrooms, stemmed
    and sliced
1/4 cup veal stock or beef broth
1 teaspoon parsley, chopped

Coat the fillet with olive oil and season with salt and pepper. Grill on a gas grill for 4 to 5 minutes per side or until the fillet flakes easily and is firm to the touch. Heat a sauté pan over medium gas heat and pour in 1/4 cup olive oil. Sauté the onion and bell peppers in the hot oil for 3 to 4 minutes. Stir in the cabbage and portobello mushroom. Cook for 3 to 4 minutes; add the shiitake mushrooms. Cook for 2 minutes longer. Stir in the stock and cook until the mixture is reduced to a sauce consistency. Season with salt and pepper. Spoon the ragout onto a serving plate and arrange the fillet over the top. Sprinkle with the parsley.—Serves 1—**Gus Silivos, Skopelos on the Bay, 1998**

Grilled Grouper with Bok Choy and Asian Barbecue Sauce

1 tablespoon olive oil
2 garlic cloves, minced
1 1/2 teaspoons minced seeded
    serrano chile
1/3 cup soy sauce
1/4 cup packed dark brown sugar
3 tablespoons unseasoned rice vinegar
3 tablespoons water
1 tablespoon Asian sesame oil

4 (7-ounce) grouper fillets
4 Japanese eggplant, cut lengthwise
    into halves
8 ribs baby bok choy, cut lengthwise
    into halves
3 tablespoons olive oil
Salt and pepper to taste
2 green onions, thinly sliced

Heat 1 tablespoon olive oil in a sauté pan over low gas heat. Add the garlic and serrano chile and cook until fragrant. Stir in the soy sauce, brown sugar, vinegar and water. Bring to a boil and boil until the brown sugar dissolves. Reduce the heat and simmer until reduced to 3/4 cup. Remove from the heat and stir in the sesame oil. Reserve 1/4 cup of the sauce. Brush the fillets, eggplant and bok choy with 3 tablespoons olive oil and season with salt and pepper. Grill the fillets, eggplant and bok choy on a gas grill for 7 to 10 minutes or until the fillets flake easily and the vegetables are the desired degree of crispness, basting with the remaining sauce occasionally. Arrange the fillets and vegetables equally on each of four serving plates and sprinkle with the green onions. Serve with the reserved 1/4 cup sauce.—Serves 4—**Gus Silivos, Skopelos on the Bay, 2006**

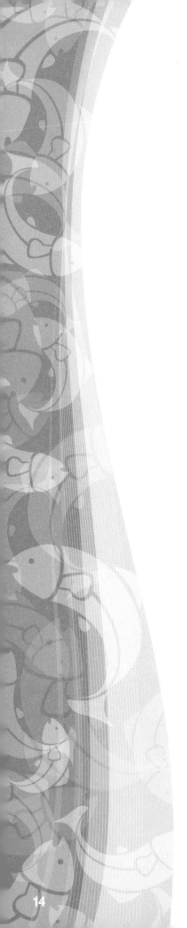

Rosemary Grilled Grouper with Grapes and Blue Cheese

2 tablespoons olive oil
Juice of 1/4 lemon
1 teaspoon chopped fresh rosemary
1 (8-ounce) grouper fillet
Salt and pepper to taste

2 tablespoons olive oil
1/4 teaspoon chopped garlic
8 to 10 seedless red grapes
1 teaspoon honey
2 ounces crumbled blue cheese

Mix 2 tablespoons olive oil, the lemon juice and rosemary in a shallow dish. Add the fillet and turn to coat. Marinate, covered, in the refrigerator for 2 to 4 hours, turning occasionally; drain, discarding the marinade. Season the fillet with salt and pepper. Grill on a gas grill until the fillet flakes easily and is firm to the touch.

Heat 2 tablespoons olive oil in a sauté pan and stir in the garlic and then the grapes. Cook until the grapes blister; mix in the honey. Arrange the fillet on a plate and top with the grape mixture. Sprinkle with the cheese and garnish with sprigs of rosemary.—Serves 1—**Gus Silivos, Gus's Shuck Shack, 2003**

Grilled Grouper Greek Style

2 (8-ounce) grouper fillets
1/4 cup extra-virgin olive oil
Juice of 1/2 lemon
1 teaspoon chopped capers
1/2 teaspoon oregano
Salt and pepper to taste
1/4 cup olive oil

1/2 cup finely chopped onion
1 pint cherry tomatoes
Pinch of oregano
1 tablespoon chopped capers
1 tablespoon chopped Greek olives
1 teaspoon minced garlic
1/4 cup crumbled feta cheese

Arrange the fillets in a single layer in a shallow dish. Mix 1/4 cup olive oil, the lemon juice, 1 teaspoon capers, 1/2 teaspoon oregano, salt and pepper in a bowl and pour over the fillets, turning to coat. Marinate, covered, in the refrigerator for 30 minutes to 2 hours, turning occasionally. Grill the fillets on a gas grill for 5 to 8 minutes per side or until the fillets flake easily and are firm to the touch. The time will vary depending on the thickness of the fillets.

Heat 1/4 cup olive oil in a sauté pan over medium gas heat. Add the onion and cook until light brown. Stir in the tomatoes and pinch of oregano and sauté for 3 to 4 minutes. Stir in 1 tablespoon capers, the olives and garlic. Season with salt and pepper. Remove to a heated bowl and stir in the cheese. Serve warm with the fillets.—Serves 2—**Gus Silivos, Skopelos on the Bay, 2008**

Grilled Marinated Grouper

8 ounces fresh peaches, chopped
3 shallots, julienned
2 semi-green tomatoes, chopped
1/4 cup red wine vinegar
1/4 cup sugar
1 tablespoon chopped parsley
1 teaspoon chopped cilantro

Salt and pepper to taste
Ground ginger to taste
3 pounds grouper fillets
1 cup sweet white wine
2 tablespoons rice vinegar
1 tablespoon ginger purée
1 teaspoon kosher salt

Mix the peaches, shallots and tomatoes in a bowl. Whisk the wine vinegar, sugar, parsley and cilantro in a bowl until the sugar dissolves. Season with salt, pepper and ground ginger to taste. Add to the peach mixture and toss to coat. Let stand for 1 hour before serving. May be prepared up to 2 days in advance.

Arrange the fillets in a large shallow dish. Mix the wine, rice vinegar, ginger purée and 1 teaspoon kosher salt in a bowl and pour over the fillets, turning to coat. Marinate in the refrigerator for 20 minutes, turning occasionally; drain. Grill on a gas grill until the fillets flake easily and are firm to the touch. Serve the fillets with the peach salsa.—Serves 6—**Alphonse Lucier IV, Eat!, 2007**

Garden Street Grouper

1/4 cup olive oil
2 tablespoons balsamic vinegar
1 teaspoon chopped garlic
Salt and pepper to taste
1 (6-ounce) grouper fillet
Olive oil for coating
1 (1/4-inch-thick) slice eggplant

1 (1/4-inch-thick) slice zucchini
1 (1/4-inch-thick) slice red bell pepper
1 (1/4-inch-thick) slice
  portobello mushroom
1 (1/4-inch-thick) slice tomato
Fresh spinach
1 teaspoon lemon juice

Whisk 1/4 cup olive oil and the vinegar in a bowl until blended. Stir in the garlic, salt and pepper. Coat the fillet with olive oil and season with salt and pepper. Coat the eggplant, zucchini, bell pepper, mushroom and tomato with olive oil. Grill the fillet and vegetable slices on a gas grill until the fillet flakes easily and the vegetables are the desired degree of crispness.

Sauté the spinach in olive oil in a skillet until wilted. Arrange the spinach in the center of a serving plate and encircle the spinach with the grilled vegetables. Top with the fillet and drizzle with the balsamic dressing and lemon juice.—Serves 1—**Jim O'Brien, O'Brien's Bistro, 2002**

Grouper Pecan

Rub Seasoning
2 teaspoons blackening seasoning
2 teaspoons black pepper
1 teaspoon cayenne pepper
1 teaspoon lemon pepper
1 teaspoon garlic powder
1/2 teaspoon red pepper flakes
1/2 teaspoon ground allspice
Pinch of ground cloves

Grouper
4 (6-ounce) grouper fillets
Olive oil

Caramel Sauce and Assembly
1/2 cup sugar
2 teaspoons corn syrup
2 tablespoons butter
1/4 cup half-and-half
1/2 cup pecans, toasted
Hot cooked saffron rice

For the rub, mix the blackening seasoning, black pepper, cayenne pepper, lemon pepper, garlic powder, red pepper flakes, allspice and cloves in a bowl.

For the grouper, coat the fillets with olive oil and then with the rub. Cook in a cast-iron skillet on a gas grill for about 15 minutes or until the fillets flake easily.

For the sauce, add the sugar and corn syrup to a heated skillet. Cook for 5 minutes or until the mixture begins to brown, stirring constantly. Be careful not to burn the caramel mixture. Whisk in the butter and half-and-half. Stir in the pecans. Arrange each fillet on a bed of hot cooked saffron rice on a serving plate. Drizzle equally with the sauce and garnish with red and yellow bell pepper strips. Serve with grilled asparagus.—Serves 4—**Tim Peck and Chris Gerlits, The Oar House, 2007**

Bamboo-Wrapped Grouper

1/2 cup mirin
1 tablespoon ginger powder
1 tablespoon soy sauce
1/2 teaspoon sesame oil
2 (6-ounce) grouper fillets
1/2 Vidalia onion, cut into 1/4-inch slices
4 bamboo leaves

1/2 cup julienned napa cabbage
1/4 cup julienned red cabbage
1 red bell pepper, thinly sliced
6 slices fresh ginger, bruised
Julienned fresh cilantro to taste
Julienned fresh basil to taste

Mix the wine, ginger powder, soy sauce and sesame oil in a bowl. Brush the fillets and onion slices with the wine mixture. Grill on a gas grill for 2 minutes per side and remove to a platter.

Overlap two bamboo leaves on a hard surface to form an "X". Arrange half the napa cabbage, half the red cabbage, half the bell pepper and half the ginger in the center of the "X". Top with one fillet, half the onion slices, cilantro and basil. Wrap the bamboo leaves to enclose and secure with wooden picks. Repeat the process with the remaining two bamboo leaves and remaining ingredients. Place the bamboo-wrapped fillets in a grill-top steamer on a gas grill and steam for 5 minutes.—Serves 2—**Jim Shirley, Fish House, 2002**

Roasted Grouper Cilantro

1/4 cup olive oil
Juice of 1 lime
1 tablespoon chopped cilantro leaves
2 (7- to 8-ounce) grouper fillets
Olive oil for coating
1 tablespoon chili powder

1 tablespoon paprika
1 teaspoon black pepper
1 teaspoon kosher salt
1 teaspoon cayenne pepper
1/2 teaspoon garlic powder

Pour 1/4 cup olive oil into a bowl. Add the lime juice gradually, whisking constantly until blended. Stir in the cilantro.

Coat the fillets with olive oil. Combine the chili powder, paprika, black pepper, salt, cayenne pepper and garlic powder in a bowl and mix well. Sprinkle on the fillets. Grill on a gas grill for 4 to 5 minutes per side or until firm to the touch. The time will vary according to the thickness of the fillets. Remove the fillets to individual serving plates and drizzle with the cilantro mixture.—Serves 2—**Gus Silivos, Skopelos on the Bay, 2000**

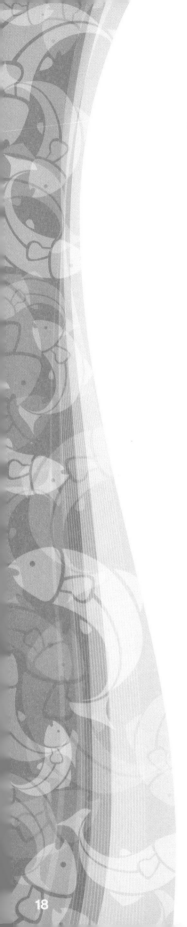

Grouper with Pesto Sauce over Angel Hair Pasta

3 1/2 cups basil leaves
1 cup pecans
Juice of 1 large lemon
1/2 cup (2 ounces) grated
   Parmesan cheese
10 to 12 garlic cloves

2 cups olive oil
2 (8-ounce) grouper fillets
6 tablespoons garlic butter, melted
1/4 cup heavy cream
8 ounces angel hair pasta, cooked
   and drained

Process the basil, pecans, lemon juice and cheese in a food processor until combined. Add the garlic and olive oil gradually, processing constantly until well blended.

Grill the fillets on a gas grill until the fillets flake easily, constantly brushing with the garlic butter. Remove the fillets to a platter and cover to keep warm. Heat the pesto quickly in a saucepan and stir in the cream. Simmer until heated through. Toss half the pesto sauce with the pasta in a bowl. Arrange equal portions of the pasta on two serving plates and top each serving with one fillet. Drizzle with the remaining pesto sauce.—Serves 2—**Ann Nina Prizzi, Annie's On The Lake, 1996**

Grouper Bayou with Sweet Hot Pecan Sauce

Sweet Hot Pecan Sauce
1/2 cup packed brown sugar
1/2 cup pecans, chopped
1/4 cup (1/2 stick) butter, melted
1/4 cup chopped red onion
2 tablespoons Worcestershire sauce
Juice of 1 lemon
1 tablespoon hot red pepper sauce
1 teaspoon crushed garlic
Salt and pepper to taste

Grouper
1 egg
1/4 cup water
1 (6- to 8-ounce) grouper fillet
Salt and pepper to taste
1/4 cup all-purpose flour
1/4 cup (1/2 stick) butter, melted

For the sauce, combine the brown sugar, pecans, butter, onion, Worcestershire sauce, lemon zest, lemon juice, hot sauce, garlic, salt and pepper in a skillet and mix well. Bring to a boil over medium gas heat, stirring occasionally. Remove from the heat and cover to keep warm.

For the grouper, whisk the egg and water in a bowl until blended. Season the fillet with salt and pepper and dust lightly with the flour. Dip the fillet in the egg mixture and dust again with the remaining flour. Pan-fry the fillet in the butter in a skillet until the fillet flakes easily. Arrange the fillet on a serving plate and drizzle with the sauce.—Serves 1—**Gustavus Myers IV, Country Club Café, 1996**

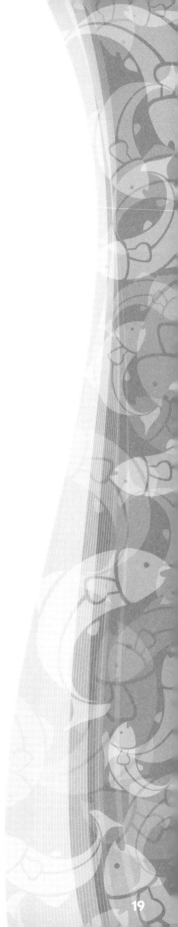

Jerry's Blackened Grouper

1/2 cup (1 stick) unsalted butter, melted
4 (8- to 10-ounce) grouper fillets,
  1/2 inch thick

6 ounces Jerry's Own
  ZydeCajun seasoning*

Heat a large cast-iron skillet over high gas heat for 10 minutes or until the skillet is red hot in the center. Pour the butter into a shallow dish. Coat both sides of the fillets with the butter and sprinkle both sides generously with the ZydeCajun seasoning.

Arrange the fillets in the hot skillet and cook for 2 minutes or until charred. Turn the fillets and cook for 2 minutes longer. The cooking times will vary depending on the temperature of the skillet.—Serves 4—**Jerry Mistretta, Jerry's Cajun Cafe, 2004**

*Available at www.jerryscajun.com

Greek-Style Grouper

4 (6-ounce) grouper fillets, skinned
1/2 cup seasoned self-rising flour
Olive oil for coating
2 tablespoons olive oil
1/2 cup julienned red bell pepper
1/2 cup julienned yellow bell pepper
1/2 cup julienned green bell pepper
1/2 cup julienned red onion

1/2 cup Greek olives
1/4 cup sherry
2 tablespoons chopped garlic
1 teaspoon fresh rosemary
1 teaspoon fresh oregano
1 teaspoon fresh basil chiffonade
1 teaspoon fresh thyme
4 ounces feta cheese, crumbled

Coat the fillets with the seasoned flour. Heat a skillet over medium gas heat and lightly coat with olive oil. Arrange the fillets in the hot skillet when the olive oil begins to smoke; cook the fillets until golden brown on both sides. Remove to a platter and cover to keep warm.

Heat 2 tablespoons olive oil in the same skillet and add the bell peppers, onion and olives. Sauté until the bell peppers are tender; stir in the wine, garlic, rosemary, oregano, basil and thyme. Sauté for 4 minutes longer. Arrange one fillet on each of four serving plates and top each serving with equal portions of the bell pepper mixture. Sprinkle equally with the feta cheese and serve with rice pilaf or roasted new potatoes.—Serves 4—**Chris Trovas, Chris' Seafood Grille, 1998**

Pan-Sautéed Grouper with Tasso, Parsnip and Roasted Corn Hash

4 (8-ounce) grouper fillets
Seasoned all-purpose flour
Canola oil
Unsalted butter
3 tablespoons bacon drippings or butter
1 cup finely chopped parsnip
1/2 cup fresh corn kernels

1/4 cup finely chopped red onion
3 tablespoons finely chopped tasso or
spiced ham
2 tablespoons water
Pinch of salt
1 teaspoon chopped fresh chives
or scallions

Coat the fillets lightly with flour. Sauté in a mixture of canola oil and butter in a skillet for 3 minutes per side or until golden brown. Remove to a platter and cover to keep warm.

Heat a sauté pan over medium gas heat; combine the bacon drippings, parsnip, corn and onion in the sauté pan. Increase the gas heat to high and cook for 3 to 4 minutes or until the vegetables caramelize or until the parsnip is tender, stirring frequently. Stir in the tasso. Add the water as the hash becomes dry. The hash will become spicy from the tasso spice coating. Season with the salt. Arrange the fillets on individual serving plates and top with the hash. Sprinkle with the chives. Serve with buttered spinach and lemon butter sauce—Serves 4—**Irv Miller, Jackson's, 1999**

Herb-Seared Grouper with Roasted Pepper and Tomato Compote

3 (8-ounce) grouper fillets
1/4 cup canola oil
1/4 cup each fresh basil, parsley, thyme
and cilantro, minced
2 tablespoons kosher salt
2 teaspoons white pepper

2 tablespoons butter
1 cup chopped seeded tomato
1/2 cup roasted red peppers, chopped
1 tablespoon chopped garlic
Salt and black pepper to taste

Coat the fillets with some of the canola oil. Mix the basil, parsley, thyme, cilantro, kosher salt and white pepper in a bowl. Press the basil mixture on both sides of the fillets. Heat a cast-iron skillet over medium-high gas heat and pour in the remaining canola oil. Cook the fillets in the hot oil until cooked halfway through and turn gently. Cook until the fillets flake easily. Remove to a platter and cover to keep warm.

Melt the butter in a heated skillet and stir in the tomato, roasted peppers, garlic, salt and black pepper. Simmer for 2 minutes. Spoon some of the warm compote on each fillet.—Serves 3—
Michael Johnson, Seville Quarter, 2003

Grouper Pinot Noir

2 cups fish fumet (flavored stock)
2 bay leaves
10 peppercorns
2 tablespoons chopped shallots
1/4 cup pinot noir
1 teaspoon cornstarch
1 tablespoon pinot noir
4 (6-ounce) grouper fillets
Salt and pepper to taste

1 cup all-purpose flour
1/2 cup vegetable oil
1/2 yellow bell pepper, julienned
1/2 red bell pepper, julienned
12 shiitake mushrooms, stemmed and
   cut into strips
6 to 8 tablespoons heavy cream
1/4 teaspoon chopped parsley
1/4 teaspoon chopped fresh chives

Mix the fish fumet, bay leaves, peppercorns, shallots and 1/4 cup wine in a saucepan and bring to a boil. Boil until reduced by one-fourth. Stir in a mixture of the cornstarch and 1 tablespoon wine and cook until of a sauce consistency. Strain the sauce into a bowl and cover to keep warm, discarding the solids.

Season the fillets with salt and pepper and coat with the flour. Heat a sauté pan and add the oil. Cook the fillets in the hot oil for 3 to 5 minutes per side or until the fillets flake easily. Remove to a platter and cover to keep warm, reserving the pan drippings. Add the bell peppers and mushrooms to the reserved pan drippings and sauté for 2 to 3 minutes. Stir in the sauce and adjust the consistency with the cream as desired. Season with salt and pepper. Spoon the sauce evenly in the center of four serving plates and arrange one fillet on each plate. Sprinkle with the parsley and chives.—Serves 4—**Gus Silivos, Skopelos on the Bay, 1995**

Pecan-Crusted Grouper with Frangelico Sauce

11/4 cup pecans, finely chopped
1/2 cup Italian-seasoned bread crumbs
4 (5-ounce) grouper fillets
All-purpose flour
1 cup milk

Vegetable oil
3/4 cup heavy cream
6 tablespoons Frangelico liquer
Salt and pepper to taste

Mix the pecans and bread crumbs in a shallow dish. Coat the fillets with flour and then the milk. Press both sides of the fillets in the pecan mixture. Heat a skillet over medium gas heat and add a small amount of oil. Add the fillets and cook for 5 to 7 minutes per side or until the fillets flake easily and are brown on both sides. Remove to a platter and cover to keep warm.

Combine the cream, liqueur, salt and pepper in a skillet and simmer for 3 to 4 minutes or until thickened. Drizzle the sauce over the fillets on serving plates. Or, drizzle the sauce in the center of each serving plate and top each serving with one of the fillets.—Serves 4—**Jim O'Brien, The Yacht Restaurant, 1995**

Provençal Grouper

1/4 cup (1/4-inch) strips green, yellow and red bell pepper medley
1 tablespoon minced onion
1 teaspoon capers
1/2 teaspoon garlic
Thyme, basil and rosemary to taste

Salt and pepper to taste
Butter
1 (8-ounce) grouper fillet or fish of choice, cut as desired
All-purpose flour
1/4 cup white wine

Sauté the bell peppers, onion, capers, garlic, thyme, basil, rosemary, salt and pepper in butter in a sauté pan over medium gas heat for 2 minutes. Coat the fillet with flour and add to the sauté pan. Sauté for 3 to 5 minutes and turn. Deglaze the pan with the wine and cook until the fillet is medium-well or the desired degree of doneness. Remove the fillet to a serving plate and spoon the bell pepper mixture over the top.—Serves 1—**Alphonse Lucier IV, Eat!, 2006**

Wasabi-Crusted Grouper

2 cups artichoke hearts
5 Roma tomatoes, cut into wedges
2 carrots, sliced
1 red onion, cut into wedges
1/4 cup olive oil

Salt and pepper to taste
1 cup wasabi powder
2 cups panko (Japanese bread crumbs)
6 (6-ounce) grouper fillets
2 tablespoons unsalted butter

Arrange the artichokes, tomatoes, carrots and onion in a single layer on a baking sheet and drizzle with the olive oil. Season with salt and pepper. Roast at 400 degrees in a gas oven for 20 minutes or until light brown, stirring occasionally. Maintain the oven temperature.

Mix the wasabi powder and bread crumbs in a shallow dish. Coat both sides of the fillets with the bread crumb mixture. Sauté the fillets in the butter in a sauté pan until brown and remove to a baking sheet. Bake until the desired degree of doneness. Serve the fillets with the roasted artichoke medley.—Serves 6—**Erika Thomas & Mark Murphy, Portabello Market, 2005**

Basil-Tomato Stewed Mahi Mahi

3 tomatoes, chopped
6 artichoke hearts, chopped
2 tablespoons chopped garlic
4 shallots, chopped
2 bunches basil, chopped
Sliced fennel to taste
2 (6- to 8-ounce) mahi mahi, black grouper or red snapper fillets
Salt and freshly ground pepper to taste
Cornmeal
Flour
Olive oil
1/4 cup chardonnay
1 1/2 cups chicken stock
1/2 cup vegetable juice cocktail

Mix the tomatoes, artichokes, garlic, shallots, basil and fennel in a bowl. Season the fillets with salt and pepper and coat with a mixture of cornmeal and flour. Sauté the fillets in a sauté pan for 2 to 3 minutes per side. Remove the fillets to a roasting pan, reserving the pan drippings. Drizzle the fillets with olive oil.

Deglaze the sauté pan with the wine and then the stock. Cook for 5 minutes or until the liquid is reduced to 1/4 cup. Stir in the tomato mixture and vegetable juice cocktail and then pour over the fillets. Roast at 375 degrees in a gas oven for 10 to 12 minutes or until the fillets flake easily.—Serves 2—**Alphonse Lucier IV, Eat!, 2007**

TIP The mahi mahi, also known as dolphin or dorado, is not the same as a porpoise. The porpoise is a mammal; mahi mahi is a fish. The Hawaiian name "mahi mahi" means "strong-strong" referring to mahi mahi as one of the fastest swimming fish in the sea.

Dorado Aguadilla

Spicy Mango Tomato Relish
2 mangoes, peeled and finely chopped
7 Roma tomatoes, finely chopped
1 purple onion, finely chopped
1/2 bunch cilantro, finely chopped
1 jalapeño chile, seeded and finely chopped
4 garlic cloves, finely chopped
1 tablespoon vegetable oil
Juice of 1 lime
1 tablespoon sugar

Mahi Mahi
2 large sweet potatoes, peeled and grated
4 (8-ounce) mahi mahi fillets
1 tablespoon vegetable oil
1/2 cup heavy cream
2 tablespoons rum
1 tablespoon butter
Salt and pepper to taste

For the relish, combine the mangoes, tomatoes, onion, cilantro, jalapeño chile and garlic in a bowl and mix well. Add the oil and toss to coat. Stir in the lime juice and sugar. Chill, covered, in the refrigerator.

For the mahi mahi, pat the grated sweet potatoes over the surface of the fillets. Heat the oil in a sauté pan and add the fillets. Cook for 4 to 5 minutes per side. Remove the fillets to a baking pan. Bake at 350 degrees in a gas oven until the fillets flake easily. Mix the cream, rum, butter, salt and pepper in a saucepan and simmer over low gas heat until heated through. Drizzle over the fillets on serving plates. Serve with the relish.—Serves 4—**Dan Dunn, Jubilee, 2003**

Curry of Mahi Mahi

Curry Sauce
8 ounces onions, cut into $1/2$-inch pieces
$1/4$ cup ($1/2$ stick) margarine
$1/2$ ounce curry powder
$1/2$ cup heavy cream
$1/2$ cup almonds, toasted and finely chopped
1 ounce chutney, coarsely chopped
1 ounce golden raisins, chopped
$1/2$ ounce shredded coconut
1 teaspoon salt
1 teaspoon pepper
1 teaspoon cornstarch
$1/4$ cup water

Sesame Batter
16 ounces fish batter mix
$1^1/2$ cups ice water
2 ounces sesame seeds, toasted
1 tablespoon garlic powder
$1/2$ teaspoon cayenne pepper

Mahi Mahi
$1^1/2$ to 2 pounds mahi mahi fillets, cut into fingers
Vegetable oil for frying

For the sauce, cook the onions in the margarine in a sauté pan until limp and light brown. Stir in the curry powder and cook for about 1 minute. Stir in the cream, almonds, chutney, raisins, coconut, salt and pepper. Reduce the gas heat and simmer for 2 to 3 minutes, stirring occasionally. Whisk the cornstarch and water in a bowl until blended and add to the curry mixture. Simmer for 2 to 3 minutes or until thickened. Remove from the heat and cover to keep warm.

For the batter, pour the batter mix into a bowl. Add the cold water all at once and whisk until no lumps remain and the mixture is smooth. Add the sesame seeds, garlic powder and cayenne pepper and stir until evenly distributed.

For the mahi mahi, dip the fingers into the batter and fry in oil in a cast-iron skillet until golden brown; drain. Serve immediately with the sauce.—Serves 8—**Jimmy McManus, Bon Appétit Waterfront Cafe, 1999**

Grilled Caribbean Mojo Mahi Mahi

1 cup canola oil
1/2 cup water
1/4 cup thawed frozen orange juice concentrate
1/4 cup lime juice
1/4 cup pineapple juice
Dash of Tabasco sauce
1 yellow onion, chopped
1 bunch cilantro, trimmed and chopped
1 ounce dry jerk seasoning
1 tablespoon chopped garlic
1 teaspoon paprika
Dash of salt
Dash of pepper
1 (8-ounce) mahi mahi fillet
Whipped cooked sweet potatoes

Whisk the canola oil, water, orange juice concentrate, lime juice, pineapple juice and Tabasco sauce in a bowl until combined. Stir in the onion, cilantro, jerk seasoning, garlic, paprika, salt and pepper. Prepare the marinade at least one day in advance and store, covered, in the refrigerator.

Pour the marinade over the fillet in a shallow dish, turning to coat. Marinate, covered, in the refrigerator for 8 to 10 hours, turning occasionally; drain. Grill the fillet on a gas grill for 4 minutes per side; grill marks should be present on both sides. Serve on a bed of whipped sweet potatoes. Garnish with fruit salad.—Serves 1—**Rodger Brown, Bayside Grill, 1998**

TIP Marinate seafood in the refrigerator and discard any used marinade to avoid bacteria from the raw juices. For basting, reserve a portion of the marinade before adding the uncooked seafood.

Grilled Thai Leaf-Wrapped Mahi Mahi with Lilikoi Reduction

Mahi Mahi
1/2 cup tamari
2 tablespoons sugar
8 large taro leaves or banana leaves
4 (6-ounce) mahi mahi fillets
1/2 cup sliced green onions,
  cut on the bias
1 1/2 cups thinly sliced Maui onions
1 cup thinly sliced carrots
1 cup thinly sliced celery
1/4 cup thinly sliced fresh ginger

2 tablespoons minced garlic
1 teaspoon salt

Lilikoi Reduction
14 ounces lilikoi purée or juice
  (Hawaiian passion fruit)
1 cup sugar
1/2 cup sake
1 tablespoon minced fresh ginger
1 teaspoon minced garlic

For the mahi mahi, mix the tamari and sugar in a small saucepan and cook over medium gas heat for 3 minutes or until reduced by half, stirring occasionally. Remove from the heat and cool slightly. Lay four of the taro leaves on a flat surface. Spoon about 1 tablespoon of the tamari reduction in the center of each leaf and top with one of the fillets. Layer one-fourth of the green onions, one-fourth of the onions, one-fourth of the carrots, one-fourth of the celery, one-fourth of the ginger, one-fourth of the garlic and one-fourth of the salt over each fillet and completely wrap the fillets inside the leaves. Wrap each fish fillet inside one of the remaining leaves and arrange seam side down on a hot gas grill. Grill for 7 minutes per side.

For the reduction, combine the lilikoi, sugar, sake, ginger and garlic in a saucepan. Cook over medium-high gas heat until the mixture is reduced by half, stirring occasionally. Remove from the heat and cool for 5 minutes before serving. To serve, spoon 1/4 cup of the reduction in the center of each of four serving plates. Unwrap the bundles and arrange the contents of each bundle on one of the plates.—Serves 4—**Keith Hoffert, Versailles, 2007**

TIP   Mahi mahi fillets have a deep pink center stripe that darkens when cooked. Trim before cooking to maintain the light color of the fillet.

Mahi Mahi Island Kabobs with Mango Beurre Blanc

2 (10-ounce) mahi mahi fillets
2 green bell peppers, cut into
   3-inch chunks
2 yellow bell peppers, cut into
   3-inch chunks
2 red bell peppers, cut into
   3-inch chunks

1 fresh pineapple, cut into 3-inch chunks
2 cups white wine
2 mangoes, cut into chunks
2 cups heavy cream
1 cup (2 sticks) unsalted butter
Lemon pepper to taste
4 cups hot cooked rice

Soak four 12-inch bamboo skewers in cold water. Cut each fillet into eight equal portions. Alternately thread the fillet portions with the bell pepper chunks and pineapple chunks on the skewers. Combine the wine and mangoes in a saucepan. Cook until the mangoes are tender, stirring occasionally. Add the cream and cook until reduced by half. Remove from the heat and add the butter gradually, stirring constantly until a beurre blanc sauce is formed.

Season the kabobs with lemon pepper. Grill on a gas grill for 10 to 12 minutes or until the fish flakes easily and the bell peppers are the desired degree of crispness. Spoon half the rice on the side of each of two serving plates. Arrange the kabobs equally over the rice and drizzle with the sauce.—Serves 2—**John Smith, Calypso!, 2002**

Redfish with Figs, Bacon and Pecans

6 slices applewood-smoked bacon
2 shallots, minced
2 garlic cloves, minced
1 teaspoon red pepper flakes
1/4 cup white wine

4 ounces fig preserves
1/4 cup pecans, toasted
2 (6-ounce) redfish fillets
Salt and pepper to taste

Fry the bacon in a cast-iron skillet; drain on paper towels, reserving the bacon drippings in the skillet. Chop the bacon into 1/2-inch pieces. Sauté the shallots, garlic and red pepper flakes in the reserved drippings over medium gas heat for 2 minutes. Add the bacon, wine, preserves and pecans and cook for 4 minutes to reduce. Pour into a heatproof bowl. Season both sides of the fillets with salt and pepper and arrange in a single layer in the cast-iron skillet. Pour the fig mixture over the fillets. Bake at 350 degrees in a gas oven for 20 minutes. Serve with your favorite rice.— Serves 2—**Jim Shirley, Fish House, 2007**

Stuffed Redfish in Banana Leaves

12 slices bacon, chopped
1/2 cup minced onion
12 ounces okra
1 teaspoon minced garlic
1 teaspoon red pepper flakes

Lemon zest to taste
4 (6-ounce) redfish steaks
Kosher salt and pepper to taste
4 banana leaves
1 lime, cut into halves

Fry the bacon in a cast-iron skillet. Add the onion and cook over medium gas heat until the onion is tender. Stir in the okra, garlic and red pepper flakes. Sauté for a few minutes. Let stand until cool. Stir in lemon zest. Make a slit in the side of each steak to form a pocket and fill the pockets equally with the okra mixture. Season the outside surface of the steaks with salt and pepper. Wrap each steak in a banana leaf and then in foil.

Grill on a gas grill for 10 minutes. Discard the foil and check for doneness. Unwrap the banana leaves and arrange the steaks on serving plates. Drizzle with a squeeze of lime. Serve with hot cooked ginger rice.—Serves 4—**Jim Shirley, Fish House, 2007**

Grilled Snapper with Mediterranean Salsa

8 ounces crumbled feta cheese
20 pitted kalamata olives, sliced
20 pimento-stuffed large green
  olives, sliced
1 small red onion, cut into 1/2-inch strips
2 large tomatoes, peeled, seeded
  and chopped
8 pepperoncini chiles, sliced

1 tablespoon extra-virgin olive oil
2 teaspoons red wine vinegar
1 tablespoon parsley, chopped
1 teaspoon mint, chopped
1 teaspoon minced garlic
4 (8-ounce) red snapper fillets
Salt and pepper to taste
2 tablespoons olive oil

Combine the cheese, olives, onion, tomatoes, pepperoncini chiles, 1 tablespoon olive oil, the vinegar, parsley, mint and garlic in a bowl and mix well. Taste and adjust the seasonings. Season the fillets with salt and pepper and coat with 2 tablespoons olive oil. Grill on a gas grill for 7 to 9 minutes or until the fillets flake easily. Arrange one fillet on each of four serving plates and top with equal portions of the salsa.—Serves 4—**Gus Silivos, Skopelos on the Bay, 1997**

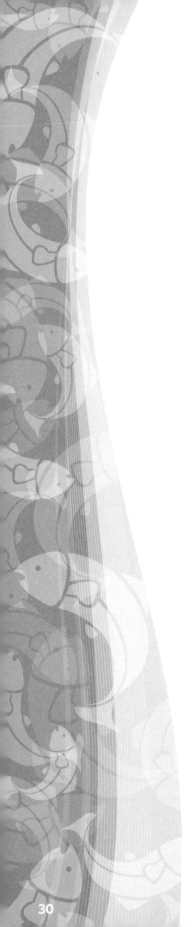

Salt-Packed Red Snapper with Citrus Herb Rub

1 (5- to 7-pound) whole red snapper
2 cups water
3 tablespoons white wine
2 lemons, sliced
1 orange, sliced
9 sprigs of thyme
3 sprigs of rosemary
1 tablespoon minced garlic
Coarse pepper to taste
Olive oil
2 cups sea salt or kosher salt

Scale and clean the fish; do not debone. Combine the water, wine, lemons, orange, thyme, rosemary and garlic in a saucepan and bring just to a simmer or until a thermometer registers 160 to 170 degrees. Remove from the heat and steep for 5 to 10 minutes. Strain, reserving the liquid and solids.

Cut a slit along the belly of the fish. Deepen the cavity, being careful not to score the flesh. Make 3-inch scores along each side of the fish, just enough to pierce the skin. Stuff the solid lemon mixture in the belly of the fish and spinkle with pepper. Arrange the fish on a large sheet of foil. Drizzle both sides with olive oil.

Mix the reserved liquid and salt in a bowl until the consistency of wet sand. Totally encrust the fish with the salt mixture and pack down tightly. Place the foil on a grill rack on a gas grill over medium heat; do not wrap the foil around the fish.

Grill until a meat thermometer registers 145 degrees. Or, bake at 350 degrees in a gas oven until a meat thermometer registers 145 degrees. Let rest for 3 to 4 minutes. Break the salt crust open and slice the fish as desired.—Serves 4—**Keith Hoffert, Vintage Gourmet, 2005**

TIP When in doubt, throw it out. Seafood should have a fresh ocean smell, not a strong fish odor.

Crispy Pan-Fried Red Snapper with Asian Cabbage and Radish Slaw

Asian Cabbage and Radish Slaw

3 cups thinly sliced napa cabbage
1 cup thinly sliced red cabbage
1 cup julienned green onions
1 cup julienned daikon
1 cup sliced red radishes
1/2 cup rice wine vinegar
1/4 cup peanut oil
3 tablespoons sugar
2 tablespoons fresh lime juice
1 tablespoon salt
1/2 teaspoon ground cumin
1/2 teaspoon coriander

Red Snapper

4 (6-ounce) red snapper fillets
Salt and pepper to taste
6 egg yolks
2 teaspoons water
1 1/2 cups cornstarch
1/2 cup all-purpose flour
Olive oil

For the slaw, toss the cabbages, green onions, daikon and radishes in a bowl. Whisk the vinegar, peanut oil, sugar, lime juice, salt, cumin and coriander in a bowl until combined. Add to the cabbage mixture and mix well. Chill, covered, for 1 hour or longer.

For the red snapper, season the fillets with salt and pepper. Whisk the egg yolks and water in a bowl until blended. Mix the cornstarch and flour in a shallow dish. Dip the fillets in the egg yolk mixture and then coat with the cornstarch mixture. Panfry the fillets in olive oil in a skillet over medium-high gas heat for 3 to 4 minutes per side; drain. Serve with the slaw.—Serves 4— **Tom McGinty, Florida Department of Agriculture and Consumer Sciences, 2001**

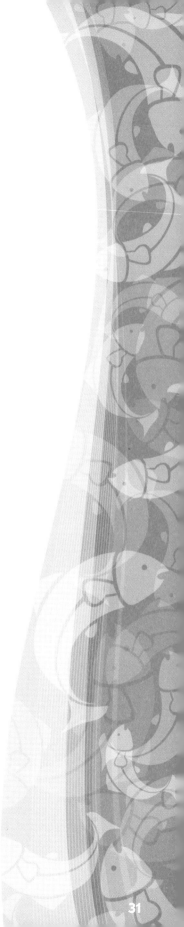

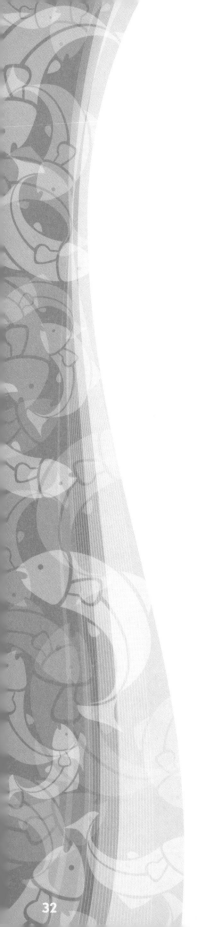

Fish Veracruz

2 (16-ounce) red snapper fillets or sea bass steaks
Salt to taste
2 limes, cut into halves
2 tablespoons extra-virgin olive oil
2 white onions, chopped
6 garlic cloves, chopped
4 large tomatoes, blanched, peeled and chopped
20 pitted large green olives, chopped
2 tablespoons capers, rinsed and drained
2 pickled jalapeño chiles, chopped
3 tablespoons pickled jalapeño chile juice
2 tablespoons chopped fresh parsley
2 sprigs of rosemary
2 sprigs of marjoram
1/2 teaspoon dried Mexican oregano
2 bay leaves
Pepper to taste
Corn tortillas, heated

Sprinkle the fillets with salt and arrange in a single layer in a shallow dish. Squeeze the limes over the fillets and place the lime halves in the dish. Marinate, covered, in the refrigerator for 1 hour.

Heat the olive oil in a large sauté pan over medium-low gas heat. Add the onions and cook for 15 minutes or until golden brown. Stir in the garlic and cook for 1 minute. Add the tomatoes and cook for 10 minutes, stirring occasionally. Stir in the olives, capers, jalapeño chiles, jalapeño chile juice, parsley, rosemary, marjoram, oregano and bay leaves. Season with salt and pepper.

Cook over low gas heat for 20 minutes. Add the fillets, marinade and lime halves. Cook, covered, for 4 minutes per side, turning once. Discard the bay leaves and limes. Serve immediately with tortillas. You may substitute one 28-ounce can whole tomatoes for the fresh tomatoes, chopping before adding.—Serves 4—**David Guardanapo, Crema Coffee and Baking Company, 2008**

Red Snapper with Black Bean Salsa

Black Bean Salsa
1¹/2 cups chopped tomatoes
1 cup chopped green and red bell peppers
1 cup cooked black beans
3/4 cup chopped cilantro
3 tablespoons lime juice
3 tablespoons red wine vinegar
1 jalapeño chile, seeded and chopped
Dash of hot red pepper sauce to taste
Salt and pepper to taste

Red Snapper
4 (6- to 8-ounce) red snapper fillets
Salt and pepper to taste
All-purpose flour
1/2 cup (1 stick) butter

For the salsa, combine the tomatoes, bell peppers, beans, cilantro, lime juice, vinegar, jalapeño chile and hot sauce in a bowl and mix well. Season with salt and pepper.

For the red snapper, season the fillets with salt and pepper and coat lightly with flour. Melt the butter in a large skillet and add the fillets. Sauté until the fillets flake easily. Arrange one fillet on each of four serving plates and top equally with the salsa. Garnish with orange zest and lime zest.— Serves 4—**Kevin Quirk, Ramada Conference Center, 1995**

TIP Snapper are caught in waters 60 to 200 feet deep with rock and limestone formations covered with coral and sponges. Snapper feed on bottom-dwelling crustaceans and small fishes. They can weigh up to thirty pounds and grow to three feet in length. Marketed both fresh and frozen, snapper have a firm-textured, mild white meat that is perfect for almost any fin fish recipe.

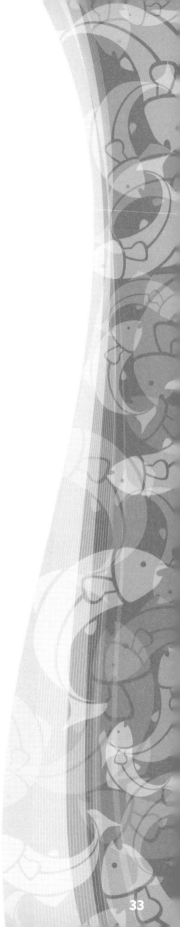

Summer Salmon

3 ears of corn, grilled
1/2 red onion, chopped
1 cup chopped Roma tomatoes
1/3 cup olive oil
2 tablespoons rice vinegar
1 tablespoon minced garlic
Salt and pepper to taste

2 cups olive oil
1 cup chopped scallions
4 (6-ounce) salmon fillets
1 tablespoon chili powder
Mashed cooked potatoes or hot cooked
   wild rice

Cut the corn kernels off the cob into a bowl using a sharp knife. Stir in the onion, tomatoes, 1/3 cup olive oil, the vinegar, garlic, salt and pepper. Let stand for 1 hour or longer. Process 2 cups olive oil, the scallions, salt and pepper in a food processor until blended.

Rub both sides of the fillets with the chili powder. Sauté in a skillet over high gas heat until a brown crust forms. Remove the fillets to a baking pan and bake at 400 degrees in a gas oven for 7 minutes. Serve the fillets over mashed potatoes. Top each with equal portions of the corn relish and drizzle with the scallion oil.—Serves 4—**Erika Thomas and Mark Murphy, Portabello Market, 2006**

Bacon-Braised Salmon with Molasses Sauce

4 slices bacon, chopped
4 (7-ounce) salmon fillets
3 cups molasses

1/4 cup red wine vinegar
1 cup pecans, toasted

Partially cook the bacon in a large ovenproof skillet. Add fillets to the skillet and sear on both sides. Mix in the molasses and vinegar. Simmer over gas heat or bake at 350 degrees in a gas oven until the fillets flake easily.

Arrange one fillet on each of four serving plates. Drizzle with the molasses sauce and sprinkle with the pecans. Serve with sweet potatoes or the starch or vegetable of your choice.—Serves 4—**Paul Pettigrew, Seville Quarter, 2001**

Teriyaki Salmon with Pineapple Papaya Salsa

Pineapple Papaya Salsa
3 tomatoes, chopped
2 jalapeño chiles, seeded and minced
1 pineapple, chopped
1 papaya, chopped
1 bunch green onions, sliced
1 bunch cilantro, chopped
3 tablespoons lemon juice
2 teaspoons salt
1 teaspoon chopped garlic

Salmon
4 (4-ounce) salmon fillets
1 cup soy sauce
1/2 cup sake
1/4 cup packed brown sugar
1 teaspoon crushed garlic
1 teaspoon minced fresh ginger
Vegetable oil

For the salsa, combine the tomatoes, jalapeño chiles, pineapple, papaya, green onions, cilantro, lemon juice, salt and garlic in a bowl and mix well. Chill, covered, in the refrigerator. Heat before serving.

For the salmon, arrange the fillets in a single layer in a shallow dish. Mix the soy sauce, sake, brown sugar, garlic and ginger in a bowl and pour over the fillets, turning to coat. Marinate in the refrigerator for 15 minutes; drain. Pat dry with paper towels.

Brush the fillets with oil and arrange in a baking pan. Broil in a gas oven or grill on a gas grill until the fillets flake easily. Arrange one fillet over 1/2 cup of heated salsa on each of four serving plates. Reserve the remaining salsa for another use.—Serves 4—**Travis Herr, Bill Hamilton and Culinary Students, Pensacola Junior College, 2005**

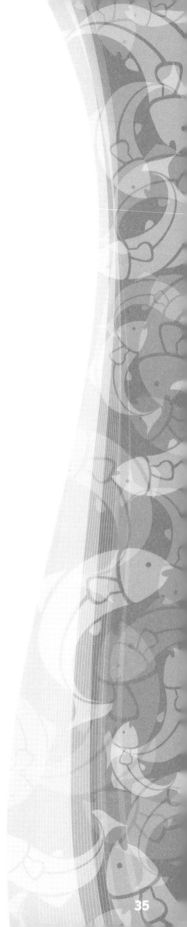

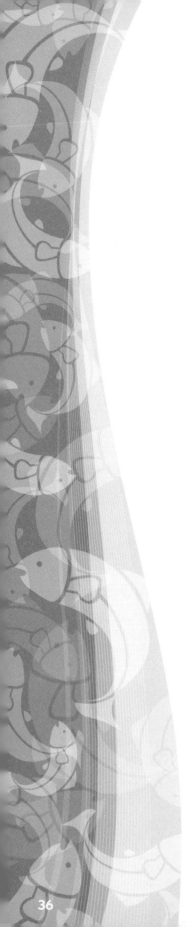

Grilled Ginger Salmon with Ginger Soy Butter Sauce

4 (6-ounce) salmon fillets
1/2 cup soy sauce
1/3 cup honey
1 tablespoon brown sugar
1 tablespoon minced garlic
1 ounce fresh ginger, grated
1 tablespoon minced shallot
1 cup (2 sticks) unsalted butter, cut into pieces
6 tablespoons olive oil
Juice of 1 orange
3 tablespoons finely chopped cilantro
2 tablespoons grated orange zest
2 tablespoons grated lemon zest
1 tablespoon ginger powder
Pepper to taste

Arrange the fillets in a single layer in a shallow dish. Bring the soy sauce, honey, brown sugar, garlic, grated ginger and shallot to a simmer in a saucepan and simmer for about 3 minutes, stirring occasionally. Remove from the heat and stir in the butter. Add the olive oil, orange juice, cilantro, orange zest, lemon zest, ginger powder and pepper and mix well. Pour half the marinade over the fillets, turning to coat.

Marinate, covered, in the refrigerator for 1 hour, turning occasionally; drain. Grill the fillets on a gas grill to medium or medium-well or to the desired degree of doneness. Drizzle the reserved marinade equally on each of four serving plates. Top each prepared plate with one of the fillets.— Serves 4—**Jim O'Brien, O'Brien's Bistro, 2000**

TIP If fish is cooked in a sauce or foil, add five minutes to the total cooking time. If you choose to cook it frozen, the cooking time should be doubled. Fish is done when the flesh becomes opaque and flakes easily at the thickest part.

Cedar-Planked Salmon with Grilled Planked Potatoes

2 potatoes
1 tablespoon extra-virgin olive oil
Salt and pepper to taste
2 (8-ounce) salmon fillets

1 onion, sliced
1 lemon, sliced
2 tablespoons barbecue butter
Sprigs of thyme or herb of choice

Blanch the potatoes in boiling water in a saucepan for 10 to 15 minutes. Drain and cool slightly. Slice the potatoes into planks and coat with the olive oil. Season with salt and pepper. Grill on a gas grill until cooked through, turning occasionally.

Soak two cedar planks in cold water. Arrange one fillet on each plank. Layer each with equal portions of the onion, lemon, barbecue butter and thyme. Wrap in foil and grill on a gas grill for 15 minutes or until the fillets flake easily. Discard the foil and serve with the potatoes.—Serves 2—**Jimmy McManus, Bon Appétit Waterfront Cafe, 1998**

Grilled Salmon with Balsamic Wilted Spinach

1/2 cup balsamic vinegar
1/4 cup sugar
1/4 cup sesame oil
1/4 cup red wine
1 teaspoon chopped garlic
1 tablespoon cornstarch
1 tablespoon water

1 (6-ounce) salmon fillet
Olive oil
Salt and pepper to taste
4 ounces fresh spinach, stemmed
4 slices red onion
2 slices red tomato
1 green onion, cut lengthwise to halves

Bring the vinegar, sugar, sesame oil, wine and garlic to a boil in a saucepan, stirring occasionally. Mix the cornstarch and water in a bowl until blended; gradually add to the vinegar mixture, stirring constantly. Cook until thickened. Remove from the heat and cover to keep warm.

Coat the fillet with olive oil and season with salt and pepper. Grill the fillet on a gas grill until medium-well or to the desired degree of doneness. Toss the spinach with just enough of the warm balsamic dressing in a bowl to coat; mound in the center of a serving plate. Arrange the fillet over the spinach and top with the red onion slices, tomato slices and green onion. Drizzle with the remaining balsamic dressing.—Serves 1—**Jim O'Brien, O'Brien's Bistro, 2006**

Hoisin-Smoked Salmon

Brine
1 gallon (16 cups) water
1 1/2 cups sugar
1 1/2 cups salt
1 orange, cut into halves
1 lime, cut into halves

Salmon
1 side of fresh salmon, skinned and bones removed
1 small bottle hoisin sauce
1 package spring roll wrappers
1 small package mixed salad greens
15 Thai basil leaves
15 mint leaves
1/2 cup soy sauce
1 tablespoon fish sauce
Juice of 1 lime

For the brine, mix the water, sugar, salt, orange and lime in a large container until the sugar and salt dissolve.

For the salmon, pour the brine over the salmon in a large container. Marinate in the refrigerator for 8 to 12 hours; drain. Soak a bag of wood chips in water. Drain and place the chips in a smoker and start the smoker. Coat one side of the salmon with the hoisin sauce and arrange sauce side up in the smoker. Smoke for 30 to 45 minutes or until the salmon flakes easily. Be careful not to overcook; the salmon should be moist and tender. Remove from the smoker and cool slightly.

Prepare the spring roll wrappers using the package directions. Layer 1 ounce of the smoked salmon, some of the salad greens, 1 basil leaf and 1 mint leaf in the center of each roll wrapper. Fold in the sides and then roll tightly to enclose the filling. Cut the rolls into halves, if desired. Mix the soy sauce, fish sauce and lime juice in a bowl and serve with the rolls. Or, serve the salmon with sushi rice and sautéed bok choy and spinach as an alternative to spring rolls.—Makes 10 to 15 spring rolls—**Dan Dunn, The Art of Catering, 2006**

Citrus Salsa-Poached Salmon

Citrus Cilantro Salsa
1¹/₂ cups green chiles, chopped
Juice of 7 oranges
Juice of 8 limes
15 garlic cloves, minced
2 tablespoons sugar
4 teaspoons ground cumin
1 teaspoon salt
³/₄ teaspoon cayenne pepper
Chopped fresh cilantro to taste

Sonoran Seasoning
1 teaspoon ground cumin
1 teaspoon paprika
1 teaspoon chili powder
1 teaspoon blackening seasoning

Salmon
4 (6-ounce) salmon fillets
Salt to taste
Hot cooked sofrito rice
1 avocado, sliced
1 red bell pepper, sliced

For the salsa, combine the green chiles, orange juice, lime juice, garlic, sugar, cumin, salt, cayenne pepper and cilantro in a bowl and mix well.

For the seasoning, mix the cumin, paprika, chili powder and blackening seasoning in a bowl.

For the salmon, season the fillets with 1 teaspoon of the Sonoran seasoning and salt. Arrange the fillets in a skillet and add 1 cup of the salsa. Bring to a boil over medium gas heat; reduce the heat. Cook for 4 minutes. Serve each fillet over a bed of hot sofrito rice on a serving plate. Top with avocado slices and bell pepper slices.—Serves 4—**Jim Shirley, The Screaming Coyote, 1997**

Poached Salmon with Mustard Lime Sauce

6 cups water
2$1/2$ cups dry white wine
Salt and white pepper to taste
2 (6- to 8-ounce) salmon fillets, skinned
$1/2$ cup sour cream
3 tablespoons Dijon mustard
2 teaspoons fresh lime juice
2 teaspoons honey
$1/2$ teaspoon sliced basil

Bring the water, wine, salt and white pepper to a simmer in a poacher and add the fillets. Poach for about 5 minutes or until the fillets flake easily. Mix the sour cream, Dijon mustard, lime juice and honey in a bowl.

Remove the fillets from the poaching liquid and arrange each fillet on a serving plate. Spoon equal portions of the sauce over the top of each fillet and top with the basil.—Serves 2— **Jim O'Brien, O'Brien's Bistro, 1999**

TIP Thaw frozen seafood in the refrigerator, never at room temperature. To use frozen seafood immediately, thaw under cold running water or in the microwave using the defrost setting.

Asian-Spiced Salmon

Asian Dressing
6 tablespoons rice vinegar
3 tablespoons soy sauce
2 tablespoons chopped fresh cilantro
2 tablespoons sesame oil
1 tablespoon finely chopped fresh ginger
1 teaspoon sugar

Salmon
1 teaspoon chili powder
1 teaspoon dry mustard
1 teaspoon curry powder
1 teaspoon salt
1 teaspoon coriander
1 teaspoon sugar
1 teaspoon ground cumin
4 (6-ounce) salmon fillets with skin
1 tablespoon vegetable oil

For the dressing, whisk the vinegar, soy sauce, cilantro, sesame oil, ginger and sugar in a bowl until combined.

For the salmon, mix the chili powder, dry mustard, curry powder, salt, coriander, sugar and cumin in a bowl. Arrange the fillets skin side down on a baking sheet with sides. Sprinkle each fillet with 1¹/2 teaspoons of the chili powder blend. Marinate, covered with plastic wrap, for 3 to 10 hours.

Heat the oil in a large heavy skillet over medium-high gas heat. Arrange the fillets skin side up in the hot skillet. Sear for about 3 minutes or until brown and crisp. Turn and sear for about 3 minutes longer or just until the fillets are cooked through. Drizzle with the dressing before serving.— Serves 4—**Angela Miller, Distinctive Kitchens Culinary Arts Center, 2007**

 After handling raw seafood, thoroughly wash knives, cutting surfaces, sponges, and hands with hot soapy water.

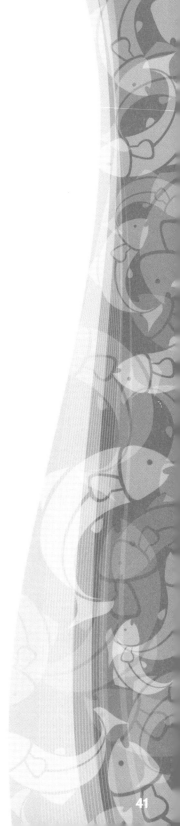

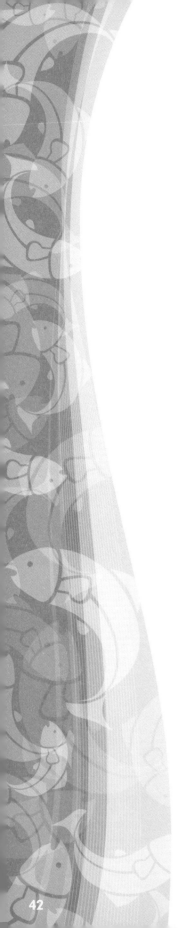

Crispy-Seared Salmon with Fennel-Green Apple Hash

Fennel-Green Apple Hash
1/4 cup sliced onion
1 tablespoon butter
1/4 cup chopped pancetta
1 cup thinly sliced napa cabbage
1 fennel bulb, thinly sliced
1 green apple, shredded
1 teaspoon fennel seeds
1 small Idaho potato, chopped and cooked
1 tablespoon chopped fresh chives
Salt and pepper to taste

Dill Nage
1 cup fish stock
1/4 cup dill weed sprigs
2 teaspoons butter, melted

Salmon
2 (6-ounce) salmon fillets with skin
Salt and pepper to taste
1 teaspoon cornstarch
1 tablespoon canola oil

For the hash, sauté the onion in the butter in a skillet. Add the pancetta and cook for 5 minutes. Stir in the cabbage, fennel bulb, apple and fennel seeds. Cook for about 4 minutes, stirring occasionally. Add the potato and chives and toss to combine. Remove from the heat and season with salt and pepper. Cover to keep warm.

For the nage, heat the stock in a saucepan. Process the warm stock, dill weed and butter in a blender until smooth.

For the salmon, season the fillets with salt and pepper and dust the skin with the cornstarch. Heat the canola oil in a skillet over high gas heat. Arrange the fillets skin side down in the hot oil and cook for 4 minutes. Reduce the gas heat to low and cook until the skin is crispy. Turn and cook until the fillets flake easily. Serve with the nage and hash.—Serves 2—**Brad Parker, Pensacola Country Club, 2001**

Pumpernickel Salmon Panade

3 tablespoons olive oil
1 (6- to 8-ounce) salmon fillet
2 tablespoons finely chopped green bell pepper
1 teaspoon finely chopped garlic
1 rib celery, finely chopped
2 tablespoons finely chopped onion
3/4 cup heavy cream
1/4 cup buttermilk
3 slices pumpernickel bread, trimmed and cut into 1/2-inch cubes
1 teaspoon Old Bay seasoning
1 teaspoon Greek seasoning
Pinch of dried dill weed
2 egg whites
1/4 cup all-purpose flour
1/2 cup panko (Japanese bread crumbs)
1 tablespoon unsalted butter

Heat the olive oil in a large sauté pan over medium gas heat; add the fillet. Sauté until brown on both sides, turning once. Remove the fillet to a plate, reserving the pan drippings. Cut the salmon into small portions. Sauté the bell pepper, garlic, celery and onion in the reserved pan drippings over medium gas heat until the onions are slightly translucent; drain.

Bring the cream and buttermilk just to a boil in a saucepan over high gas heat. Reduce the gas heat to low and fold in the bread, being careful not to tear or crumble the cubes. Soak until the bread is saturated and most of the cream mixture has been absorbed. Drain to remove any excess cream mixture. Fold the salmon, bread, bell pepper mixture, Old Bay seasoning, Greek seasoning and dill weed together in a bowl, making sure the ingredients are not too moist or dry.

Whisk the egg whites in a bowl until medium peaks form; chill. Shape the salmon mixture into silver dollar–size cakes. Dust with the flour, dip in the egg whites and then coat with the bread crumbs. Heat the butter in a large nonstick skillet over medium-high gas heat until melted. Add the salmon cakes and cook until golden brown on both sides; drain. Serve immediately.—Serves 1—
Alphonse Lucier IV, Pensacola Country Club, 2003

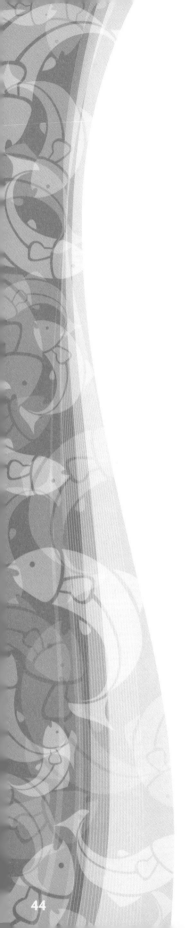

Grilled Sea Bass with Pineapple and Cranberry Compote

Pineapple and Cranberry Compote
2 cups fresh or frozen cranberries
1/2 cup finely chopped pineapple
1/4 cup chopped cilantro leaves
1/4 cup peach schnapps
2 small serrano chiles, seeded and finely chopped
1 tablespoon apple cider
1 tablespoon sugar
1/2 teaspoon roasted habanero chile paste
Salt to taste

Sea Bass
4 (6-ounce) sea bass fillets
1/2 cup teriyaki sauce
2 tablespoons sesame oil
1 green onion, finely chopped
1 teaspoon grated fresh ginger
1 tablespoon olive oil

For the compote, simmer the cranberries in a saucepan for 15 minutes. Let stand until cool. Finely chop the cranberries and add to a bowl. Stir in the pineapple, cilantro, schnapps, serrano chiles, apple cider, sugar, habanero chile paste and salt.

For the sea bass, arrange the fillets in a shallow dish. Mix the teriyaki sauce, sesame oil, green onion and ginger in a bowl and pour over the fillets, turning to coat. Marinate, covered, in the refrigerator for 2 hours, turning occasionally.

Heat the olive oil in a sauté pan and add the fillets. Sear until golden brown on both sides. Arrange each fillet on a serving plate and top equally with the compote.—Serves 4—
James Ammons, Seville Quarter, 2007

Poached Sea Bass Chinoise

1 (6-ounce) package wild rice
2 tablespoons butter, softened
Salt and pepper to taste
2 cups julienned zucchini, squash and carrot medley
4 (6- to 7-ounce) sea bass fillets, skinned
4 green onions, cut into 3-inch lengths
4 cups water
Lemon juice to taste
Peppercorns to taste
1 bay leaf
Sliced fresh ginger
2 tablespoons cornstarch
4 egg yolks, beaten
1/4 cup lemon juice
Soy sauce to taste

Cook the rice using the package directions. Stir in the butter and season with salt and pepper. Cover to keep warm. Blanch the vegetable medley in a small amount of water in a saucepan until al dente; drain. Cover to keep warm.

Make two slits in each fillet and press the green onions into the slits. Bring the water, lemon juice to taste, peppercorns, bay leaf and ginger to a boil in a poacher. Gently arrange the fillets in the poaching liquid and poach for 7 to 8 minutes. Remove the fillets to a platter and cover to keep warm, reserving the poaching liquid. Discard the bay leaf and ginger.

Gradually add the cornstarch to the reserved poaching liquid, whisking constantly until blended. Cook until thickened, stirring constantly. Remove from the heat and whisk in the egg yolks, 1/4 cup lemon juice and soy sauce. Mound the rice equally on each of four serving plates and arrange one fillet over each serving. Drizzle with the sauce and top with the vegetable mixture. If you are concerned about using raw egg yolks, use egg yolks from eggs pasteurized in their shells, which are sold at some specialty food stores, or use an equivalent amount of pasteurized egg substitute.—
Serves 4—**Klaus Bertram, Executive Club, 1998**

Sautéed Sea Bass over Wilted Frisée with Thai Dressing

Thai Dressing
3 garlic cloves, minced
1 small onion, minced
1 sprig of rosemary, minced
1/2 teaspoon minced dried Thai chile or
    jalapeño chile
1/4 cup rice wine vinegar
Juice of 1 lemon
2 tablespoons soy sauce
1 can coconut milk
2 scallions, finely sliced

Sea Bass
4 (6-ounce) sea bass fillets, cut 3/4 inch
    thick on the bias
3 tablespoons olive oil
2 tablespoons white sesame seeds
1/2 cup white wine
2 tablespoons fresh lemon juice
1/4 cup (1/2 stick) butter
1 yellow bell pepper, julienned
1 green bell pepper, julienned
2 bunches frisée
24 small plum tomatoes, cut into halves

For the dressing, place the garlic, onion, rosemary and Thai chile in a blender. Begin processing at high speed and add the vinegar, lemon juice and soy sauce. Gradually add the coconut milk, processing constantly at low speed until blended. Pour the dressing into a bowl and whisk in the scallions.

For the sea bass, brush the tops of the fillets with some of the olive oil. Coat the tops evenly with the sesame seeds. Heat the remaining olive oil in a skillet over medium-high gas heat and add the fillets sesame seed side down. Sauté until golden brown. Turn the fillets and deglaze the skillet with the wine and lemon juice. Cook, covered, over low gas heat for 4 to 5 minutes.

Heat the butter in a sauté pan over medium gas heat until almost melted. Add the bell peppers and frisée to the butter and cook just until the frisée wilts. Remove from the heat and add the dressing, tossing to coat. Arrange the bell pepper mixture equally in the center of four serving plates. Top each serving with one of the fillets and top with the tomato halves.—Serves 4—**Andrew Selz, Chef Selz Collection, 2004**

Grilled Sheepshead with Orange Fennel Salsa

Orange Fennel Salsa
3 tablespoons white wine vinegar
2 tablespoons olive oil
2 tablespoons chopped cilantro
2 teaspoons soy sauce
2 teaspoons minced fresh ginger
2 teaspoons sugar
3 oranges
1 fennel bulb, trimmed and julienned
1/2 red onion, thinly sliced
Salt and pepper to taste

Sheepshead
3 tablespoons olive oil
1 tablespoon soy sauce
1 garlic clove, thinly sliced
4 (6- to 8-ounce) sheepshead fillets
Salt and pepper to taste

For the salsa, whisk the vinegar, olive oil, cilantro, soy sauce, ginger and sugar in a bowl until combined. Peel the oranges and discard the white pith. Hold the oranges over the bowl to catch the juices and cut between the membranes to release the orange sections into the bowl. Add the fennel and onion and toss gently. Season with salt and pepper. Chill, covered, in the refrigerator. The salsa may be prepared up to 3 hours in advance.

For the sheepshead, mix the olive oil, soy sauce and garlic in a shallow dish. Add the fillets and turn to coat. Season the fillets with salt and pepper. Grill over medium-high gas heat for about 3 minutes per side or until the fillets are opaque in the center. Remove the fillets to serving plates and top evenly with the salsa.—Serves 4—**William Guthrie, Guthrie's Dining Designs, 2008**

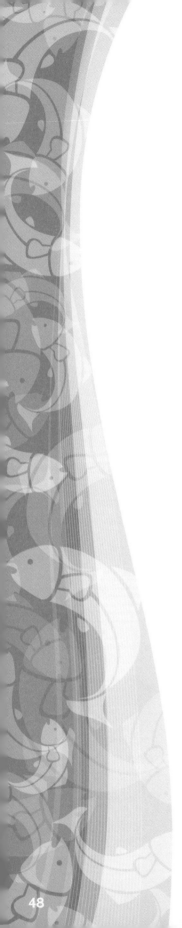

Grilled Swordfish with Smoked Salmon-Cracked Pepper Linguini

Salmon-Cracked Pepper Linguini
All-purpose flour
2 cups semolina flour
3 eggs
3/4 cup puréed smoked salmon
1 tablespoon freshly cracked pepper

Swordfish
4 (7- to 8-ounce) swordfish fillets
Olive oil
1 cup white wine
1 cup sea clam juice
1 tablespoon minced shallots
1 cup (2 sticks) unsalted butter, chopped
2 tablespoons drained capers

For the linguini, dust a hard surface lightly with all-purpose flour. Mound 2 cups semolina flour on the hard surface and make a well in the center. Add the eggs to the well and beat with a fork, gradually working the eggs into the flour. Knead for 15 minutes or longer. Roll the dough on the hard surface and spread with the salmon purée and cracked pepper. Fold the dough into a log and roll out. Continue the folding and rolling process until the purée and pepper are evenly incorporated. If the dough crumbles, add a small amount of water until the dough comes together. If the dough becomes sticky, sprinkle with additional semolina flour until of a drier consistency. Roll out the dough using the pasta machine instructions. Cook in boiling water in a saucepan until al dente; drain.

For the swordfish, brush the fillets with olive oil. Grill over medium gas heat until the fillets flake easily. Remove to a platter and cover to keep warm. Cook the wine and clam juice in a saucepan over medium gas heat until reduced by half. Add the shallots and cook until of a syrupy consistency. Reduce the gas heat to low and gradually add 6 tablespoons of the butter, stirring constantly.

Simmer until the butter melts. Remove from the heat and stir in the capers and the remaining 10 tablespoons of butter. Swirl the sauce until no butter pieces remain, but do not allow the butter to melt completely. Do not break the sauce. Arrange the linguini equally on four serving plates. Top each serving with one fillet and drizzle evenly with the sauce.—Serves 4—**Chuck Morgan, Scotto's Ristorante Italiano, 1995**

Grilled Swordfish with Horseradish Mustard

2 (10-ounce) swordfish steaks
1 cup horseradish
1 cup Dijon mustard
1/2 cup dry white wine
Juice of 2 lemons
1 teaspoon crushed pepper
2 tablespoons capers

Arrange the steaks in a single layer in a shallow dish. Combine the horseradish, Dijon mustard, wine, lemon juice and pepper in a bowl and mix well. Pour the horseradish mixture over the steaks and turn to coat.

Marinate, covered, in the refrigerator for 1 hour, turning occasionally. Grill the steaks on a gas grill until medium-rare. Top with the capers.—Serves 2—**Ann Nina Prizzi, Annie's on the Lake, 1996**

TIP Store seafood in leak-proof containers at 34 to 38 degrees in the coldest part of the refrigerator for up to three days, or freeze for up to ten months. Shelf life will vary depending upon product form and species.

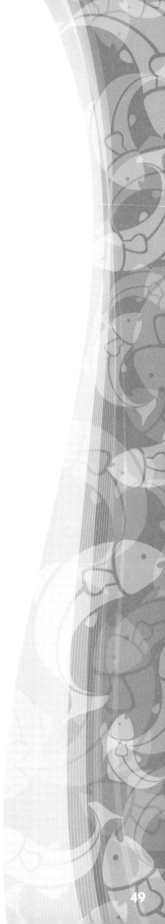

Citrus-Crusted Swordfish Steak with Mango Sauce

Mango Sauce
2 tablespoons white wine
1 tablespoon lime juice
2 tablespoons mango purée
2 tablespoons orange juice
1 tablespoon butter

Swordfish
1 teaspoon lime zest
1 teaspoon lemon zest
1 teaspoon orange zest
1/4 cup bread crumbs
1 (6-ounce) swordfish fillet
2 tablespoons all-purpose flour
1/4 cup egg wash
1 teaspoon canola oil
1 yuca, peeled
Salt and pepper to taste
Garlic to taste
1 plantain
Canola oil for frying

For the sauce, combine the wine, lime juice, mango purée and orange juice in a saucepan and mix well. Cook over low gas heat until reduced by half. Remove from the heat and swirl in the butter. Cover to keep warm.

For the swordfish, mix the lime zest, lemon zest, orange zest and bread crumbs in a shallow dish. Dust the fillet with the flour and then dip in the egg wash. Coat both sides evenly with the zest mixture. Heat 1 teaspoon canola oil in a skillet and add the fillet. Sear on both sides until the fillet flakes easily.

Boil the yuca in water seasoned with salt, pepper and garlic in a saucepan; drain. Fry the plantain in canola oil in a skillet; drain. Serve the fillet with the yuca, plantain and sauce.—Serves 1—
Kevin Faoutas, The Veranda at Henderson Park Inn, 1996

Grilled Triggerfish with Peppers and Garlic Mayonnaise

Garlic Mayonnaise
2 tablespoons sour cream
2 tablespoons mayonnaise
1 tablespoon chopped garlic
1 teaspoon chopped parsley
Dash of Tabasco sauce

Triggerfish
1 whole triggerfish, dressed
1/2 cup soy sauce

1/4 cup red wine
2 tablespoons chopped fresh ginger
1 red bell pepper, sliced
1 green bell pepper, sliced
1 yellow bell pepper, sliced
1 purple onion, sliced
1 tablespoon olive oil

For the mayonnaise, combine the sour cream, mayonnaise, garlic, parsley and Tabasco sauce in a bowl and mix well. Chill, covered, in the refrigerator.

For the triggerfish, place the fish in a large shallow dish. Mix the soy sauce, wine and ginger in a bowl and let stand for 10 minutes. Pour over the fish, turning to coat. Marinate in the refrigerator, turning occasionally. Grill on a gas grill until the fish flakes easily. Baste the peppers and onion with the olive oil and grill until the desired degree of crispness. Serve the fish with the grilled peppers, grilled onion and mayonnaise. For variety, brush the fish with the soy sauce mixture after grilling instead of marinating in the mixture.—Serves 4—**Jim O'Brien, New World Landing, 1997**

Grilled Triggerfish with Roasted Garlic Vinaigrette

1/2 cup balsamic vinegar
2 tablespoons roasted garlic purée
1 tablespoon basil pesto
1 teaspoon salt
1/2 teaspoon ground black pepper

11/2 cups vegetable oil
4 (6- to 8-ounce) triggerfish fillets
Salt and white pepper to taste
12 fresh tomato slices

Mix the vinegar, garlic purée, pesto, 1 teaspoon salt and the black pepper in a bowl. Add the oil gradually, whisking constantly until the oil is emulsified to form a vinaigrette. If the vinaigrette is too sharp, thin with some water. Season the fillets with salt and white pepper to taste. Spray with nonstick cooking spray. Grill on a gas grill until the fillets flake easily. Arrange the fillets on a bed of the sliced tomatoes on a platter. Drizzle each fillet with 2 tablespoons of the vinaigrette and garnish with a chiffonade of fresh basil and chopped kalamata olives.—Serves 4—**Anthony Redfield, Perdido Bay Restaurant, 1995**

Red Chile-Crusted Triggerfish with Avocado Corn Salsa

Avocado Corn Salsa
2 ripe avocados, chopped
3 to 4 ears roasted sweet white corn
2 red bell peppers, chopped
1 large Bermuda onion, chopped
3 small tomatillos, peeled and chopped
1/2 cup rice wine vinegar
1/2 cup Key West lime juice
1 tablespoon minced garlic
Salt and pepper to taste

Red Chile Sauce
4 or 5 red New Mexico or Anaheim
  chiles, roasted and seeded

3 very ripe Roma tomatoes, peeled
  and seeded
1 tablespoon roasted garlic
1 tablespoon red wine vinegar
1 tablespoon sugar
Salt and pepper to taste
1 cup extra-virgin olive oil

Triggerfish
4 (7- to 8-ounce) triggerfish fillets
Salad greens or mesclun mix

For the salsa, cut the kernels from the ears of corn into a bowl using a sharp knife. Combine the corn, avocados, bell peppers, onion, tomatillos, vinegar, lime juice, garlic, salt and pepper in a bowl and mix well. Chill, covered, for 1 hour.

For the sauce, combine the New Mexico chiles, tomatoes, garlic, vinegar, sugar, salt and pepper in a food processor and process until of a paste consistency. Add the olive oil gradually, processing constantly until the desired consistency.

For the triggerfish, remove the gill fat from the fillets. Coat the fillets with the sauce. Marinate in the sauce for 20 to 30 minutes for added heat. Grill on a gas grill for 2 to 3 minutes per side or until the fillets are opaque. Mound salad greens on four serving plates. Arrange the fillets on the outside edge of the greens. Serve warm or at room temperature with the salsa.—Serves 4—
Chuck Morgan, Dharma Blue, 1997

Sautéed Triggerfish with Guajillo Beurre Blanc

2 guajillo chiles, seeded
4 (6-ounce) triggerfish fillets
All-purpose flour
Olive oil
4 garlic cloves, chopped
2 tablespoons chopped shallots

3 peppercorns
1 bay leaf
1 tablespoon coriander seeds
2 cups (4 sticks) butter, softened
1/2 cup heavy cream
1/4 cup riesling

Soak the guajillo chiles in hot water in a bowl. Drain and chop. Coat the fillets in flour and sauté in olive oil in a skillet until the fillets flake easily. Remove to a platter and cover to keep warm.

Combine the guajillo chiles, garlic, shallots, peppercorns, bay leaf, coriander seeds and 2 tablespoons of the butter in a saucepan. Add the cream and cook until thickened, stirring frequently. Cook over high gas heat for 2 minutes. Stir in the wine and cook until reduced to one-third. Reduce the heat and gradually whisk in the remaining chopped butter. Strain through a chinois into a bowl, discarding the solids. Serve over the fillets.—Serves 4—**Jim Shirley, Fish House, 1998**

Triggerfish Del Sol

1 cup pineapple juice
1/2 cup white wine
Heavy cream to taste
1/2 cup (1 stick) butter, chopped
1/2 cup shelled sunflower seeds
1/2 cup bread crumbs

2 cups milk
2 eggs
1 (6-ounce) triggerfish fillet
1/2 cup all-purpose flour
1/4 cup vegetable oil
2 pineapple spears, grilled

Cook the pineapple juice and wine in a saucepan until almost reduced to dry. Stir in cream. Add the butter gradually and cook over low gas heat until blended and of a sauce consistency. Remove from the heat and cover to keep warm. Process the sunflower seeds in a food processor until ground and toss with the bread crumbs in a bowl. Whisk the milk and eggs in a bowl until blended.

Dust the fillet with the flour and dip in the egg mixture. Coat with the bread crumb mixture and pat lightly. Heat the oil in a sauté pan. Sauté the fillet in the hot oil until the fillet flakes easily, turning once. Serve with the sauce and pineapple.—Serves 1—**Kevin Faoutas, The Veranda at Henderson Park Inn, 1995**

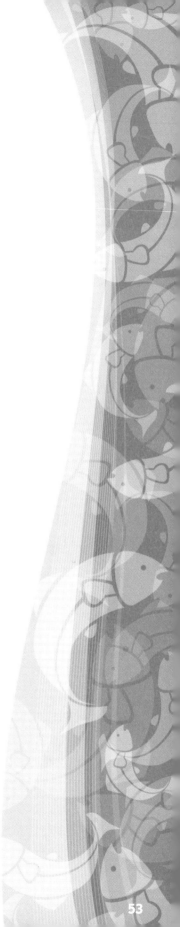

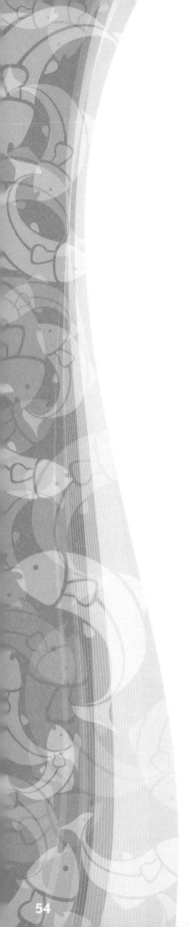

Pecan-Crusted Triggerfish

2 cups milk
3 eggs
2 cups all-purpose flour
1 1/2 cups crushed pecan pieces
2 tablespoons salt
2 tablespoons onion powder

1 tablespoon garlic powder
1 teaspoon pepper
4 (8-ounce) triggerfish fillets
1/4 cup olive oil
Splash of white wine

Whisk the milk and eggs in a bowl until blended. Mix the flour, pecans, salt, onion powder, garlic powder and pepper in a shallow dish. Dust the fillets with the flour mixture and then dip in the egg mixture. Repeat the process with the remaining flour mixture and the remaining egg mixture for double breading.

Heat the olive oil in a large ovenproof sauté pan and add the fillets. Cook for 3 to 4 minutes per side or until golden brown. Drizzle with a splash of wine. Bake at 400 degrees in a gas oven for 4 minutes.—Serves 4—**David Oreskovich and Pasco Gibson, Oyster Bar/Nichols Seafood, 2003**

Tuna Ceviche

1/2 cup fresh lemon juice
1/2 cup fresh lime juice
1/4 cup orange juice
1/4 cup pineapple juice
Leaves of 6 sprigs of parsley, chopped
Leaves of 6 sprigs of cilantro, chopped
2 tablespoons salt
1 tablespoon pepper
1 tablespoon Tabasco sauce

1 tablespoon ground cumin
1 1/2 pounds sushi-grade tuna
1 kiwifruit, chopped
1/4 pineapple, chopped
1/4 cantaloupe, chopped
1/4 honeydew melon, chopped
1/4 red bell pepper, chopped
1/4 green bell pepper, chopped

Mix the lemon juice, lime juice, orange juice and pineapple juice in a bowl. Stir in the parsley and cilantro. Add the salt, pepper, Tabasco sauce and cumin and mix well. Cut the tuna into 3/8-inch pieces and add to the lemon juice mixture. Stir in the kiwifruit, pineapple, cantaloupe, honeydew melon and bell peppers. Marinate, covered, in the refrigerator for 5 hours. Serve chilled as a appetizer, entrée or salad.—Serves 6—**Alphonse Lucier IV, Pensacola Country Club, 2003**

Tempura-Crusted Spicy Tuna Roll with Ginger Coconut Sauce

1/4 cup wasabi paste
6 asparagus spears
12 slices red bell pepper
4 ounces sushi-grade tuna
3 cups cooked sushi rice
6 sheets nori
1 can coconut milk
1/4 cup white wine
1/4 cup water
3 tablespoons ginger essence
2 tablespoons soy sauce
1 teaspoon curry powder
1 teaspoon salt
Vegetable oil
3 cups tempura batter

Enclose equal portions of the wasabi, asparagus, bell pepper and tuna in the rice in the order listed and wrap with the nori. Chill in the refrigerator.

Combine the coconut milk, wine, water, ginger essence, soy sauce, curry powder and salt in a saucepan and mix well. Cook over medium gas heat for 5 minutes, stirring constantly.

Heat oil in a deep skillet to 350 degrees. Cut the rolls into halves and coat with the batter. Fry the rolls in the hot oil until golden brown on all sides; drain. Serve with the sauce.—Serves 4—**Alphonse Lucier IV, Eat!, 2004**

Black Pepper and Sesame-Crusted Tuna with Fried Southwest Ravioli

Mango Jalapeño Salsa
1 mango, cut into 1/2-inch pieces
2 fresh jalapeño chiles, cut into
    1/2-inch pieces
1 red bell pepper, cut into
    1/2-inch pieces
1/2 purple onion, cut into
    1/2-inch pieces
2 tablespoons rice wine vinegar
2 tablespoons honey
1 tablespoon soy sauce
2 teaspoons chopped cilantro
Salt and pepper to taste

Tuna
1/4 to 1/2 cup cracked black pepper
1/4 to 1/2 cup sesame seeds, toasted
1 (28- to 32-ounce) tuna loin
2 to 3 tablespoons olive oil
3 to 4 cups corn oil or canola oil
Southwest-flavored ravioli
8 ounces mesclun mix

For the salsa, combine the mango, jalapeño chiles, bell pepper and onion in a bowl and mix well. Whisk the vinegar, honey, soy sauce and cilantro in a bowl until combined and season with salt and pepper. Add to the mango mixture, tossing to coat.

For the tuna, mix the pepper and sesame seeds in a shallow dish. Rub the surface of the tuna with some of the olive oil and coat with the pepper mixture. Heat the remaining olive oil in a large sauté pan over high gas heat. Sear both sides of the tuna until a crust forms. Cut the tuna into four 7- to 8-ounce steaks. Grill the steaks on a gas grill for 3 to 5 minutes or until medium rare or slightly pink in the center. Remove to a platter and cover to keep warm.

Heat the corn oil in a large saucepan to 350 degrees. Fry raviolis in the hot oil until golden brown on all sides. Remove to paper towels to drain. Divide the mesclun mix evenly among four serving plates. Arrange one steak on each serving and top equally with the salsa. Serve with the fried raviolis.—Serves 4—**Chuck Morgan, Dharma Blue, 1996**

Blushing Lady Tuna

Garlic Mayonnaise Sauce
1 cup mayonnaise
1 cup sour cream
1/4 cup minced garlic
1/4 cup chopped green onions
2 teaspoons Worcestershire sauce
1 teaspoon hot red pepper sauce
Salt and coarsely ground pepper
    to taste

Red Pepper Coulis
6 large red bell peppers, chopped
6 tomatoes, seeded and chopped
1 cup chicken stock

1 teaspoon basil
1 teaspoon coarsely ground pepper
Salt to taste
Dash of hot red pepper sauce (optional)
1/2 cup (1 stick) butter, softened

Tuna
1/2 cup (1 stick) butter
1 teaspoon lemon juice
1 teaspoon Worcestershire sauce
1 teaspoon hot red pepper sauce
1 (8-ounce) tuna steak, swordfish steak
    or any fish steak

For the sauce, combine the mayonnaise, sour cream, garlic, green onions, Worcestershire sauce, hot sauce, salt and pepper in a bowl and mix well. Chill, covered, for 30 minutes.

For the coulis, combine the bell peppers, tomatoes, stock, basil, pepper, salt and hot sauce in a saucepan and bring to a boil. Reduce the gas heat and simmer for about 10 minutes or until the liquid is reduced by half. Combine the bell pepper mixture and butter in a blender or food processor and process until blended.

For the tuna, melt the butter in a saucepan and stir in the lemon juice, Worcestershire sauce and hot sauce. Brush the steak with the butter mixture. Grill on a gas grill or panfry in a skillet for 4 to 6 minutes per side or to the desired degree of doneness. Heat the coulis in a saucepan and spread just enough over the bottom of a serving plate to cover. Top with the steak and the desired amount of the sauce.—Serves 1—**Gustavus Myers IV, New England House of Seafood, 1995**

Carbie Tuna Napoleon with Pink Peppercorn Vinaigrette

Pink Peppercorn Vinaigrette
3/4 cup olive oil
1/4 cup raspberry vinegar
1/4 cup minced fresh cilantro
2 tablespoons soy sauce
2 tablespoons pink peppercorns
1 teaspoon grated fresh ginger
1/2 teaspoon brown sugar

Tuna
4 (6-ounce) tuna steaks
Olive oil
Carribean spice blend to taste
2 jumbo sweet potatoes, baked and cut into 8 thick medallions
Sections of 1 lemon
Sections of 1 lime
Sections of 1 orange

For the vinaigrette, combine the olive oil, vinegar, cilantro, soy sauce, peppercorns, ginger and brown sugar in a jar with a tight-fitting lid and seal tightly. Shake to mix.

For the tuna, coat the steaks with olive oil and sprinkle with Carribean spice blend. Grill on a gas grill until medium-rare.

Rub the sweet potato medallions with olive oil and grill on a gas grill. Stack one sweet potato medallion, one steak and then another sweet potato medallion on a serving plate and drizzle with 1/4 cup of the vinaigrette. Arrange some of the lemon sections, lime sections and orange sections around the napoleon. Repeat the process with the remaining ingredients. Garnish with sprigs of cilantro.—Serves 4—**Jimmy McManus, Bon Appétit Waterfront Cafe, 1997**

Crusted Tuna Medallions with Vegetable Salad

Creole Vinaigrette
2 tablespoons safflower oil
2 tablespoons mineral water
1 tablespoon rice wine vinegar
2 teaspoons minced shallots
2 teaspoons minced chives
2 teaspoons Creole mustard
1 garlic clove, minced
Dash of soy sauce

Vegetable Salad
8 ounces carrots, julienned
4 ounces spicy sprouts
4 ounces napa cabbage, shredded

4 ounces daikon, julienned
1/2 ounce pickled ginger, minced
1 teaspoon sesame seeds
   (natural and black)

Tuna
2 tablespoons black sesame seeds
2 tablespoons freshly cracked pepper
2 tablespoons natural sesame seeds
1 tablespoon grated fresh ginger
11/2 to 2 pounds center-cut tuna
Olive oil
1 teaspoon minced garlic
Salt to taste

For the vinaigrette, combine the safflower oil, mineral water, vinegar, shallots, chives, Creole mustard, garlic and soy sauce in a jar with a tight-fitting lid and seal tightly. Shake to combine. Chill in the refrigerator.

For the salad, toss the carrots, sprouts, cabbage, daikon, ginger and sesame seeds in a bowl. Add half the vinaigrette and mix until coated.

For the tuna, mix the black sesame seeds and pepper in a shallow dish. Mix the natural sesame seeds and ginger in a shallow dish. Rub the tuna with olive oil and the garlic and season with salt. Press opposite sides of the tuna in the black mixture and press the remaining two sides with the white mixture.

Sear the tuna on all sides on a gas grill until the desired degree of doneness. If you prefer tuna that is medium-well to well, finish cooking in a gas oven. Let the tuna rest; cut into 1/2-inch medallions. Mound the salad equally on each of six serving plates and top with the medallions. Drizzle with the remaining vinaigrette.—Serves 6—**Scott Wilson, Radley's Deli After Dark, 1995**

Tuna with Ratatouille and Black Olive Vinaigrette

Black Olive Vinaigrette
1/2 cup olive oil
1/4 cup red wine vinegar
1/2 cup pitted niçoise olives
2 garlic cloves, chopped
1 tablespoon honey
1 teaspoon Creole mustard
Salt and pepper to taste

Ratatouille and Tuna
1 large eggplant, cut lengthwise
   into quarters
3 onions, cut into quarters
2 zucchini, cut lengthwise into quarters

2 yellow squash, cut lengthwise
   into quarters
3 green bell peppers, cut into halves
3 red bell peppers, cut into halves
3 yellow bell peppers, cut into halves
Extra-virgin olive oil for coating
Salt and pepper to taste
8 garlic cloves, chopped
1/4 cup extra-virgin olive oil
5 tomatoes, seeded and chopped
6 to 8 ounces fresh basil, trimmed
   and chopped
4 (6- to 8-ounce) tuna steaks

For the vinaigrette, combine the olive oil, vinegar, olives, garlic, honey and Creole mustard in a blender or food processor and process until smooth. Season with salt and pepper.

For the ratatouille and tuna, toss the eggplant, onions, zucchini, yellow squash and bell peppers with olive oil for coating in a bowl and season with salt and pepper. Grill the cooked vegetables on a gas grill until grill marks appear on all sides. Let stand until cool; chop the grilled vegetables into large chunks. Toss together in a large bowl.

Heat a large sauté pan and add the garlic and 1/4 cup olive oil. Cook until the garlic is fragrant and then add the grilled vegetables. Cook until heated through. Do not overcook the vegetables. Add the tomatoes and cook for 1 minute. Remove from the heat and stir in the basil.

Grill the steaks on a gas grill to the desired degree of doneness. Spoon the ratatouille equally in the center of four serving plates and top each serving with one steak. Drizzle with the vinaigrette and garnish with sprigs of fresh basil.—Serves 4—**John Huggins, McGuire's Irish Pub, 2004**

Mediterranean Tuna

2 (6- to 8-ounce) tuna steaks,
   1 1/2 inches thick
Olive oil
Salt and pepper to taste
1 tablespoon finely chopped
   yellow onion
1 tablespoon finely chopped red
   bell pepper
1 tablespoon finely chopped green
   bell pepper

1 tablespoon sliced black olives
1 tablespoon sliced green olives
1 tablespoon finely chopped
   Roma tomato
1 tablespoon chopped garlic
2 tablespoons white wine
1 tablespoon lemon juice
Pinch of oregano
Pinch of salt
3 tablespoons unsalted butter, chopped

Coat the steaks with olive oil and season with salt and pepper to taste. Grill on a gas grill for 3 to 4 minutes per side for medium. Remove the steaks to a platter and cover to keep warm.

Sauté the onion and bell peppers in olive oil in a skillet for 1 minute. Stir in the olives, tomato and garlic and sauté for 30 seconds. Add the wine, lemon juice, oregano and a pinch of salt and cook until the mixture is reduced by half. Add the butter gradually and cook until incorporated, swirling the pan frequently. Arrange each steak on a serving plate and top evenly with the sautéed vegetable mixture.—Serves 2—**Buzz Valadao, Ryan's Catch, 1999**

Tuna Stack

1 (4-ounce) tuna steak
1 tablespoon olive oil
Salt and pepper to taste
3 slices green tomato
All-purpose flour
1 egg, beaten
2 tablespoons water

1/2 cup ground pecans
1/4 cup bread crumbs
Vegetable oil
3 tablespoons honey
1 tablespoon horseradish
1 teaspoon chopped parsley
Spring salad mix

Coat the steak with the olive oil and season with salt and pepper. Grill on a gas grill over high heat to the desired degree of doneness; slice. Coat the tomato slices with flour and dip in a mixture of the egg and water. Coat with the pecans and bread crumbs.

Fry the tomato slices in vegetable oil in a skillet for about 2 minutes or until light brown; drain. Mix the honey, horseradish and parsley in a bowl. Mound spring mix in the center of a serving plate. Alternate the tomato slices with the tuna slices over the spring mix. Drizzle with the honey glaze and garnish with toasted pecan halves.—Serves 1—**Jim O'Brien, O'Brien's Bistro, 2002**

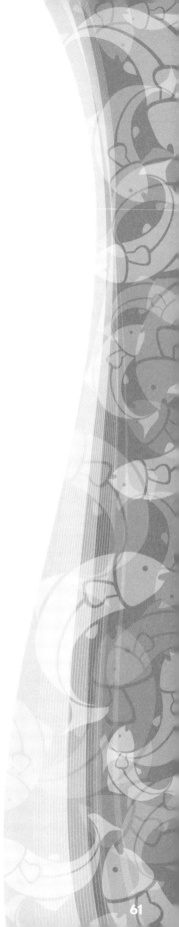

Grilled Pesto Tuna Steak with Balsamic Pan Sauce

Tuna
2 (7-ounce) tuna steaks
1/2 cup balsamic vinaigrette
1/4 cup olive oil
Salt and pepper to taste
1 bunch thyme
8 fingerling potatoes, cut into halves
3 Roma tomatoes, cut into wedges
2 to 3 tablespoons pesto

Balsamic Pan Sauce and Assembly
3/4 cup balsamic vinaigrette
Juice of 2 lemons
1 tablespoon chopped shallot
1 teaspoon minced garlic
1 teaspoon minced kalamata olives
1 teaspoon rinsed capers
16 ounces fresh spinach
1 bunch basil, julienned

For the tuna, arrange the steaks in a shallow dish and pour the vinaigrette over the steaks, turning to coat. Marinate, covered, in the refrigerator for 2 hours, turning occasionally. Coat the bottom of a baking pan with the olive oil. Sprinkle with salt, pepper and the thyme. Arrange the potatoes cut side down and the tomatoes in the seasoned oil. Roast at 375 degrees in a gas oven for 30 minutes. Remove the potatoes and tomatoes to a plate. Drain the steaks. Grill the steaks on one side on a gas grill over medium-high gas heat. Turn and spread generously with the pesto. Grill to the desired degree of doneness.

For the sauce, bring the vinaigrette to a simmer in a saucepan and add the lemon juice, shallot, garlic, olives and capers. Simmer to the desired consistency. Toss the spinach with 2 tablespoons of the sauce in a bowl. Mound the desired amount of spinach on two serving plates and top each serving with one of the steaks. Arrange the roasted potatoes and tomatoes evenly on the plates. Spoon the remaining sauce over the steaks and top with the basil.—Serves 2—**Irv Miller, Jackson's, 2004**

Tuna Confit Salad with Fried Zucchini

Fused Herb Oil
4 cups olive oil
2 ounces Vidalia onion, chopped
1 fennel bulb, thinly sliced
2 bay leaves
2 garlic cloves
Black peppercorns to taste
2 sprigs of basil
2 sprigs of thyme

Tuna Salad
1 red bell pepper
1 tablespoon capers
2 tablespoons balsamic vinegar
1 (10-ounce) tuna steak
1 tablespoon kosher salt
1 zucchini, julienned lengthwise
Seasoned all-purpose flour
Vegetable oil
2 cups mixed baby salad greens
8 asparagus spears, blanched
2 hard-cooked eggs, sliced or cut into wedges
2 tablespoons chopped red onion

For the oil, combine the olive oil, onion, fennel, bay leaves, garlic, peppercorns, basil and thyme in a saucepan and bring to a simmer. Simmer for 30 minutes, stirring occasionally. Strain, discarding the solids.

For the tuna, roast the bell pepper over a gas flame until charred; cool slightly. Peel and seed. Process the bell pepper, capers, vinegar and 1/4 cup of the herb oil in a blender until puréed. Sprinkle the steak with the salt and let stand for 10 to 15 minutes. Poach the steak in the remaining herb oil in a skillet to the desired degree of doneness. Dust the zucchini with seasoned flour and fry in oil in a skillet until light brown; drain.

Mound the salad greens evenly on two serving plates. Slice the tuna as desired and arrange over the greens. Drizzle with the bell pepper dressing. Top with the zucchini, asparagus, eggs and onion.—Serves 2—**Travis Herr, Bill Hamilton and Culinary Students, Pensacola Junior College, 2003**

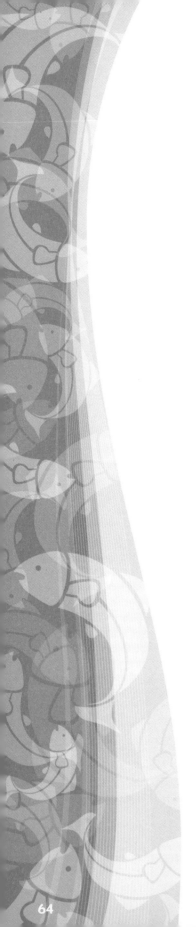

Grilled Yellowfin Tuna with Black Bean and Mango Salsa

Black Bean and Mango Salsa
6 ounces canned black beans, drained and rinsed
1 mango, finely chopped
1 red bell pepper, finely chopped
1/4 cup olive oil
2 tablespoons lime juice
2 tablespoons chopped garlic
2 tablespoons vinegar
1 tablespoon chopped fresh parsley
1 tablespoon chopped fresh cilantro
Salt and pepper to taste

Tuna
4 (4-ounce) yellowfin tuna steaks
2 tablespoons salt and pepper blend
2 tablespoons olive oil

For the salsa, combine the beans, mango, bell pepper, olive oil, lime juice, garlic, vinegar, parsley and cilantro in a bowl and mix well. Season with salt and pepper.

For the tuna, season the steaks with the salt and pepper blend and coat with the olive oil. Sear on a gas grill over high heat for 1¹/2 minutes per side or until medium-rare. Thinly slice the tuna and arrange equally on four serving plates. Top each serving with one-fourth of the salsa.—Serves 4—**Jim O'Brien, O'Brien's Bistro, 2004**

TIP Tuna is traditionally cooked to rare or medium-rare in the center. For a rare center, cook for 2 minutes per side; for a medium center, cook for 3 to 5 minutes per side; and for a well-done center, cook for 5 to 8 minutes per side.

Banana-Crusted Yellowfin Tuna

Asian Slaw
5 cups shredded napa cabbage
3 cups chopped bok choy
1 cup golden raisins, minced
1 cup almonds, sliced
1 cup shredded carrots
1/4 cup fresh cilantro, minced
1 tablespoon ginger
1 cup vegetable oil
1/2 cup mirin
1/2 cup white vinegar
1/2 cup confectioners' sugar

Soy Orange Sauce
1 cup orange marmalade
1/2 cup vegetable oil

1/3 cup red wine vinegar
1/3 cup soy sauce
2 teaspoons lemon oil
2 teaspoons lime oil

Tuna and Assembly
5 eggs
1/2 cup milk
4 (8-ounce) yellowfin tuna fillets
2 cups all-purpose flour
2 cups banana chips, ground
Clarified butter

For the slaw, toss the cabbage, bok choy, raisins, almonds, carrots, cilantro and ginger in a bowl. Whisk the oil, wine, vinegar and confectioners' sugar in a bowl until blended. Add to the cabbage mixture and mix until coated.

For the sauce, process the marmalade, vegetable oil, vinegar, soy sauce, lemon oil and lime oil in a blender until puréed.

For the tuna, whisk the eggs and milk in a bowl until blended. Coat the fillets with the flour and then dip in the egg mixture. Press the banana chips over both sides of the fillets. Sauté the fillets in clarified butter in a skillet for 2 minutes per side for medium-rare or to the desired degree of doneness. Spoon some of the sauce over the bottom of each of four serving plates and top each serving with one fillet. Serve the slaw on the side.—Serves 4—**Stephen Gamble and Stephen Barber, Pensacola Yacht Club, 2005**

TIP Yellowfin tuna can weigh up to 300 pounds, but average weights in commercial catches are between 20 and 100 pounds. In Florida yellowfin are commercially harvested exclusively with hook-and-line, which makes the fishery "dolphin safe."

Red Hot Chile and Sesame-Seared Tuna with Jasmine Rice Cakes

Tahini Sauce
10 ounces tahini
2 tablespoons cane syrup
1 tablespoon roasted garlic
1 tablespoon grated fresh ginger
5 tablespoons soy sauce
1/4 cup rice wine vinegar
2 tablespoons Worcestershire sauce
2 teaspoons sesame oil

Sweet Red Chile Sauce
1 1/2 cups apple cider or white vinegar
1 cup sugar
1 cup corn syrup
1/2 cup chopped hot chiles or crushed
   red pepper

Sesame Red Chile Dust
1 cup whole Thai chiles

1 cup untoasted sesame seeds
1 teaspoon kosher salt

Jasmine Rice Cakes
4 cups jasmine rice, cooked and cooled
3 eggs, lightly beaten
1/2 cup finely chopped red bell pepper
1/4 cup finely chopped fresh chives
1/2 cup all-purpose flour
Salt and pepper to taste
1/4 cup canola oil

Tuna and Assembly
1 (10-ounce) yellowfin tuna steak
Canola oil
2 ounces sesame seaweed salad
1 vegetable spring roll, fried and cut
   into halves on the bias
1 tablespoon soy reduction

For the tahini sauce, combine the tahini, syrup, garlic and ginger in a food processor and process for 20 seconds or until the mixture begins to bind and resemble the consistency of peanut butter. Add the remaining ingredients and process until blended. Spoon into a squeeze bottle.

For the chile sauce, combine the apple cider, sugar and corn syrup in a saucepan and bring to a boil. Boil for 5 minutes or until the sugar dissolves. Stir in the hot peppers and cook for 1 minute.

For the pepper dust, spread the chiles on a baking sheet. Bake at 250 degrees in a gas oven for 8 to 10 minutes. Remove to a plate and let stand until cool. Process the chiles in a food processor until finely chopped. Add the sesame seeds and salt. Pulse to combine. Store in an airtight container.

For the rice cakes, combine the rice, eggs, bell pepper, chives, flour, salt and pepper in a bowl and mix well. Shape the rice mixture into small patties. Sauté in the canola oil in a skillet until golden brown on both sides; drain. Remove to a platter and cover to keep warm.

For the tuna, coat the steak with 4 ounces of the pepper dust. Sear the steak on both sides in canola oil in a skillet over high gas heat for about 30 seconds, turning once. Remove to a paper towel to drain. Arrange the rice cakes in the center of a serving plate. Cut the steak on the bias into halves and place over the rice cakes. Mound 1 ounce of the seaweed salad on each side of the steak. Arrange the spring roll next to the steak. Drizzle 2 tablespoons of the tahini sauce, 2 tablespoons of the chile sauce and the soy reduction on and around the steak. Garnish with thinly sliced red bell pepper curls and green onions curls that have soaked in ice water for 1 hour. Spear the spring roll halves with fresh chives.—Serves 1—**Scott Weichbrodt, Jackson's, 2000**

Grilled Wahoo with Gazpacho Sauce

3 tablespoons extra-virgin olive oil
1 cup finely chopped seeded tomato
1/2 cup finely chopped yellow onion
1/2 cup finely chopped yellow or green
  bell pepper
1/4 cup finely chopped seeded cucumber
1 teaspoon finely chopped garlic
2 1/2 cups Bloody Mary mix
Fresh lime juice to taste

4 (7-ounce) wahoo steaks
Olive oil for coating
Kosher salt and cracked pepper to taste
1/4 teaspoon ground cumin
1/4 teaspoon minced fresh or dried
  dill weed
1/4 teaspoon minced fresh or
  dried savory
Sour cream (optional)

Heat 3 tablespoons olive oil in a skillet over medium gas heat and add the tomato, onion, bell pepper, cucumber and garlic. Sauté for 2 minutes or just until the vegetables are tender. Stir in the Bloody Mary mix and lime juice.

Brush the steaks with olive oil for coating and sprinkle with salt, pepper, cumin, dill weed and savory. Grill the steaks on a gas grill to the desired degree of doneness. Arrange one steak on each of four serving plates. Top each with 1/4 cup of the gazpacho sauce and a dollop of sour cream. Serve with hot cooked rice and grilled vegetables.—Serves 4—**Irv Miller, Jackson's, 2008**

Jazz on the Grill

1/4 cup (1/2 stick) butter, melted
1/4 cup olive oil
1/2 cup finely chopped pineapple
1/4 cup finely chopped seeded
  jalapeño chiles

1/4 cup honey
4 (8-ounce) fish fillets or steaks
  (salmon, bass, halibut, mahi mahi,
  yellowtail or lingcod)
Green leaf lettuce

Mix the butter and olive oil in a bowl. Combine the pineapple, jalapeño chiles and honey in a bowl and mix well. Brush both sides of the fillets with the olive oil mixture. Sear on both sides on a gas grill over high heat, basting with the remaining olive oil mixture before and after turning. Reduce the gas heat to low and cover with the lid. Grill for several minutes and then drizzle with the pineapple mixture. Grill, covered, until the desired degree of doneness. Do not overcook. Adjust grilling times based on the thickness of the fillets. Arrange the fillets on a bed of lettuce on a platter. —Serves 4—**Keith Hoffert, Versailles, 2007**

Local Fish in Foil with Grilled Pineapple Salsa

Grilled Pineapple Salsa
1 pineapple
1/2 red onion, sliced
1 teaspoon olive oil
1 red bell pepper, chopped
2 teaspoons brown sugar
1 bunch scallions, chopped
2 tablespoons chopped cilantro
Juice of 1 lime
2 tablespoons red wine vinegar

Local Fish
1 (8- to 10-ounce) fish fillet of choice
2 tablespoons extra-virgin olive oil
1 plum tomato, chopped
2 garlic cloves, crushed
Fresh basil to taste
Fresh oregano to taste
Fresh parsley to taste
Salt and pepper to taste

For the salsa, cut the pineapple lengthwise into 1/4-inch slices, avoiding the tough core. Grill the slices on a gas grill over medium-high heat for a few minutes on each side. Chop the pineapple into small pieces and place in a bowl. Sweat the onion in the olive oil in a sauté pan. Stir in the bell pepper and brown sugar and add to the pineapple. Add the scallions, cilantro, lime juice and vinegar and mix well. Let stand at room temperature for 1 hour. May also serve with chicken, pork or shrimp.

For the fish, place the fillet on a sheet of foil large enough to enclose. Top with the olive oil, tomato, garlic, basil, oregano, parsley, salt and pepper. Wrap with the foil to completely enclose. Grill on a gas grill for 10 to 15 minutes or until the fillet flakes easily. Unwrap the fillet and place on a serving plate. Serve with the salsa.—Serves 1—**Jimmy McManus, Bon Appétit Waterfront Cafe, 1998**

Clams, Oysters & Scallops

Oysters by the sack from world-famous Apalachicola or, if you're lucky and the weather is right, from the even-more-local East Bay beds off Santa Rosa County. Scallops, the succulent bay or the "diver," harvested by hand from the depths of the Gulf of Mexico. Clams, sweet and tasty, from Cedar Key. All these bivalves play a role on the menus of chefs in the Pensacola area.

The oysters from Apalachicola are known worldwide, but in recent years savvy local chefs have been taking advantage of oysters from our "local" waters of East Bay. These beds, privately farmed and closely tended, offer up some of the most succulent, saltiest oysters to be found anywhere along the Emerald Coast of Northwest Florida. Eaten "nude," (cracked open and served raw on-the-half-shell) may be the way to show off oysters at their pearly best, but local chefs have also found any number of other ways to bring the "erster" into play. Fried, char-grilled, steamed, or broiled, the oyster magically takes on different characteristics—texture, intensity of flavor—depending on how they are utilized. And then there is oyster bisque or stew, oysters with pasta, oysters en brochette, and oysters in seafood gumbo. However they are prepared and consumed, the oyster remains at the pinnacle of our area's seafood.

With July comes the eagerly anticipated arrival of the bay scallop season, a three-month-long window when the sweet-tasting scallops can be harvested in waters from Bay County to Pasco County along Florida's "Big Bend." The tasty, bite-sized morsels, mild and fresh, can become a welcome ingredient in pasta dishes, flash-fried whole, or broiled. The larger "diver" scallops, some as large as a hamburger patty, can constitute a meal by themselves. Local chefs love to sear them quickly over a hot grill and then serve them simply so their unique, briny flavor comes through.

Mahogany Clams with Chorizo and Chiles

1 pound Yukon potatoes, cut into quarters
1 tablespoon vegetable oil
4 pounds mahogany clams (small steamers)
1 cup water
3 ounces chorizo, chopped
Juice of 1 lime
1 tablespoon chopped ancho chiles
4 Roma tomatoes, chopped
1 cup (2 sticks) butter, chopped
1 tablespoon chopped cilantro
Salt and pepper to taste

Toss the potatoes with the oil in a bowl. Arrange the potatoes in a single layer on a baking sheet. Roast at 350 degrees in a gas oven for about 20 minutes or until light brown. Cool slightly and place in a large serving bowl.

Scrub the clams under cold running water. Combine the clams, water, chorizo, lime juice and ancho chiles in a large sauté pan and bring to a simmer. Simmer, covered, until the clams open. Discard any clams that do not open. Stir in the tomatoes, butter, cilantro, salt and pepper. Simmer until heated through. Pour the clam mixture over the potatoes and serve with French bread or sliced baguette.—Serves 6—**Dan Dunn, Lou Michael's Downtown, 2001**

TIP Clams should never be exposed to sudden temperature change. Do not place live clams directly on ice or immerse in water for storage purposes.

Steamed Mahogany Clams over Pole Bean and Red Onion Salad

Pole Bean and Red Onion Salad
4 ounces fresh pole beans, cut into
   4-inch pieces
1/4 cup olive oil
1/4 teaspoon white wine vinegar
1 garlic clove, chopped
1/4 teaspoon Dijon mustard
Salt and pepper to taste
1 red onion, thinly sliced
4 black olives, sliced
1 1/2 teaspoons chopped parsley

Mahogany Clams
3 dozen mahogany clams
Salt to taste
3 tablespoons butter
2 tablespoons chopped garlic
2 tablespoons chopped shallots
3 fresh bay leaves
1 sprig of thyme
4 peppercorns
Salt and pepper to taste
1/4 cup dry white wine
1/4 cup water
1 1/2 teaspoons chopped parsley

For the salad, steam or boil the beans in a saucepan for 5 minutes. Drain and immediately plunge the beans into a bowl of ice water to stop the cooking process. Drain and pat dry with paper towels. Whisk the olive oil, vinegar, garlic, Dijon mustard, salt and pepper in a bowl until combined. Add the beans, onion and olives and mix until coated. Stir in the parsley. Chill, covered, in the refrigerator.

For the clams, scrub the clams under cold running water and then soak in a bowl of salt water for 1 hour to purge the grit. Drain and chill. Melt the butter in a heavy saucepan and stir in the garlic, shallots, bay leaves, thyme, peppercorns, salt and pepper.

Cook for 4 to 5 minutes; stir in the clams. Mix in the wine and water. Cook, covered, over high gas heat until the clams open; drain. Discard any clams that do not open. Spoon the desired amount of the bean salad on each of two serving plates. Add equal portions of the clams to the plates and sprinkle with the parsley.—Serves 2—**Brad Parker, The Grille at Osceola, 2002**

TIP Live clams should close tightly when the shell is tapped. Discard clams that do not close. Shucked clams will keep up to seven days in the refrigerator.

Oysters Eros

1 cup sake
1 (2-inch) piece fresh ginger, cut into
 1/4-inch slices
2 shallots, minced
1 cup (2 sticks) butter, thinly sliced
 and softened
1 dozen fresh spinach leaves

1 tablespoon sake
1 teaspoon sesame oil
1 dozen oysters on the half shell
3 ounces prosciutto, thinly sliced
 into 12 (3/4-inch) strips
1/2 cup chopped chives

Heat 1 cup sake in a saucepan over medium gas heat. Bruise the ginger slices with the handle of a knife and add to the wine with the shallots. Cook until the liquid is reduced to 2 tablespoons. Remove from the heat and gradually whisk in the butter. Strain through a chinois into a bowl, discarding the solids. Cover to keep warm.

Wilt the spinach in a sauté pan with 1 tablespoon sake and the sesame oil. Remove the oysters from the shells and wrap each oyster with one spinach leaf and one strip of prosciutto. Return the oysters to the shells. Arrange the oysters in a baking pan. Broil in a gas oven for 6 to 10 minutes or until the prosciutto begins to crisp. Drizzle with the warm sake butter and sprinkle with the chives. Asian pear-infused sake is recommended for this recipe.—Serves 2—**Jim Shirley, Fish House, 2000**

Cornmeal-Crusted Oysters with Turnip Greens and Vidalia Onion Sauce

1 teaspoon olive oil
1 Vidalia onion, finely chopped
2 cups heavy cream
2 tablespoons butter
Salt and pepper to taste
1 cup milk

1 egg
20 select oysters, shucked
1 cup all-purpose flour
1 cup white cornmeal
1 cup vegetable oil
2 cups frozen turnip greens, thawed

Heat the olive oil in a saucepan and add the onion. Reduce the gas heat and cook until the onion is tender but not brown. Stir in the cream and cook until reduced to 3/4 cup or to a sauce consistency. Pour into a blender and add the butter. Process until puréed and season with salt and pepper.

Whisk the milk and egg in a bowl until blended. Season the oysters with salt and pepper. Coat the oysters with the flour, dip in the egg mixture and then coat with the cornmeal. Heat the vegetable oil in a deep skillet; add the oysters. Fry for 3 to 5 minutes or to the desired crispness; drain.

Heat the turnip greens in a saucepan and season with salt and pepper. Spoon the turnip greens evenly on each of two serving plates and arrange ten oysters on each plate. Drizzle the sauce around the greens.—Serves 2—**Gus Silivos, Skopelos on the Bay, 1997**

Semolina-Fried Oyster Po-Boy with Homemade Pickles

Homemade Pickles
1¹/2 cups white vinegar
1 cup sugar
1 teaspoon mustard seeds
1 teaspoon peppercorns
1 teaspoon salt
3 cups sliced cucumbers
2 white onions, thinly sliced

Oyster Po-Boy
2 cups semolina flour
1 tablespoon garlic powder
1 tablespoon onion powder
Salt and pepper to taste
3 cups vegetable oil
10 oysters, shucked
1 po-boy bun, split
Mayonnaise to taste
Shaved cabbage

For the pickles, heat the vinegar, sugar, mustard seeds, peppercorns and salt in a saucepan until the sugar dissolves. Pour over the cucumbers and onions in a heatproof bowl. Marinate, covered, in the refrigerator for 24 to 48 hours.

For the po-boy, mix the semolina flour, garlic powder, onion powder, salt and pepper in a shallow dish. Heat the oil in a deep skillet to 350 degrees. Coat the oysters with the flour mixture and fry in the hot oil until golden brown; drain. Spread the bun with mayonnaise and arrange the oysters on the bottom half. Top with the pickles, cabbage and the remaining bun half.—Serves 1—
Brian Culleton, Dharma Blue, 2008

TIP Along Florida's Gulf Coast, oysters are harvested commercially from small boats by fishermen using large, long-handled tongs to scoop the oysters from the sandy bottom beds.

Tropical Scallop Ceviche with Plantain Planks

Scallop Ceviche
2 pounds shucked calico scallops
3 cups fresh lime juice
1 cup chopped mango
1/2 cup chopped red onion
1/2 cup chopped red bell pepper
1/2 cup orange sections
1/2 cup grapefruit sections
1 tablespoon minced jalapeño chile
1 cup cilantro, chopped
1/2 cup chopped seeded tomato
Salt and pepper to taste

Plantain Planks
2 green plantains
Peanut oil
Salt to taste
Ground cumin to taste
Coriander to taste

For the ceviche, combine the scallops, lime juice, mango, onion, bell pepper, orange sections, grapefruit sections and jalapeño chile in a large nonreactive bowl and mix well. Marinate, covered, in the refrigerator for 2 hours, stirring occasionally. Stir in the cilantro, tomato, salt and pepper. Serve chilled.

For the planks, slice the plantains lengthwise into very thin slices. Fry in 375-degree peanut oil in a deep skillet for about 3 to 4 minutes or until crisp. Drain on paper towels. Season with salt, cumin and coriander. Serve hot with the ceviche.—Serves 4 to 6—**Tom McGinty, Florida Department of Agriculture and Consumer Sciences, 2001**

 TIP Scallops do not close their shells tightly. Therefore, they are shucked soon after harvesting to prevent moisture loss in the meat.

Dove's Nest

Nest
1 chicken breast, pounded thin
1/4 cup olive oil
Salt and pepper to taste

Bay Scallop Filling
1 onion, finely chopped
Olive oil
1 red bell pepper, finely chopped
1 green bell pepper, finely chopped
1 yellow bell pepper, finely chopped
1 tablespoon chopped garlic
4 ounces bay scallops or sea scallops
1 large tomato, seeded and chopped
1 teaspoon basil
Dash of hot red pepper sauce (optional)
Salt and pepper to taste
Shredded Cheddar cheese
Hot cooked rice
2 teaspoons chopped parsley

   For the nest, invert a small soup bowl on a hard surface. Cover with foil to form a small mold. Place the foil mold on a baking sheet and line with the chicken. Brush the chicken with the olive oil and season with salt and pepper. Bake at 450 degrees in a gas oven for about 15 minutes. Let stand until cool; remove from the foil.

   For the filling, sauté the onion in olive oil in a skillet. Add the bell peppers and garlic and sauté over high gas heat for about 5 minutes. Stir in the scallops and sauté for 6 minutes. Mix in the tomato, basil, hot sauce, salt and pepper. Cook over low gas heat until heated through.

   Spoon the filling into the nest. Sprinkle with cheese and place on a baking sheet. Bake at 300 degrees in a gas oven just until heated through. Serve on a bed of hot cooked rice. Sprinkle with the parsley.—Serves 1—**Gustavus Myers IV, New England House of Seafood, 1995**

Bacon and Scallop-Stuffed Mushrooms with Roasted Roma Cream

Roasted Roma Cream
8 Roma tomatoes, cut into halves
Pinch of salt
Pinch of pepper
Dried basil to taste
1 cup heavy cream

Stuffed Mushrooms
4 ounces bacon, finely chopped
1/4 cup minced red bell pepper
1/4 cup minced red onion
1 tablespoon minced garlic

8 ounces medium bay scallops,
    coarsely chopped
2 tablespoons sherry
1/4 cup chopped parsley
Kosher salt and pepper to taste
1 egg, beaten
1/2 to 3/4 cup Italian-seasoned
    bread crumbs
8 button mushroom caps
Melted butter to taste
White wine to taste

For the cream, arrange the tomatoes cut side up on a baking sheet and sprinkle with the salt, pepper and basil. Roast at 200 degrees in a gas oven for 2 hours. Combine the tomatoes and cream in a nonreactive saucepan and bring to a boil. Reduce the gas heat to low and simmer for 15 to 20 minutes, stirring occasionally. Season to taste. Remove from the heat and cover to keep warm.

For the mushrooms, cook the bacon in a skillet until crisp. Remove the bacon to a paper towel to drain, reserving 2 tablespoons of the bacon drippings in the skillet. Sauté the bell pepper and onion in the reserved bacon drippings over medium gas heat for 2 to 3 minutes or until tender. Add the garlic and cook for 1 minute. Increase the gas heat to high and add the scallops. Sauté for 2 minutes. Stir in the sherry and cook for 1 minute. Add the parsley, salt and pepper and cook until the liquid is reduced by half. Remove from the heat and let stand until cool. Stir in the bacon.

Add the egg to the cooled scallop mixture and mix well. Stir in the bread crumbs. Mound the scallop mixture in the mushroom caps and arrange the mushrooms stuffing side up in a baking pan. Add butter and wine to the baking pan. Bake at 350 degrees in a gas oven for 12 to 16 minutes or until heated through and brown. Drizzle with the cream and serve immediately.—Makes 8 stuffed mushrooms—**Michael Johnson, Seville Quarter, 2003**

Sea Scallops en Papillote

1 ounce carrots, julienned
1 ounce leeks, julienned
1 ounce yellow squash, julienned
6 ounces fresh sea scallops

2 tablespoons butter
2 tablespoons white wine
Juice of 1 lemon
1 sprig of tarragon

Cut a sheet of baking parchment into a heart shape large enough to enclose the scallop mixture. Place the carrots, leeks and squash on the parchment paper. Top with the scallops, butter, wine, lemon juice and tarragon. Wrap the parchment paper around the mixture until tightly enclosed.

Arrange the packet on a baking sheet and bake at 350 degrees in a gas oven for 10 to 15 minutes or until the scallops are opaque and slightly firm. Remove the scallops and vegetables to a serving plate, discarding the baking parchment.—Serves 1—**Jim O'Brien, New World Landing, 1997**

Grilled Scallops with Portobello Mushroom

4 large sea scallops
1 large portobello mushroom cap
Olive oil
Salt and pepper to taste
Mesquite seasoning to taste
1/2 cup heavy cream

3 tablespoons sherry
1/2 teaspoon chopped garlic
1/2 teaspoon chopped shallot
1 tablespoon grated Parmesan cheese
Pinch of chopped parsley

Coat the scallops and mushroom cap with olive oil and season with salt and pepper. Lightly dust the scallops with mesquite seasoning. Grill the scallops and mushroom cap over medium gas heat until the scallops are opaque and slightly firm and the mushroom is tender. Remove to a platter and cover to keep warm.

Combine the cream, sherry, garlic, shallot, salt and pepper in a small saucepan and cook until reduced, thickened and of a sauce consistency, stirring frequently.

Slice the mushroom as desired and arrange on a serving plate. Arrange the scallops over and around the mushroom slices. Drizzle with the sauce and sprinkle with the cheese and parsley.—Serves 1—**Jim O'Brien, O'Brien's Bistro, 2006**

Grilled Bacon-Wrapped Scallop Kabobs with Pineapple and Sweet Potato

Hoisin Soy Marinade
1¹/4 cups honey
1 cup soy sauce
1 cup vegetable oil
1 cup hoisin sauce
1 cup sesame seeds
1 tablespoon minced garlic
1 tablespoon hot dry mustard

Sea Scallops
Snow peas, blanched
1 pound (31- to 35-count) sea scallops
Bacon slices, partially cooked and cut into halves
1 sweet potato, boiled and cut into chunks
1 pineapple, cut into chunks
1 green bell pepper, cut into chunks

For the marinade, combine the honey, soy sauce, oil, hoisin sauce, sesame seeds, garlic and dry mustard in a nonreactive container and stir until the honey dissolves. Chill, covered, in the refrigerator.

For the scallops, wrap one snow pea around a scallop, pressing to seal. Wrap one piece of bacon around the snow pea. Arrange seam side down on a sheet pan lined with plastic wrap. Repeat the process with the remaining scallops, snow peas and bacon slices. Chill, covered, in the refrigerator.

Soak about fifteen 7- to 8-inch wooden skewers in water in a bowl; drain. Thread one sweet potato chunk, one wrapped scallop, one pineapple chunk, one wrapped scallop and one bell pepper chunk in the order listed on each skewer. Arrange the kabobs in a single layer in a shallow dish and drizzle with the marinade, turning to coat. Drain, reserving the marinade. Grill the kabobs on both sides on a gas grill for 10 to 12 minutes or until the scallops are opaque and slightly firm, basting frequently with the reserved marinade.—Makes about 15 kabobs—**Jimmy McManus, Bon Appétit Waterfront Cafe, 1999**

Grilled Stuffed Scallops

12 spinach leaves, chopped
1 teaspoon minced onion
1/4 teaspoon chopped garlic
Vegetable oil
1/2 cup crumbled feta cheese

1 ounce smoked salmon, sliced
12 to 14 ounces fresh sea scallops
1/2 cup balsamic vinegar
1 tablespoon Dijon mustard

Sauté the spinach, onion and garlic in oil in a large skillet for a few seconds. Remove from the heat and let stand until cool. Stir in the cheese.

Lay the salmon slices on a hard surface and place 1 teaspoon of the cheese mixture on each slice. Wrap the salmon around the cheese mixture to enclose. Make a small slit in the side of one of the scallops to form a pocket and stuff one of the salmon packets in the pocket. Repeat the process with the remaining scallops and remaining salmon packets.

Grill the stuffed scallops on both sides on a gas grill for 3 to 4 minutes or until the scallops are opaque and slightly firm. Mix the vinegar and Dijon mustard in a bowl and drizzle over the scallops. Serve immediately.—Serves 4—**Jim O'Brien, The Yacht Restaurant, 1995**

Pesto-Marinated Sea Scallops

1/2 cup extra-virgin olive oil
1/2 cup chopped basil
1/4 cup pine nuts
1 tablespoon chopped garlic

Juice of 1 lemon
1/2 teaspoon kosher salt
Pinch of pepper
1 pound (20- to 30-count) sea scallops

Process the olive oil, basil, pine nuts, garlic, lemon juice, salt and pepper in a food processor until smooth, scraping the side as needed. Combine the pesto and scallops in a bowl and mix until evenly coated. Marinate, covered, in the refrigerator for 4 hours or longer.

Arrange the scallops on the rack of a gas grill. Grill for 2 to 3 minutes per side or until the centers are opaque. Serve warm or chilled. You may prepare the pesto several days in advance and store, covered, in the refrigerator.—Serves 3 to 4—**Gus Silivos, Skopelos on the Bay, 2008**

Grilled Sea Scallops with Mixed Greens and Orange Balsamic Vinaigrette

Juice of 1 large orange
1/2 cup balsamic vinegar
1/4 cup extra-virgin olive oil
1 to 2 pounds large sea scallops

Olive oil for coating
Salt and white pepper to taste
1 bunch salad greens, trimmed

Simmer the orange juice in a saucepan until reduced by half. Pour into a bowl and chill. Combine the vinegar and 1/4 cup olive oil in a jar with a tight-fitting lid and seal tightly. Shake to combine. Add the chilled orange juice and shake to combine. Chill in the refrigerator.

Brush the scallops with olive oil for coating and season with salt and white pepper. Grill on a hot gas grill for about 1 minute per side or until the scallops are opaque and slightly firm. Arrange the salad greens in the center of each of four serving plates and top evenly with the scallops. Drizzle with the chilled vinaigrette.—Serves 4—**Chris Tingle, Gauthier's, 1998**

Sea Scallops with Lemon Grass Ginger Sauce

11/2 pounds sea scallops
Salt and pepper to taste
1 tablespoon unsalted butter
1 tablespoon vegetable oil
1 tablespoon unsalted butter
2 tablespoons minced shallots

1 tablespoon minced lemon grass
  (use tender inner bulb)
1 tablespoon minced fresh ginger
1/4 cup vermouth
2/3 cup heavy cream

Season the scallops with salt and pepper. Heat 1 tablespoon butter and the oil in a skillet over high gas heat until the butter melts. Add the scallops and cook for 3 minutes or until a nice crust forms. Turn the scallops and cook for 2 minutes. Remove the scallops to a platter and cover to keep warm.

Drain the skillet and then add 1 tablespoon butter. Heat over medium gas heat until the butter melts; stir in the shallots, lemon grass and ginger. Cook for about 3 minutes. Mix in the vermouth and cook until most of the vermouth evaporates. Stir in the cream and scrape the bottom of the skillet to release any browned bits. Cook until thickened and of a sauce consistency, stirring frequently. Season with salt and pepper. Serve the sauce with the scallops.—Serves 4—**Angela Miller, Distinctive Kitchens Culinary Arts Center, 2008**

Sautéed Scallops with Grape Tomatoes and Feta Cheese

2 tablespoons virgin olive oil
1¹/₂ pounds large (20- to 30-count) sea scallops
Kosher salt and pepper to taste
1 tablespoon virgin olive oil
Tops and bulbs of 4 green onions, chopped separately
12 ounces grape tomatoes
3 tablespoons chopped fresh Italian parsley
3 tablespoons lemon juice
¹/₂ teaspoon Spanish paprika
6 ounces feta cheese, crumbled
1 tablespoon chopped fresh Italian parsley
1 tablespoon virgin olive oil

Heat a sauté pan over gas heat and add 2 tablespoons olive oil. Season the scallops with salt and pepper. Sauté the scallops in the olive oil until brown on both sides. Remove the scallops to a platter, reserving the pan drippings.

Heat 1 tablespoon olive oil with the reserved pan drippings. Sauté the green onion bulbs in the hot oil. Add the tomatoes and green onion tops and sauté until the tomatoes blister. Stir in 3 tablespoons parsley, the lemon juice and paprika. Return the scallops to the skillet and cook until heated through. Season with salt and pepper. Remove the scallops to a platter and sprinkle with the cheese and 1 tablespoon parsley. Drizzle with 1 tablespoon olive oil.—Serves 4—
Gus Silivos, Skopelos on the Bay, 2006

TIP Fresh shucked scallops should be chilled on ice at 32 degrees for up to 2 days, or frozen at 0 degrees for up to 4 months. Thaw frozen scallops in the refrigerator or under cold running water.

Sea Scallops with Rigatoni, Sun-Dried Tomatoes and Prosciutto

3 to 5 tablespoons olive oil
3 ounces prosciutto, julienned
1 pound (20- to 30-count) sea scallops
1 tablespoon chopped shallot
2 teaspoons chopped garlic
1/4 cup white wine
1/4 cup seafood stock
2 ounces sun-dried tomatoes, reconstituted
1 tablespoon basil pesto
1 teaspoon dried oregano
Salt and pepper to taste
8 ounces cooked rigatoni

Heat a skillet until very hot and add the olive oil. Brown the prosciutto in the hot oil. Add the scallops and sear quickly. Mix in the shallot and garlic. Stir in the wine and stock. Add the tomatoes, pesto, oregano, salt and pepper and mix well.

Cook until heated through, stirring occasionally. Spoon the scallop mixture over hot cooked rigatoni on a serving platter. Garnish with grated Romano cheese and serve with hot crusty French bread.—Serves 4—**Anthony Redfield, Perdido Bay Restaurant, 1995**

TIP Scallops are cooked through when the center is opaque and white; test by cutting a scallop into halves. Overcooking will cause toughness and valuable weight loss. Depending on their size, scallops will cook in three to four minutes by any method.

Seared Sea Scallops with Mushrooms and Roasted Garlic Beurre Blanc

Mushrooms

1/2 cup (about) canola oil
24 ounces mixed mushrooms, trimmed
1/4 cup minced garlic
1/4 cup minced shallots
1/4 cup minced fresh herbs (such as
   parsley, tarragon, chives and basil)
Kosher salt and freshly ground pepper
   to taste

6 peppercorns
2 bay leaves
4 sprigs of thyme
1/2 cup heavy cream
4 cups (8 sticks) butter, cubed
   and chilled
Kosher salt and freshly ground pepper
   to taste
Honey (optional)

Roasted Garlic Beurre Blanc

4 cups white wine, muscadet preferred
4 shallots, finely chopped
Juice of 2 lemons
8 ounces roasted garlic

Sea Scallops

12 jumbo sea scallops
1 cup (about) canola oil
2 teaspoons kosher salt
2 teaspoons freshly ground pepper

For the mushrooms, add enough of the canola oil to cover the bottom of a sauté pan. Heat over high gas heat until light wisps of smoke appear. Add the mushrooms and sauté until partially cooked. Stir in the garlic and shallots and sauté just until the mushrooms are tender. Stir in the herbs and season with salt and pepper. Remove from the heat and cover to keep warm.

For the beurre blanc, combine the wine, shallots, lemon juice, garlic, peppercorns, bay leaves and thyme in a small saucepan and bring to a boil. Boil until the liquid is reduced to 2 tablespoons, stirring occasionally. Reduce the gas heat to low and mix in the cream. Add the butter one cube at a time, cooking until the butter is incorporated after each addition and whisking constantly. Strain through a fine mesh strainer into a heatproof bowl, discarding the solids. Season with salt and pepper. Add honey if the sauce is too acidic. Cover to keep warm.

For the scallops, gently toss the scallops with 1/2 cup of the canola oil in a bowl. Season both sides of the scallops with the salt and pepper. Add just enough of the remaining canola oil to cover the bottom of a large sauté pan. Heat the oil over high gas heat until light wisps of smoke appear. Arrange the scallops in a single layer in the hot oil; do not allow the scallops to touch.

Sauté until the scallops are deep golden brown on both sides. Continue cooking at 350 degrees in a gas oven until the desired degree of doneness, if desired. Serve the scallops with the mushrooms and drizzle evenly with the beurre blanc.—Serves 3—**James Ammons, Seville Quarter, 2007**

Crab, Crawfish, Lobster & Shrimp

Consider the crustacean: shrimp, crab, lobster, crawfish.

In the Pensacola area our waters teem with shrimp and shrimp boats. With their "doors out" and nets trailing behind, shrimpers can still be seen working the bays or the deep waters of the Gulf of Mexico. Whether it's the local brown or white shrimp, either of which turn bright pink when cooked, or the ever-so-sweet Royal Reds (pulled from depths of 1,500 feet or deeper), shrimp in Pensacola are an everyday food. Local chefs boil them for peel-and-eat parties. They fry them, broil them, chargrill them or use them as a tasty garnish for other dishes, sauce them, make them into a salad, or search out the perfectly fried shrimp po' boy.

Across the bays and in Santa Rosa Sound, telltale plastic floats mark the locations of crab traps baited and waiting to snare one of the Gulf Coast's great delicacies, the blue crab. Blue crab, with its mild, sweet flavor, remains a favorite with local chefs for its taste, delicacy and versatility. From crab claws sautéed in a garlic-cream sauce, flaky crab cakes, the rare and delicious soft-shell crabs to traditional deviled crabs, nothing says Gulf Coast seafood quite like it.

Lobster plays a role in our local chefs' stocks of favorite recipes. Even though they have a short local season, live lobster imported from Maine or lobster tails imported from South Florida ensure they are readily available in Pensacola. Whether in surf 'n' turf, broiled, boiled, stuffed, or in a bisque, lobster has a richness prized in local cooking.

And crawfish, the legendary "mud bug," are plentiful when the spring season brings them in 50- and 100-pound sacks from Mississippi and Louisiana. Local chefs eagerly await the crawfish for their sweet taste and use it primarily to garnish other dishes or fry the tails as "Cajun popcorn."

Crab and Corn Beignets with Herbed Mayonnaise

Herbed Mayonnaise
1 cup mayonnaise
2 tablespoons lemon juice
2 tablespoons chopped fresh basil
2 tablespoons chopped fresh cilantro
1 teaspoon chopped fresh tarragon
2 teaspoons Dijon mustard
Salt and pepper to taste

Beignets
1/2 cup all-purpose flour
2 tablespoons cornmeal
3/4 teaspoon kosher salt
1/2 teaspoon baking powder
1/4 teaspoon coarse pepper
1/3 cup milk
1 egg, beaten
8 ounces claw crab meat
1/2 cup frozen corn
1/2 cup roasted red bell pepper, chopped
1 green onion, minced
Vegetable oil

For the mayonnaise, blend the mayonnaise, lemon juice, basil, cilantro, tarragon, Dijon mustard, salt and pepper in a bowl. Chill, covered, in the refrigerator.

For the beignets, whisk the flour, cornmeal, salt, baking powder and pepper in a bowl. Add the milk and egg and stir until blended. Fold in the crab meat, corn, bell pepper and green onion. Let stand for 10 minutes.

Heat oil in a deep-fat fryer to 350 degrees. Drop the batter by rounded teaspoonfuls into the hot oil. Fry for 1 minute per side or until golden brown. Drain on a wire rack and arrange the beignets in a single layer on a baking sheet. Keep warm in a 200-degree gas oven. Serve warm with the mayonnaise.—Serves 4—**Keith Hoffert, Vintage Gourmet, 2005**

Crab Cakes

2 tablespoons finely chopped red
bell pepper
2 tablespoons finely chopped yellow
bell pepper
2 tablespoons finely chopped green
bell pepper
Butter
1/4 cup cooked black-eyed peas
1/4 cup panko (Japanese bread crumbs)

1/4 cup mayonnaise
1 or 2 eggs, beaten
2 teaspoons Old Bay seasoning
1 teaspoon Tabasco sauce
1 teaspoon sea salt
1 pound lump crab meat, shells removed
1/4 cup yellow cornmeal
1 cup collard greens, julienned and fried

Sauté the bell peppers in butter in a sauté pan until tender. Let stand until cool. Combine the bell peppers, black-eyed peas, bread crumbs, mayonnaise, egg, Old Bay seasoning, Tabasco sauce and salt in a bowl and mix well. Fold in the crab meat, being careful not to break up the lumps.

Shape the crab meat mixture into sixteen 2-ounce cakes and dust lightly with the cornmeal. Sauté in butter in a sauté pan over medium gas heat until golden brown on both sides. Serve the crab cakes over the collard greens on serving plates.—Makes 16 crab cakes—**Alphonse Lucier IV, Pensacola Yacht Club, 2002**

Miller's Crab Cakes

2 tablespoons unsalted butter
1/4 cup minced red onion
2 tablespoons minced red bell pepper
2 tablespoons minced yellow
bell pepper
1 pound jumbo lump crab meat, shells
removed
1/4 cup heavy whipping cream
1 egg

1 tablespoon Old Bay seasoning
1 tablespoon Louisiana hot sauce
2 tablespoons dry mustard
1/2 cup Italian-seasoned bread crumbs
1 cup all-purpose flour
1 teaspoon salt
1/2 teaspoon pepper
3 tablespoons vegetable oil
Small pat of butter

Heat a sauté pan over medium gas heat and add 2 tablespoons butter. Heat until the butter begins to bubble; add the onion and bell peppers. Sauté for 2 minutes or until the vegetables are tender. Remove the onion mixture to a plate and let stand until cool. Place the crab meat in a medium bowl and top with the cooled onion mixture.

Whisk the cream and egg in a bowl until blended. Stir in the Old Bay seasoning, hot sauce and dry mustard. Pour over the crab meat mixture and mix gently. Mix in the bread crumbs. Shape the crab meat mixture into six 3-ounce cakes. Dust with a mixture of the flour, salt and pepper. Heat a sauté pan or griddle over medium gas heat and add the oil and small pat of butter. Sauté the crab cakes in the oil mixture for 3 minutes per side or until golden brown and firm.—Makes 6 (3-ounce) crab cakes—**Irv Miller, Jackson's, 1999**

McGuire's Crab Cakes

1 pound jumbo lump crab meat, shells removed
3/4 cup bread crumbs
1 egg, beaten
Salt and pepper to taste
1/2 cup all-purpose flour
1/4 cup olive oil
2 cups spring salad mix
1 cup rémoulade sauce
8 piquanté chiles, sliced

Combine the crab meat, bread crumbs, egg, salt and pepper in a bowl and mix gently. Shape into four to six cakes and dust lightly with the flour. Heat the olive oil in a sauté pan. Brown the crab cakes on both sides in the hot oil; drain. Place the spring mix equally in the center of four to six serving plates. Arrange one crab cake on the side of each plate and drizzle with the rémoulade sauce. Serve with the piquanté chiles and garnish with lemon twists.—Makes 4 to 6 crab cakes—
Chris Tingle, McGuire's Irish Pub, 2005

Panéed Crab Cakes

2 tablespoons minced red bell pepper
2 tablespoons minced green bell pepper
2 tablespoons minced yellow
   bell pepper
1 tablespoon minced red onion
Butter
1/2 cup mayonnaise
1/2 cup panko (Japanese bread crumbs)
2 eggs, beaten
2 teaspoons Old Bay seasoning
1 teaspoon sea salt
1 pound lump crab meat, shells removed
1/4 cup all-purpose flour

Sauté the bell peppers and onion in butter in a sauté pan until tender. Let stand until cool. Combine the bell pepper mixture, mayonnaise, bread crumbs, eggs, Old Bay seasoning and salt in a bowl and mix well. Fold in the crab meat, being careful not to break up the lumps. Shape into ten 2-ounce cakes and dust lightly with the flour. Sauté the crab cakes in butter in a sauté pan over medium gas heat until golden brown on both sides. Serve immediately.—Makes 10 crab cakes—
Alphonse Lucier IV, Pensacola Yacht Club, 2001

Big Sexy Risotto Crab Cakes with Roasted Red Pepper Aïoli

Roasted Red Pepper Aïoli
2 red bell peppers
1/2 cup olive oil
2 tablespoons chopped garlic
Salt and pepper to taste

Crab Cakes
6 to 8 cups water
2 tablespoons crab base or
   crab bouillon
1/2 cup sliced red onion
1/2 cup chopped celery
1/3 cup chopped green bell pepper
1/3 cup chopped red bell pepper

1/3 cup chopped garlic
2 tablespoons Paul Prudhomme's
   Seafood Magic
1/2 cup olive oil
16 ounces arborio rice
1 pound lump crab meat, shells removed
1 pound claw crab meat, shells removed
2/3 cup grated Parmesan cheese
1 piece boursin cheese, chopped
1/2 cup sliced green onions
Grated zest and juice of 1 lemon
1 tablespoon chopped lemon grass
Kosher salt and freshly cracked pepper
   to taste

For the aïoli, roast the bell peppers over a gas flame until charred. Place in a bowl and cover with plastic wrap. Steam for 5 minutes. Peel, seed and chop the bell peppers. Process the bell peppers, olive oil, garlic, salt and pepper in a blender until puréed.

For the crab cakes, mix the water and crab base in a large bowl for the crab stock. Sauté the onion, celery, bell peppers, garlic and Seafood Magic seasoning in the olive oil in a 3- to 5-quart saucepan until tender. Add the rice and stir until evenly coated. Add two-thirds of the crab stock and bring to a simmer. Reduce the gas heat and cook until the rice is tender and creamy, adding only enough additional crab stock to keep the rice from sticking to the bottom of the saucepan. Fold in the crab meat, Parmesan cheese, boursin cheese, green onions, lemon zest, lemon juice, lemon grass, salt and pepper.

Spread the crab risotto on a baking sheet. Chill in the refrigerator for 1 to 2 hours. Shape the crab risotto into cakes of the desired size and shape. Cook in a nonstick skillet or on an electric griddle for about 2 minutes on each side or until golden brown. Serve the crab cakes topped with the aïoli.—Serves 6—**John Murphy and Chris Kimberl, Nooner Cafe, 2008**

Gulf Crab and Chorizo Fritters with Chipotle Cream Sauce

Chipotle Cream Sauce
1 cup crème fraîche
1 tablespoon chopped canned chipotle chile in adobo sauce
1/2 teaspoon salt
1/4 teaspoon pepper

Crab and Chorizo Fritters
1 cup water
1/2 cup (1 stick) butter
1 1/4 teaspoons salt
1 cup all-purpose flour
1 teaspoon ground cumin
4 eggs
1/2 cup finely chopped dry-cured link chorizo, cooked (about 2 1/2 ounces)
4 scallions, finely chopped
2 tablespoons sofrito*
8 ounces lump crab meat
Canola oil

For the sauce, mix the crème fraîche, chipotle chile, salt and pepper in a bowl.

For the fritters, bring the water, butter and salt to a boil in a medium heavy saucepan and boil until the butter melts and the salt dissolves. Whisk in the flour and cumin and cook for 3 minutes, whisking constantly. Remove from the heat and cool slightly. Add the eggs one at a time, blending well after each addition. Stir in the sausage, scallions and sofrito. Fold in the crab meat.

Pour enough canola oil into a large heavy skillet to measure 3 inches. Heat to 375 degrees over medium gas heat. Working in batches, spoon the batter by tablespoonfuls into the hot oil, slightly flattening with the back of a metal spatula. Fry the fritters for 5 minutes or until cooked through and brown, turning once and adding canola oil as needed. Drain on paper towels and serve immediately with the sauce.—Makes 30 fritters—**William Guthrie, Guthrie's Dining Designs, 2008**

 TIP *Sofrito is a Caribbean cooking base usually made of tomato paste, onions, peppers, and spices. It is available in Cuban markets or may be purchased at www.goya.com.

Jumbo Lump Crab Tostadas with Goat Cheese

Calypso Black Beans
1¹/2 cups dried black beans
1 yellow onion, chopped
1 green bell pepper, chopped
1 jalapeño chile, chopped
1 tablespoon chopped garlic
2 bay leaves
Salt and pepper to taste

Crab Tostadas
8 tostada shells
1 pound jumbo lump Dungeness or blue crab meat, shells removed
3 ripe avocados, chopped
2 Roma tomatoes, chopped
1 small log goat cheese, crumbled
1/4 cup sour cream
2 sprigs of cilantro, chopped
Juice of 1 lime

For the beans, sort and rinse the beans. Soak the beans using package directions; drain. Combine the beans, onion, bell pepper, jalapeño chile, garlic, bay leaves, salt and pepper with enough water to generously cover in a stockpot. Bring to a boil over high gas heat; reduce the heat to low. Simmer for 2 hours, adding water as needed. Discard the bay leaves. Drain and slightly mash the beans.

For the tostadas, arrange the shells in a single layer on a baking sheet. Spread each with some of the mashed beans and layer with the crab meat, avocados and tomatoes. Sprinkle with the cheese.

Bake at 350 degrees in a gas oven for 8 to 10 minutes or until the cheese melts. Top each tostada with a dollop of sour cream and sprinkle with the cilantro. Drizzle with the lime juice and serve.—Serves 4—**Dan Dunn, The Art of Catering, 2006**

TIP Blue crabs are sold live or steamed, or the meat is picked and packaged ready to eat.

Dungeness Crab

2 whole Dungeness crabs
24 cups (6 quarts) water
1 red onion, cut into quarters
1/2 cup salt
1/4 cup cayenne pepper

2 bags Zatarain's crab boil
1 cup Old Bay seasoning
2 lemons, cut into quarters
Old Bay seasoning to taste

To clean the crabs, hold one side of legs in your right hand and, using your left hand, gently remove the top shell; do not discard the top shell. Scrape everything out, leaving only the body and legs and replace the top shell. Repeat the process with the remaining crab.

Combine the water, onion, salt, cayenne pepper, crab boil, 1 cup Old Bay seasoning and the lemons in a large stockpot and bring to a rolling boil. Add the crabs and boil for 7 to 10 minutes. Remove the crabs using tongs and arrange on a serving plate. Remove the top shells and lightly dust the crabs with Old Bay seasoning to taste. Replace the top shells and garnish with lemon wedges and tropical fruit wedges. Serve immediately with boiled new potatoes and corn on the cob.—Serves 1—**Ian Barber, Crabs We Got 'Em, 2005**

Andouille-Crusted Soft-Shell Crabs

1 cup heavy cream
4 eggs
1 pound andouille
1 tablespoon olive oil
1 cup panko (Japanese bread crumbs)
1 tablespoon minced parsley

1 tablespoon minced garlic
1 tablespoon Cajun spice
Salt and pepper to taste
6 large soft-shell crabs
2 cups all-purpose flour
Vegetable oil

Whisk the cream and eggs in a bowl until blended. Chill in the refrigerator. Heat the sausage with the olive oil in a saucepan until warm; drain. Process the sausage in a food processor until minced. Drain on paper towels. Mix the sausage, bread crumbs, parsley, garlic, Cajun spice, salt and pepper in a bowl.

Coat the crabs one at a time with the flour; dip in the egg wash and then coat with the sausage mixture. Heat oil in a deep-fat fryer to 300 degrees. Fry the crabs in the hot oil until golden brown on all sides; drain. Serve with aïoli or your favorite sauce.—Serves 6—**Alphonse Lucier IV, Eat!, 2004**

Crawfish Cheesecake

1 pound crawfish tails, chopped
1 red bell pepper, finely chopped
1 yellow bell pepper, finely chopped
1/2 purple onion, finely chopped
1 garlic clove, minced
3 tablespoons butter
32 ounces cream cheese, softened
5 eggs
2 tablespoons Creole seasoning
2 tablespoons dried cilantro
1 tablespoon cayenne pepper

Sauté the crawfish, bell peppers, onion and garlic in the butter in a sauté pan until the vegetables are tender. Remove from the heat and let stand until cool. Beat the cream cheese in a mixing bowl until light and fluffy. Add the eggs one at a time, beating constantly at high speed until blended after each addition. Stir in the Creole seasoning, cilantro and cayenne pepper. Fold in the crawfish mixture.

Spread the crawfish mixture in a 9-inch springform pan. Bake at 200 degrees in a gas oven for 2 hours. Serve with assorted party crackers. You may cut the recipe in half and bake in a 6-inch springform pan.—Serves 40 to 50—**David Penniman and Katie Batchelor, Classic City Catering, 2006**

TIP If using a marinade, allow fish to soak up flavor for at least 30 minutes. Refrigerate while soaking in marinade.

Crawfish Beignets with Sun-Dried Tomatoes and Roasted Corn Tartar Sauce

Roasted Corn Tartar Sauce
1/2 cup corn kernels
Olive oil
1 cup mayonnaise
1/4 cup chopped sun-dried tomatoes
2 tablespoons chopped green onions
1 teaspoon chopped garlic

Crawfish Beignets
1 pound crawfish tails, chopped
1/2 cup chopped yellow onion
1/4 cup chopped green or red
  bell pepper

1/4 cup chopped green onions
1 tablespoon chopped garlic
1 tablespoon olive oil
Salt and pepper to taste
31/4 cups all-purpose flour
2 teaspoons baking powder
11/2 cups milk
3 eggs, beaten
1 tablespoon chopped parsley
Vegetable oil

For the sauce, sauté the corn in olive oil in a small skillet until golden brown. Combine the corn, mayonnaise, tomatoes, green onions and garlic in a bowl and mix well. Chill, covered, in the refrigerator.

For the beignets, sauté the crawfish, yellow onion, bell pepper, green onions and garlic in the olive oil. Season with salt and pepper and let stand until cool. Mix the flour and baking powder in a bowl. Whisk the milk and eggs in a bowl until blended and add to the flour mixture, whisking until smooth. Season with salt and pepper. Fold in the crawfish mixture and parsley. Chill for 1 hour.

Heat oil in a deep-fat fryer to 365 degrees. Drop the batter by tablespoonfuls into the hot oil and deep-fry for 3 to 4 minutes or until golden brown on all sides; drain. Serve the beignets with the sauce or spread the sauce over the bottom of serving plates and top with the beignets.
—Makes 2 dozen beignets—**Jim O'Brien, O'Brien's Bistro, 2000**

Cajun Spring Rolls

8 ounces crawfish tails
Salt and pepper to taste
Soy sauce to taste
1 small carrot, peeled and julienned
1 zucchini, peeled and julienned
1 crookneck squash, peeled and julienned
6 collard green leaves, deveined and julienned
8 thin spring roll wrappers
2 tablespoons cornstarch
1 tablespoon water
Canola oil

Devein the crawfish and season with salt, pepper and a spritz of soy sauce. Let stand for 30 minutes; drain. Combine the crawfish, carrot, zucchini, squash and collard leaves in a bowl and mix well.

Spread the wrappers on a hard surface and place one-eighth of the crawfish mixture in the 4 o'clock to 8 o'clock position on each wrapper. Mix the cornstarch and water in a bowl until blended and spread on the top point of each wrapper. Roll the wrappers to the halfway point and fold 3 o'clock and 9 o'clock corners to the middle. Finish rolling.

Heat canola oil in a deep skillet to 325 degrees. Fry the rolls in the hot oil until golden brown on all sides or bake at 400 degrees in a gas oven for 15 minutes. You may cover the rolls with damp paper towels and store in the refrigerator until just before frying.—Makes 8 spring rolls—
Alphonse Lucier IV, Pensacola Yacht Club, 2002

TIP Prevent cross-contamination between raw seafood products and clean surfaces or other foods. Always wash your hands before and after handling raw seafood.

Blackened New York Strip Steak with Crawfish Succotash

Crawfish Succotash
2 tablespoons clarified butter
1¹/2 ounces green beans
2 tablespoons corn kernels
1¹/2 teaspoons minced shallot
¹/4 teaspoon chopped garlic
Pinch of red pepper flakes
1¹/2 ounces crawfish tails
2 tablespoons chopped Roma tomato
Salt and black pepper to taste
2 tablespoons white wine
2 tablespoons shrimp stock

New York Strip Steak
1 (8-ounce) New York strip steak
2 ounces blackening seasoning
2 tablespoons clarified butter

For the succotash, melt the clarified butter in a heated skillet. Add the beans, corn, shallot, garlic and red pepper flakes and sauté for 1 minute. Stir in the crawfish and tomato and sauté for 1 minute. Season with salt and black pepper. Deglaze the skillet with the wine and stock. Simmer for about 3 minutes, stirring occasionally.

For the steak, coat the steak with the blackening seasoning. Melt the clarified butter in a heated skillet. Sear the steak on both sides in the butter to the desired degree of doneness. Serve with the succotash.—Serves 1—**Anthony Wilson, Bayside Grill, 2000**

Ragin' Cajun Combo

4 (8-ounce) New York strip steaks
4 ounces blackening seasoning
4 ounces green bell peppers, sliced
4 ounces red bell peppers, sliced
4 ounces yellow bell peppers, sliced
4 ounces purple onion, sliced
2 ounces garlic, chopped

Olive oil
2 ounces blackening seasoning
1 ounce fresh basil, chopped
8 ounces crawfish tail meat, cooked
1/2 cup chardonnay
1 cup heavy cream
1/2 cup (1 stick) salted butter

Heat a large cast-iron skillet over high gas heat until very hot. Coat the steaks with 4 ounces blackening seasoning and arrange in the hot skillet. Cook to the desired degree of doneness. Remove the steaks to a platter and cover to keep warm.

Sauté the bell peppers, onion and garlic in olive oil in a skillet until the bell peppers and onion are tender. Stir in 2 ounces blackening seasoning and the basil and continue to cook. Add the crawfish and cook until heated through. Remove the crawfish mixture to a bowl and cover to keep warm. Deglaze the skillet with the wine and cook until reduced by two-thirds. Stir in the cream and butter and cook until the sauce coats the back of a spoon. Pool the sauce evenly in the middle of four serving plates and arrange one steak on each plate. Top with the crawfish mixture.—Serves 4—
Chris Trovas, Chris' Seafood Grille, 1998

Crawfish and Sausage Frittata

1/2 cup thinly sliced red onion
2 tablespoons olive oil
1 zucchini, thinly sliced
Salt and pepper to taste
5 eggs, beaten
1/2 cup chopped andouille

8 ounces crawfish
1 tablespoon julienned basil
1 tablespoon chopped parsley
2 tablespoons butter
1/4 cup crumbled goat cheese

Sauté the onion in the olive oil in a large skillet over medium gas heat until the onion is tender. Add the zucchini and cook for 7 to 8 minutes or until the zucchini is light brown. Season with salt and pepper. Drain on paper towels.

Combine the onion mixture, eggs, sausage, crawfish, basil and parsley in a bowl and mix well. Heat the butter in an ovenproof sauté pan over medium gas heat until melted. Add the egg mixture to the hot pan and tilt to cover evenly. Reduce the gas heat and cook until the bottom is set. Remove from the heat and sprinkle with the cheese. Broil at 350 degrees in a gas oven until set. Invert onto a plate and slice. Serve immediately.—Serves 6—**Alphonse Lucier IV, Eat!, 2006**

Blackened Bayou Chicken with Crawfish Tasso Sauce

3 tablespoons julienned tasso
1 tablespoon chopped green onions
1 tablespoon salted butter
1/4 cup unseasoned crawfish

1/2 teaspoon Cajun spice
1/2 cup heavy cream
1 (10 1/2-ounce) chicken breast

Heat a skillet until hot and add the tasso, green onions and butter. Cook for 2 minutes or until the tasso is rendered. Stir in the crawfish and Cajun spice and sauté for 1 minute. Add the cream and simmer until reduced to a sauce consistency, stirring frequently. Blacken the chicken on both sides in a hot skillet until cooked through. Cut the chicken vertically into halves and arrange in a bowl or on a rimmed serving plate. Top with the crawfish sauce and serve.—Serves 1—**Robbie Catton, Copeland's, 2004**

Crawfish Fettuccini

2 tablespoons butter
1 pound crawfish tail meat
1 teaspoon minced garlic
1 cup chopped green onions
2 tablespoons Jerry's Own
   ZydeCajun seasoning*
1 teaspoon basil
1 teaspoon thyme
1/2 teaspoon Jerry's habanero sauce*,
   or to taste
2 cups half-and-half

1 cup (4 ounces) shredded
   provolone cheese
1/4 cup (1 ounce) grated
   Parmesan cheese
4 cups drained cooked fettuccini
Dash of Jerry's Own
   ZydeCajun seasoning*
Finely shredded provolone cheese
   to taste
Dash of Jerry's Own
   ZydeCajun seasoning*

Heat the butter in a skillet over medium gas heat for 2 to 4 minutes. Stir in the crawfish, garlic and some of the green onions. Sauté for about 5 minutes. Add 2 tablespoons ZydeCajun seasoning, the basil, thyme and habanero sauce and reduce the gas heat. Stir in the half-and-half. Sprinkle with 1 cup provolone cheese and the Parmesan cheese and toss until evenly distributed.

Cook until the cheese melts and the mixture is of a sauce consistency, stirring frequently. Add the pasta, some more of the remaining green onions and a dash of ZydeCajun seasoning and mix well. Cook until heated through and to the desired consistency, stirring frequently. Add additional half-and-half if the sauce is too thick, or add more cheese if the sauce is too thin. Spoon into bowls and top with provolone cheese to taste, the remaining green onions and a dash of ZydeCajun seasoning.—Serves 2—**Jerry Mistretta, Jerry's Cajun Cafe, 2002**

 TIP *Available at www.jerryscajun.com

Crawfish Hebert

1/4 cup (1/2 stick) butter
1 pound crawfish tail meat
2 tablespoons finely chopped green onions
2 tablespoons Jerry's Own ZydeCajun seasoning*
1 teaspoon minced garlic
Dash of Jerry's habanero sauce*
1 tablespoon cornstarch
1 cup (about) hot water
1/2 teaspoon basil
1/2 teaspoon thyme
2 tablespoons finely chopped green onions
Hot steamed rice

Heat the butter in a skillet over medium gas heat until melted. Add the crawfish and sauté for about 5 minutes. Stir in 2 tablespoons green onions, the ZydeCajun seasoning, garlic and habanero sauce and reduce heat. Mix the cornstarch and some of the hot water in a bowl until blended. Add to the crawfish mixture with the basil and thyme and mix well.

Cook until thickened and of a sauce consistency, adding a mixture of additional cornstarch and hot water as needed for the desired consistency. Mix in 2 tablespoons green onions. Serve over hot steamed rice. Garnish with additional chopped green onions.—Serves 4—**Jerry Mistretta, Jerry's Cajun Cafe, 1999**

TIP *www.jerryscajun.com

Crab, Crawfish, Lobster & Shrimp

Lobster and Mango Summer Rolls

2 limes, peeled and separated into sections
1 tablespoon fish sauce
1 teaspoon light brown sugar
8 ounces pea sprouts (such as radish or bean)
16 fresh sweet basil leaves
Salt and pepper to taste
8 (6- to 8-inch) round rice paper wrappers
2 lobster tails, cooked
1 large mango, cut into 16 thin strips
1 red bell pepper, cut into 48 thin strips

Combine the limes, fish sauce and brown sugar in a bowl and mix well, breaking up the lime sections. Add the pea sprouts and basil and toss lightly. Season with salt and pepper.

Soak the wrappers in warm water in a bowl for 2 to 3 minutes or until pliable. Drain on a clean tea towel, turning each wrapper once.

Cut the lobster meat lengthwise into eight equal portions. Arrange the wrappers on a hard surface. Place 1/4 cup of the lime filling on the lower third of each wrapper. Layer each with one portion of the lobster, two mango strips and six bell pepper strips. Roll as tight as possible to enclose the filling and arrange seam side down on a platter. Let stand for 2 minutes. Mound the remaining lime filling equally on each of four serving plates. Cut the rolls on the bias into halves. Arrange two rolls on each serving. Serve with Chef Selz Collection spice mango peanut sauce*—Serves 4—
Andrew Selz, Chef Selz Collection, 2004

 TIP *www.chefselz.com.

Portobello Mushroom Timbale with Lobster and Fresh Herb Cream Reduction

Marinated Mushrooms
2 large portobello
   mushrooms, stemmed
3 tablespoons water
1 tablespoon soy sauce
Worcestershire sauce to taste
Red wine to taste
Granulated garlic to taste
Freshly ground pepper to taste
Olive oil

Timbale
3 cups water
1 (1- to 2-pound) lobster
1 cup white wine
2 celery tops
1/2 small onion
1 tablespoon chopped fresh garlic
1/2 cup heavy cream
1 tablespoon chopped fresh herbs (such
   as thyme, basil and chives)
Salt and pepper to taste

For the marinade, arrange the mushrooms stem side up in a shallow dish. Whisk the water, soy sauce, Worcestershire sauce, wine, garlic and pepper in a bowl and pour over the mushrooms. Marinate for 10 minutes or longer. Drain, reserving the marinade. Drizzle the mushrooms with olive oil. Grill on a gas grill or bake in a gas oven until tender, basting with the reserved marinade frequently. Remove the mushrooms to a cutting board. Cut the mushrooms diagonally into thin slices.

For the timbale, bring the water to a boil in a medium stockpot and add the lobster. Steam, covered, for 6 minutes. Remove the lobster to a platter and let stand until cool, reserving the cooking liquid. Separate the lobster between the body and tail. Remove and chop the legs. Crack the lobster tail carefully and remove the meat, reserving the shells. Add the reserved lobster shells, chopped lobster legs, wine, celery tops, onion and garlic to the reserved cooking liquid. Bring to a boil. Reduce the heat and cook for about 30 minutes or until the liquid is reduced to 1/2 cup. Strain, discarding the solids.

Return the strained liquid to the stockpot and stir in the cream. Cook until the mixture is reduced and slightly thickened. Chop the lobster tail meat and knuckle meat and stir into the sauce. Add the fresh herbs, salt and pepper and mix well. Cook until the desired consistency, stirring occasionally.

Line a timbale mold with some of the mushroom slices overlapping about 1/2 inch. Fill with some of the lobster sauce and then fold the remaining mushrooms over the top. Invert the mold onto a serving plate and drizzle with the remaining sauce. Crack the lobster claws and remove the cartilage, being careful not to tear the claws. Garnish the timbale with the lobster claws.—Serves 2 to 4—**Chris Tingle, Gauthier's, 1997**

Crab, Crawfish, Lobster & Shrimp

Lobster and Sweet Corn Chowder

Lobster Corn Stock
1 whole lobster
2 tablespoons canola oil
24 cups (6 quarts) water
2 ears of roasted corn, kernels removed
1 bay leaf
Pinch of kosher salt
Pinch of pepper

Chowder
2 ears of sweet corn with husks
3/4 cup (1 1/2 sticks) unsalted butter

1 Vidalia onion, coarsely chopped
3/4 cup dry sherry
2 1/2 cups all-purpose flour
1 pound russet potatoes, peeled,
  coarsely chopped and steamed
  or boiled
1 (14-ounce) can coconut milk
1 cup heavy whipping cream
Salt and pepper to taste

For the stock, steam the lobster in a steamer for 8 to 10 minutes; immediately plunge in a bowl of ice water to stop the cooking process. Drain. Split the lobster lengthwise into halves and discard the head sacs and tomalley. Remove the tail, claw and leg meat and store in the refrigerator until needed, reserving the shells.

Sear the reserved shells in the canola oil in a stockpot over medium gas heat for 2 to 3 minutes. Add the water, corn cobs, bay leaf, salt and pepper and bring to a boil. Reduce the gas heat to low and simmer for 40 minutes. Strain, discarding the solids and reserving the stock.

For the chowder, pull the corn husks back, leaving the husks attached at the base of the cob. Remove the silk and reposition the husks. Arrange the corn on a baking sheet and roast at 350 degrees in a gas oven for 30 minutes. Let stand until cool and then cut the corn kernels into a bowl using a sharp knife.

Heat the butter in a large stockpot over medium gas heat. Sauté the onion in the butter for 3 minutes. Deglaze the stockpot with the sherry and sprinkle in the flour. Cook for 3 minutes, stirring constantly. Whisk in the reserved stock and bring to a boil.

Simmer for 30 minutes or until slightly thickened. Stir in the potatoes and roasted corn kernels. Add the coconut milk and cream and simmer until heated through; do not allow to boil. Season with salt and pepper. Ladle into soup bowls and top with the reserved lobster meat. Garnish with chopped fresh chives.—Serves 12—**Irv Miller, Jackson's, 2001**

Lobster Salad with Spicy Key Lime Dressing

Spicy Key Lime Dressing
1/4 cup fresh Key lime juice
3/4 teaspoon chili garlic sauce, strained
1 tablespoon plus 2 teaspoons soy sauce
1 teaspoon freshly ground pepper
1/2 teaspoon finely grated fresh garlic
1/2 teaspoon finely grated fresh ginger
1/4 cup plus 2 teaspoons grapeseed oil

Lobster Salad
1 (2 1/2-pound) fresh whole lobster
1 teaspoon sea salt
1 cup vegetable oil
2 garlic cloves, thinly sliced
5 medium to large shiitake mushrooms, stemmed
3 ounces assorted baby field greens

For the dressing, combine the lime juice, chili garlic sauce, soy sauce, pepper, garlic and ginger in a bowl and whisk until combined. Add the grapeseed oil gradually, whisking constantly until emulsified.

For the salad, bring enough water to a boil in a stockpot to cover the lobster and add the lobster and salt. Boil for 10 minutes. Immediately plunge the lobster into a bowl of ice water to stop the cooking process and let stand until chilled; drain. Remove the claws and the tail meat and cut the tail meat into 1/2-inch pieces.

Heat the oil in a small saucepan to 320 degrees. Add the garlic to the hot oil and deep-fry until crisp. Remove to a paper towel to drain. Lightly grill the mushroom caps on a gas grill or sauté in a sauté pan over gas heat just until tender. Toss the field greens with the lobster tail meat and dressing in a bowl. Mound the greens mixture evenly on each of four serving plate. Encircle the greens with the garlic chips, grilled mushrooms and lobster claws.—Serves 4—**Andrew Selz, Chef Selz Collection, 2004**

TIP Store fresh lobster in the refrigerator at 32 degrees Fahrenheit and use within 2 days. Freeze lobster at 0 degrees Fahrenheit for up to 6 months. Thaw frozen lobster in the refrigerator or under cold running water.

Sun-Ripened Tomatoes and Asian-Style Lobster Salad

1 (1¹/4-pound) whole lobster
2 tablespoons sliced scallions, cut on the bias
4 teaspoons rice vinegar
1 tablespoon chopped fresh cilantro
1 teaspoon grated fresh ginger
1 teaspoon sugar
1/2 teaspoon sesame oil
Pinch of kosher salt
Pinch of cracked pepper
4 ounces napa cabbage leaves, rolled and sliced into julienne strips
2 sun-ripened tomatoes, thickly sliced
1 avocado, coarsely chopped
1 teaspoon black and toasted white sesame seeds

Steam the lobster in a steamer for 9 minutes. Shock the lobster in a bowl of ice water to stop the cooking process; drain. Split the lobster lengthwise into halves. Carefully remove the tail meat from the lobster and coarsely chop. Place in a chilled bowl. Crack the lobster claws and remove the meat. Add the meat to the chilled bowl. Add the scallions, vinegar, cilantro, ginger, sugar, sesame oil, salt and pepper and mix with a fork until combined.

Arrange the cabbage evenly over the bottoms of four serving plates and overlap with the sliced tomatoes. Mound the lobster salad over the tomatoes and top with the avocado and sesame seeds. Garnish with fresh cilantro leaves.—Serves 4—**Irv Miller, Jackson's, 2001**

 TIP Whole lobsters or lobster tails should have a mild sea breeze aroma, firm flesh, and tightly adhering shells free of black spots.

Grilled Lobster Salad with Blood Orange Vinaigrette and Mango Saffron Coulis

Blood Orange Vinaigrette
2 cups blood orange juice
1/2 cup corn syrup
1/4 cup red wine vinegar
1 tablespoon lime juice
1 tablespoon raspberry vinegar
2 teaspoons Greek seasoning
1/2 cup olive oil

Mango Saffron Coulis
1 pound fresh or frozen
  mangoes, chopped

1/4 cup corn syrup
1 teaspoon saffron
Slurry as needed (mixture of cornstarch
  and water)

Lobster Salad
4 cups spring salad mix
2 cups arborio rice, cooked and shaped
  into 4 cakes
4 (6-ounce) lobster tails, grilled

For the vinaigrette, combine the orange juice, corn syrup, wine vinegar, lime juice, raspberry vinegar and Greek seasoning in a food processor and process until blended. Add the olive oil gradually, processing constantly until emulsified.

For the coulis, process the mangoes in a food processor until puréed. Combine the purée with the corn syrup and saffron in a saucepan and mix well. Cook until heated through. Add the desired amount of slurry and cook until thickened and of a sauce consistency, stirring frequently. Remove from the heat and let stand until cool.

For the salad, mound 1 cup of the salad mix on each of four serving plates. Top each with one rice cake and one lobster tail. Drizzle with the vinaigrette and coulis. Garnish each serving with three edible orchids.—Serves 4—**Alphonse Lucier IV, Pensacola Yacht Club, 2001**

TIP One pound of cooked lobster meat yields 4 servings; a one pound whole lobster yields 1/3 pound cooked meat.

Grilled Ginger Garlic Lobster Tails

Asian Guacamole
2 Haas avocados, chopped
1/2 cup finely chopped Maui or Vidalia onion
1/2 cup finely chopped tomato
1/4 cup sliced scallions
2 tablespoons minced pickled ginger
2 tablespoons chopped cilantro
Juice of 2 limes
1 teaspoon garlic chile paste or sriracha
1 teaspoon sesame seeds, toasted
1/2 teaspoon sesame oil

Lobster Tails
2 lobster tails, shells removed
1/4 cup rice wine vinegar
3 tablespoons ketchup or chili sauce
3 tablespoons sesame oil
3 tablespoons dark soy sauce
1 tablespoon grated lime zest or lemon zest
1 tablespoon minced garlic
1 tablespoon fish sauce
1 tablespoon sambal oelek (red chili paste)
2 teaspoons grated fresh ginger
2 to 4 steaks, grilled

For the guacamole, combine the avocados, onion, tomato, scallions, ginger and cilantro in a bowl and mix well. Add the lime juice, chile paste, sesame seeds and sesame oil and stir to the desired consistency. Serve immediately or apply plastic wrap directly to the surface of the guacamole and store, covered, in the refrigerator for 8 to 10 hours.

For the lobster, split the tail meat lengthwise into halves and thread on metal or soaked wooden skewers. Arrange on a rimmed baking sheet. Combine the vinegar, ketchup, sesame oil, soy sauce, lime zest, garlic, fish sauce, sambal oelek and ginger in a saucepan and mix well. Simmer for 5 minutes, stirring frequently. Pour the marinade over the lobster meat, turning to coat.

Marinate in the refrigerator for 1 hour or longer, turning occasionally. Drain, reserving the marinade. Set the gas grill on medium-high heat. Arrange the skewers on an oiled grill rack over indirect heat. Grill for about 5 minutes, brushing with the reserved marinade occasionally. Arrange the grilled lobster and guacamole on the steaks on serving plates.—Serves 2 to 4—
Irv Miller, Jackson's, 2008

Blackened Shrimp in Beer Butter Sauce

2 tablespoons olive oil
24 (21- to 25-count) shrimp,
   peeled and deveined
1/4 cup blackening seasoning
1/4 cup chopped tomato

2 tablespoons chopped green onions
2 cups beer
2 tablespoons unsalted butter
Salt and pepper to taste
12 slices crusty French bread

Heat the olive oil in a medium skillet until almost smoking. Add the shrimp and blackening seasoning to the hot oil and sauté until the shrimp are almost cooked through. Stir in the tomato and green onions and sauté for 2 minutes longer. Stir in the beer and remove from the heat. Swirl in the butter and season with salt and pepper. Divide the shrimp equally among four serving plates. Add three slices of bread to each plate to sop up the sauce and serve immediately.—Serves 4 as an appetizer—**Paul Pettigrew, Seville Quarter, 2001**

Garlic and Sherry Shrimp on Grilled French Bread

10 slices country loaf or baguette
2 tablespoons extra-virgin olive oil
1 cup (2 sticks) unsalted butter, cut into
   tablespoons and chilled
20 (21- to 25-count) shrimp, peeled
   and deveined

1/2 cup dry sherry
2 tablespoons minced fresh garlic
3 tablespoons heavy whipping cream
Squeeze of lemon juice
1 cup packed fresh spinach, wilted

Brush the bread slices with the olive oil and grill on a gas grill until toasted on both sides. Melt 2 tablespoons of the butter in a medium skillet and then add the shrimp. Cook until the shrimp turn pink. Remove the shrimp to a platter using a slotted spoon, reserving the pan drippings.

Add the sherry and garlic to the reserved pan drippings and mix well. Cook over medium gas heat for 3 to 5 minutes or until the liquid is reduced and concentrated. Stir in the cream and lemon juice and cook over low gas heat until thickened, stirring frequently. Gradually whisk in the remaining chilled butter and cook until the sauce is thickened. Top each grilled bread slice with wilted spinach and two of the shrimp. Drizzle with the sauce.—Serves 10 as an appetizer—**Irv Miller, Jackson's, 2007**

Chocolate Shrimp

Infused Oil
3 tablespoons minced fresh ginger
2 teaspoons minced fresh garlic
1 habanero chile, thinly sliced
1/2 cup canola oil

Orange Chocolate Sauce
Juice of 1 orange
2 tablespoons sherry
1 ounce unsweetened chocolate, finely chopped

Shrimp
3 tablespoons all-purpose flour
1 teaspoon salt
1 teaspoon coarsely ground pepper
8 jumbo shrimp, peeled, deveined and butterflied
Fresh lime juice to taste

For the oil, sauté the ginger, garlic and habanero chile in the canola oil in a sauté pan over medium-high gas heat for 3 minutes. Remove from the heat and let stand for 10 minutes. Strain, discarding the solids. Return the oil to the sauté pan.

For the sauce, bring the orange juice and sherry to a boil in a saucepan over medium gas heat. Stir in the chocolate and remove from the heat.

For the shrimp, mix the flour, salt and pepper in a shallow dish. Coat the shrimp with the seasoned flour. Heat the infused oil in a sauté pan over medium-high gas heat until hot. Add the shrimp to the hot oil and sauté for 2 minutes on each side or until brown; drain. Toss the shrimp with the sauce in a bowl. Divide the shrimp evenly between two plates and drizzle with lime juice. Serve immediately.—Serves 2 as an appetizer—**Jim Shirley, Atlas Oyster House, 2003**

TIP Shrimp are sized by the number of shrimp per pound. Less than twenty per pound is jumbo; twenty to thirty per pound is large; thirty to forty per pound is medium; more than forty per pound is small.

Shrimp Lettuce Wraps

8 ounces fresh ginger, minced
2 cups canola oil
1/4 cup sesame oil
1/2 cup soy sauce
1/4 cup minced cilantro
1/4 cup minced basil
6 garlic cloves, minced

1 (2-inch) piece fresh ginger, minced
2 pounds medium shrimp, peeled
    and deveined
Julienned carrots to taste
Julienned onions to taste
Julienned bell peppers to taste
Crisp iceberg lettuce leaves

Combine 8 ounces minced ginger and the canola oil in a saucepan. Simmer over low gas heat for 2 hours. Let stand until cool; strain. Stir in the sesame oil. Reserve the infused oil. Mix the soy sauce, cilantro, basil, garlic and minced 2-inch piece of ginger in a bowl.

Heat a wok until very hot and add 1 tablespoon of the infused oil, 2 teaspoons of the soy sauce mixture and a handful of the shrimp. Sauté for about 3 minutes or until the shrimp turn pink. Remove the shrimp to a platter. Repeat the process with the infused oil, soy sauce mixture and remaining shrimp until all of the shrimp are cooked. Reserve any remaining infused oil for another recipe.

Add 1 tablespoon of the remaining infused oil, 2 teaspoons of the remaining soy sauce mixture, carrots, onions and bell peppers to the hot wok. Sauté until the vegetables are the desired degree of crispness. Stuff lettuce leaves with the shrimp and vegetables and roll to enclose the filling. Serve as an appetizer or entrée.—Variable servings—**Jim Shirley, Atlas Oyster House, 2004**

Shrimp Tortellini Maria

2 cups cheese tortellini
1/4 cup olive oil
2 tablespoons unsalted butter
1 pound medium shrimp, peeled
    and deveined

1 tablespoon capers
1 garlic clove, minced
Salt and pepper to taste

Cook the pasta using the package directions until al dente; drain. Cover to keep warm. Heat the olive oil and butter in a skillet until hot. Add the shrimp and cook for 1 to 2 minutes or until the shrimp turn pink; do not overcook. Stir in the capers, garlic, salt and pepper. Immediately spoon the shrimp mixture over the hot pasta on serving plates.—Serves 4 as an appetizer—**Travis Herr, Bill Hamilton and Culinary Students, Pensacola Junior College, 2005**

Chilled Gazpacho with Ginger-Lime Marinated Shrimp

Gazpacho
1 pound tomatoes, peeled, seeded and chopped
1 small bell pepper, finely chopped
1 small purple onion, finely chopped
1 small cucumber, peeled, seeded and finely chopped
1 1/2 cups tomato juice
2 tablespoons red wine vinegar
Juice of 1 lime
1 tablespoon olive oil
2 teaspoons Tabasco sauce
Salt and freshly ground pepper to taste

Shrimp and Assembly
2 tablespoons grated fresh ginger
1/4 cup reduced-sodium soy sauce
1/4 cup white wine
2 tablespoons olive oil
Juice of 1 lime
Freshly ground pepper to taste
18 large shrimp, peeled and deveined
12 (1/2-inch-thick) slices French bread
Garlic-flavor olive oil for brushing

   For the gazpacho, combine the tomatoes, bell pepper, onion and cucumber in a nonreactive bowl and mix well. Stir in the tomato juice, vinegar, lime juice, olive oil, Tabasco sauce, salt and pepper. Chill, covered, for 8 to 10 hours. Taste and adjust seasonings.

   For the shrimp, combine the ginger, soy sauce, wine, 2 tablespoons olive oil, the lime juice and pepper in a bowl and mix well. Mix in the shrimp and marinate in the refrigerator for 30 minutes; drain. Grill the shrimp on a gas grill until the shrimp turn pink. Remove to a bowl and chill in the refrigerator.

   Brush the bread slices with garlic-flavor olive oil and grill until light brown and crisp on both sides. Ladle the gazpacho into chilled soup bowls and top each serving with two grilled bread slices. Arrange three shrimp on each serving and garnish with julienned cucumber.—Serves 6—
Scott Wilson, Radley's Deli After Dark, 1995

Grecian Shrimp Salad

12 medium shrimp, peeled and deveined
2 tablespoons olive oil
1 teaspoon leaf oregano
Salt and pepper to taste
1/4 cup extra-virgin olive oil
2 tablespoons red wine vinegar

1 cucumber, peeled
1 large tomato, cut into wedges
1/2 small red onion, cut into slivers
1/2 cup feta cheese chunks
1 teaspoon chopped parsley

Brush the shrimp with 2 tablespoons olive oil. Sprinkle with the oregano and season with salt and pepper. Grill the shrimp on a gas grill for 2 to 3 minutes per side or until the shrimp turn pink. Whisk 1/4 cup olive oil and the vinegar in a bowl until blended.

Cut the cucumber lengthwise into halves, remove the seeds and then cut into half-moons. Arrange the cucumber, tomato and onion in a decorative pattern on one or two serving plates. Place the shrimp on the prepared plates and drizzle with the olive oil vinaigrette. Sprinkle with the cheese and parsley.—Serves 1 or 2—**Gus Silivos, Skopelos on the Bay, 2000**

Grilled Avocado with Shrimp and Fire-Roasted Tomato Salad

1 bag of Zatarain's crab boil
12 shrimp
1 tomato
Vegetable oil
2 avocados, cut into halves
3 tablespoons mayonnaise
3 tablespoons sour cream

1/4 cup cilantro, finely chopped
3 tablespoons minced red onion
1 teaspoon Old Bay seasoning
1 tablespoon grated lime zest or
   lemon zest
2 tablespoons pine nuts, toasted
2 tablespoons chopped scallions

Bring the crab boil and enough water to generously cover the shrimp to a boil in a stockpot. Add the shrimp and return to a boil. Boil until the shrimp turn pink; drain. Peel and devein the shrimp. Chill, covered, in the refrigerator. Lightly coat the tomato with oil and grill on a gas grill over medium-high heat for 10 minutes or until charred on all sides. Peel, seed and chop the tomato. Place in a bowl and chill in the refrigerator.

Clean the grill rack with an oiled towel. Grill the avocados cut side down on the grill rack until grill marks appear. Arrange each half grilled side up on a serving plate. Mix the mayonnaise, sour cream, cilantro, onion and Old Bay seasoning in a bowl. Fold in the shrimp, tomato and lime zest. Mound equal portions of the shrimp salad in each avocado half and sprinkle with the pine nuts and scallions.—Serves 4—**Irv Miller, Jackson's, 2006**

Shrimp and Black-Eyed Pea Salad

24 shrimp, peeled and deveined
1 tablespoon olive oil
2 teaspoons sugar
Juice of 2 limes
Salt and pepper to taste
2 cups drained cooked black-eyed peas
2 onions, finely chopped
2 tomatoes, chopped
2 cucumbers, chopped
1 bell pepper, chopped
1 bunch parsley, minced
2 garlic cloves, minced
Salt and pepper to taste
Lettuce leaves

Sauté the shrimp in the olive oil in a sauté pan until the shrimp turn pink. Stir in the sugar, lime juice, salt and pepper and toss to coat. Remove the shrimp to a bowl using a slotted spoon, reserving the olive oil dressing. Chill the shrimp and olive oil dressing separately in the refrigerator.

Toss the peas, onions, tomatoes, cucumbers, bell pepper, parsley, garlic, salt and pepper in a bowl. Add the chilled olive oil dressing and mix well. Line four serving plates with lettuce leaves and top each with equal portions of the pea salad. Arrange six shrimp on each salad and garnish with additional minced parsley.—Serves 4—**Stephen Gamble and Stephen Barber, Pensacola Yacht Club, 2005**

TIP Store cooked shrimp in serving-size packets or small containers in the refrigerator or freezer within one hour after cooking. Leftovers can be refrigerated for two days or stored in the freezer for up to one year.

Roasted Corn and Teriyaki Shrimp Salad

4 fresh ears of corn,
   Silver Queen preferred
1 1/2 pounds medium shrimp,
   peeled and deveined
1/4 cup plus 1 tablespoon teriyaki sauce
3/4 cup sliced green onions

3/4 cup chopped red bell pepper
1/2 cup minced cilantro
1/3 cup reduced-calorie mayonnaise
1/3 cup fat-free sour cream
1/2 teaspoon ground cumin
Mixed lettuce leaves

Discard the husks and silk from the ears of corn and trim the ends. Coat the corn with butter-flavor nonstick cooking spray. Arrange on a baking sheet and roast at 400 degrees in a gas oven for 20 minutes, turning occasionally. Thread the shrimp on water-soaked wooden skewers. Brush the shrimp with 1/4 cup of the teriyaki sauce. Grill on a gas grill for 3 to 4 minutes per side or until the shrimp turn pink.

Brush the corn with the remaining 1 tablespoon teriyaki sauce. Grill on a gas grill for 5 minutes or until slightly charred. Let stand until cool. Cut the kernels into a bowl using a sharp knife. Add the shrimp, green onions, bell pepper and cilantro and mix well. Mix the mayonnaise, sour cream and cumin in a bowl and then stir into the shrimp mixture. Spoon about 1 cup of the shrimp salad onto each of six lettuce-lined serving plates.—Serves 6—**Scott Wilson, Radley's Deli After Dark, 1996**

Shrimp Sandwiches with Tarragon Caper Mayonnaise

1/4 cup mayonnaise
1 tablespoon plus 1 teaspoon drained
   capers, finely chopped
1 tablespoon grated sweet onion
2 teaspoons chopped fresh tarragon
1/8 teaspoon celery seeds
1/4 teaspoon hot red pepper sauce,
   or to taste
1/3 cup finely chopped celery heart
   with leaves

Salt and pepper to taste
2 tablespoons butter, softened
8 small soft sandwich rolls, split, or
   6 hot dog buns, split horizontally
10 2/3 ounces large shrimp, cooked,
   peeled and deveined
Sliced tomatoes (optional)
Sliced avocados (optional)
Thinly sliced butter lettuce leaves
   (optional)

Mix the mayonnaise, capers, onion, tarragon, celery seeds and hot sauce in a bowl. Stir in the celery and season to taste with salt, pepper and additional hot sauce. Lightly butter the cuts sides of the rolls. Heat a griddle or large nonstick skillet over medium gas heat. Arrange the rolls cut side down on the griddle and cook for 1 to 2 minutes or until golden brown. Spread the mayonnaise mixture over the bottom of each roll. Cut each shrimp horizontally into halves. Layer the roll bottoms with the shrimp, tomatoes, avocados, lettuce and roll tops to form sandwiches.—Makes 6 to 8 sandwiches—**Angela Miller, Distinctive Kitchens Culinary Arts Center, 2008**

Applewood Barbecued Shrimp

12 jumbo (16- to 20-count) shrimp, peeled and deveined
4 thin slices applewood-smoked bacon, cut into thirds
1 teaspoon Cajun seasoning
1/4 red bell pepper, julienned
1/4 green bell pepper, julienned
1/4 yellow onion, julienned
1 garlic clove, minced
1 tablespoon butter
1/2 cup smoke-flavor barbecue sauce
1 tablespoon Worcestershire sauce
1 tablespoon red hot pepper sauce
Hot cooked rice

Wrap each shrimp with one piece of bacon and secure. Arrange the shrimp seam side down on one side of a foil-lined baking sheet and sprinkle with the Cajun seasoning. Mix the bell peppers, onion, garlic and butter in a bowl and arrange on the other side of the baking sheet.

Bake at 425 degrees in a gas oven until the bacon is brown and the shrimp are pink. Mix the barbecue sauce, Worcestershire sauce and hot sauce in a bowl. Drizzle over the shrimp. Toss the vegetables and continue baking until the shrimp are glazed and the vegetables are caramelized. Arrange the shrimp over hot cooked rice on serving plates. Top with the vegetables.—Serves 3 to 4—**John Flaningam, Angus, 2006**

 TIP   Skewer small shellfish such as shrimp or scallops on metal or water-soaked wooden skewers or cook them in a grill basket.

Barbecued Shrimp

1/2 cup (1 stick) butter
1/4 cup chopped garlic
1/4 cup minced purple shallots
1/4 cup sliced green onions
1/4 cup sliced red bell pepper
24 (21- to 25-count) shrimp with heads
1 tablespoon chopped basil
1 tablespoon chopped thyme
1/4 cup Worcestershire sauce
1 bottle Abita amber beer
Salt and black pepper to taste
Louisiana gold pepper sauce to taste
1/2 cup (1 stick) butter, cut into tablespoons and chilled

Melt 1/2 cup butter in a 14-inch cast-iron skillet over medium-high gas heat. Add the garlic, shallots, green onions and bell pepper and sauté for 3 to 5 minutes or until the vegetables are tender. Stir in the shrimp, basil, thyme and Worcestershire sauce.

Simmer for 3 to 5 minutes or until the shrimp curl and turn pink. Mix in the beer, salt, black pepper and pepper sauce. Cook until the liquid is reduced by half, stirring frequently. Add 1/2 cup butter 2 to 3 tablespoons at a time and cook until the butter is incorporated after each addition, swirling the skillet constantly. Serve four shrimp per person with equal portions of the sauce and hot crusty French bread.—Serves 6—**John Folse, Lafitte's Landing Restaurant, 1996**

Barbecued Shrimp over Grits

4 slices bacon, chopped
1/4 cup chopped red onion
2 tablespoons chopped garlic
1/2 cup white wine
2 cups chopped Roma tomatoes

1 cup stewed tomatoes
1 cup barbecue sauce
1 pound (16- to 20-count) shrimp
   with tails, peeled
Hot cooked grits or mashed potatoes

Cook the bacon in a sauté pan over low gas heat until the fat is rendered and the bacon is light brown. Add the onion and garlic and sauté until the onion is tender. Deglaze the sauté pan with the wine. Cook until the wine is reduced by half. Stir in the chopped tomatoes and sauté until tender. Add the stewed tomatoes and barbecue sauce and mix well.

Simmer over low gas heat for 20 minutes, stirring occasionally. Add the shrimp and simmer for 5 minutes or until the shrimp are cooked through. Spoon the shrimp and sauce over hot cooked grits on serving plates.—Serves 2 to 4—**Erika Thomas and Mark Murphy, Portabello Market, 2006**

Marinated Barbecued Shrimp

2 cups white wine
4 cups (8 sticks) butter, melted
2 cups olive oil
2 tablespoons Worcestershire sauce
6 tablespoons lemon juice
6 tablespoons paprika

4 teaspoons thyme
4 teaspoons black pepper
4 teaspoons cayenne pepper
1 1/2 teaspoons oregano
3 bay leaves
5 pounds shrimp, peeled and deveined

Combine the wine, butter, olive oil, Worcestershire sauce, lemon juice, paprika, thyme, black pepper, cayenne pepper, oregano and bay leaves in a large baking dish and mix well. Add the shrimp and stir until coated. Marinate, covered, in the refrigerator for 8 to 10 hours, stirring occasionally. Bake at 400 degrees in a gas oven until the shrimp turn pink. Discard the bay leaves and serve the shrimp with the sauce.—Serves 5 to 6—**Keith Barber, The Big Easy, 2001**

Barbecued Shrimp over White Rice

2 tablespoons butter
4 (10- to 15-count) shrimp
1 teaspoon minced garlic
1/4 cup beer

1 tablespoon blackening seasoning
1/2 cup barbecue sauce
1/4 cup honey
1 cup hot cooked white rice

Melt the butter in a saucepan and then add the shrimp and garlic. Cook over medium-high gas heat until the shrimp start to turn pink. Add the beer and blackening seasoning and bring to a boil.

Boil until the liquid is reduced by half. Stir in the barbecue sauce and honey and simmer for 1 minute. Mound the rice in the center of a serving plate and surround with the shrimp. Drizzle the sauce over the top.—Serves 1—**David Oreskovich and Pasco Gibson, Oyster Bar/Nichols Seafood, 2003**

Big Sexy-Style Barbecued Shrimp

3 pounds large fresh shrimp
3 tablespoons black pepper
1 tablespoon kosher salt
2 teaspoons Paul Prudhomme's Seafood
    Magic
2 teaspoons red pepper flakes
1 teaspoon chopped fresh rosemary

3 tablespoons chopped garlic
1 tablespoon olive oil
1/3 cup Worcestershire sauce
Grated zest and juice of 2 lemons
1/2 (12-ounce) bottle amber beer
11/2 cups (3 sticks) butter

Devein the shrimp and place in a bowl. Mix the black pepper, salt, Seafood Magic seasoning, pepper flakes and rosemary in a bowl and sprinkle over the shrimp. Add the garlic and olive oil and mix well. Marinate in the refrigerator for 12 to 15 minutes, stirring occasionally.

Sauté the shrimp mixture in a large skillet over high gas heat until the shrimp are three-fourths cooked through or just until opaque. Remove the shrimp to a bowl using a slotted spoon, reserving the pan juices in the skillet. Add the Worcestershire sauce, lemon zest, lemon juice and beer to the reserved pan juices and mix well. Cook until the liquid is reduced. Add the butter and cook until a thick sauce forms, stirring frequently. Return the shrimp to the skillet and simmer until the shrimp turn pink. Serve equal portions of the shrimp and sauce in large bowls. Garnish with additional grated lemon zest and lemon juice. Serve with hot crusty French bread.—Serves 6—**John Murphy and Chris Kimberl, Nooner Cafe, 2008**

Jamaican Barbecued Shrimp

10 shrimp
1 tablespoon jerk seasoning
1 yam, julienned
2 cups vegetable oil for frying
1/4 cup Jamaican barbecue sauce

Sprinkle the shrimp with the jerk seasoning. Grill on a gas grill until the shrimp turn pink. Fry the yam in the oil in a deep skillet until brown; drain. Spread the barbecue sauce over the bottom of a serving plate. Stack the yam in the center of the plate, forming a nest, and arrange the shrimp around the nest. Serve with additional Jamaican barbecue sauce.—Serves 1—**Kevin Faoutas, The Veranda at Henderson Park Inn, 1995**

Asian Almond Shrimp

6 (21- to 25-count) shrimp, peeled, deveined and butterflied
Seasoned all-purpose flour
Buttermilk
Vegetable oil
1/2 cup shredded cabbage
1/4 cup duck glaze (stir-fry sauce and honey)
1 tablespoon sweet chili glaze
2 tablespoons almonds
1 tablespoon chopped Asian herbs (such as cilantro, basil and green onions)

Coat the shrimp with seasoned flour and shake to remove any excess. Dip the shrimp in buttermilk and then again in seasoned flour. Fry the shrimp in hot oil in a deep skillet until golden brown on all sides; drain. Mound the cabbage in the center of a serving plate and arrange the shrimp tail side up on top of the cabbage. Drizzle the duck glaze and chili glaze evenly over the shrimp. Sprinkle with the almonds and herbs and serve.—Serves 1—**Hans Limburg and Alan Turner, Zea Restaurant, 2005**

Most Excellent Fried Shrimp

Orange Sauce
1 cup orange marmalade
1 tablespoon prepared horseradish
1 teaspoon soy sauce

Fried Shrimp
1 cup all-purpose flour
1 teaspoon white pepper
1 teaspoon kosher salt
1 teaspoon garlic powder
1 teaspoon onion powder
1 cup milk
1 egg
2 pounds jumbo shrimp, peeled and deveined
1 cup panko (Japanese bread crumbs)
3 cups vegetable oil

For the sauce, combine the marmalade, horseradish and soy sauce in a saucepan and mix well. Cook over medium gas heat until heated through. Remove from the heat and cover to keep warm.

For the shrimp, mix the flour, white pepper, salt, garlic powder and onion powder in a shallow dish. Whisk the milk and egg in a bowl until blended. Coat the shrimp with the flour mixture and then dip in the egg mixture. Coat with the bread crumbs. Arrange the shrimp in a single layer on a baking sheet and chill for 30 minutes.

Heat the oil in a deep skillet to 375 degrees. Fry the shrimp four at a time in the hot oil until they come to the surface; remove with a slotted spoon to drain. Serve with the warm sauce.—Serves 4—
Jim Shirley, Atlas Oyster House, 2004

TIP To devein shrimp, make a shallow slit down the back of a peeled shrimp with a sharp knife. Locate the black vein and remove with the tip of the knife.

Crab, Crawfish, Lobster & Shrimp

Chipotle Shrimp

1/2 white onion, coarsely chopped
4 chipotle chiles
4 garlic cloves
1 tablespoon balsamic vinegar
1 tablespoon corn syrup
1 teaspoon salt
Pinch of pepper
1 cup olive oil
2 pounds jumbo shrimp, peeled and deveined

Combine the onion, chipotle chiles, garlic, vinegar, corn syrup, salt and pepper in a food processor and process until smooth. Add the olive oil gradually, processing constantly until emulsified.

Toss the chipotle chile mixture with the shrimp in a bowl. Marinate, covered, in the refrigerator for 2 hours, stirring occasionally. Grill the shrimp on a gas grill for 4 minutes or until the shrimp turn pink.—Serves 2 to 4—**Jim Shirley, The Screaming Coyote, 1997**

TIP One pound of raw, headless shrimp in the shell will yield approximately three-fourths pound of cooked, peeled, deveined shrimp. Shrimp may be cooked with the shell on or off, and the cooking time is about the same.

Grilled Gulf Shrimp with Black Bean Cakes and Roasted Red Pepper Coulis

Roasted Red Pepper Coulis
1 large red bell pepper
Olive oil
1 teaspoon chopped fresh garlic
1/2 cup chicken stock
1/2 teaspoon Worcestershire sauce
Pinch of cayenne pepper
Salt and black pepper to taste

Black Bean Cakes and Shrimp
Olive oil
1 tablespoon chopped fresh garlic

1/4 cup chopped red bell pepper
1/4 cup chopped green bell pepper
1/4 cup chopped onion
16 ounces cooked black beans, drained
4 or 5 sun-dried tomatoes, chopped
2 dashes of Tabasco sauce
Salt and pepper to taste
1/4 cup all-purpose flour or
   bread crumbs
1 egg, beaten
All-purpose flour for dusting
10 to 12 large Gulf shrimp

For the coulis, char the bell pepper over a gas flame until blackened. Let stand until cool. Peel the bell pepper and discard the seeds. Process the bell pepper in a blender until puréed. Heat olive oil in a saucepan over medium gas heat and add the garlic. Sauté until the garlic is light brown. Stir in the puréed bell pepper, stock, Worcestershire sauce, cayenne pepper, salt and black pepper. Simmer for 5 minutes. Taste and adjust the seasonings. Process the bell pepper mixture in a blender until smooth.

For the cakes, heat olive oil in a skillet and add the garlic. Sauté until the garlic is light brown and then stir in the bell peppers and onion. Sauté for 1 minute. Remove from the heat and stir in the beans, tomatoes, Tabasco sauce, salt and pepper. Add 1/4 cup flour and the egg and mix well.

Divide the bean mixture into equal portions and place the portions one at a time on a plate lightly dusted with flour. Shape each portion into a cake. Sauté the bean cakes in olive oil in a sauté pan until crisp; drain. Remove to a baking sheet and bake at 350 degrees in a gas oven until cooked through. Brush the shrimp with olive oil and season with salt and pepper. Grill on a gas grill until the shrimp turn pink. Arrange the bean cakes evenly on two to three serving plates and top with equal portions of shrimp and coulis.—Serves 2 to 3—**Chris Tingle, Gauthier's, 1997**

Grilled Gulf Shrimp with Cashew and Lime Butter Sauce

Grilled Shrimp
12 jumbo shrimp, peeled and deveined
2 tablespoons olive oil
Freshly cracked pepper to taste

Cashew and Lime Butter Sauce
1/2 cup cashews, finely chopped
1 tablespoon olive oil
1/2 cup heavy cream
1/4 cup white wine
2 tablespoons lime juice
2 tablespoons chopped shallots
1 tablespoon chopped garlic
1 cup (2 sticks) unsalted butter, cut into cubes and softened

For the shrimp, coat the shrimp with the olive oil and season with pepper. Grill on a gas grill until the shrimp turn pink.

For the sauce, sauté the cashews in the olive oil in a medium saucepan until golden brown. Stir in the cream, wine, lime juice, shallots and garlic. Cook until the liquid is reduced by two-thirds, stirring frequently. Remove from the heat and cool slightly. Add the butter gradually, whisking constantly until combined. Serve immediately with the shrimp.—Serves 4—**Jim O'Brien, O'Brien's Bistro, 2004**

TIP To grill shrimp, place in a grill basket or thread on skewers and grill over medium gas heat. Be careful not to overcook shrimp. Overcooking toughens the shrimp and causes a loss in taste and appearance.

Rim Pesto Shrimp

Pesto and Shrimp
2 cups fresh basil
1/2 cup peanuts
1/2 cup cilantro
1/2 cup sesame oil
1/4 cup lime juice
1/4 cup garlic cloves
2 tablespoons chopped fresh mint
2 teaspoons crushed red pepper flakes
1 teaspoon fish sauce
Salt and black pepper to taste
14 jumbo shrimp, peeled and deveined

Green Tomatoes and Okra
1/2 cup all-purpose flour
1 teaspoon garlic powder
1 teaspoon onion powder
1 teaspoon salt
1/2 teaspoon white pepper
1/2 cup finely chopped pecans
1/2 cup half-and-half
1 egg
2 green tomatoes, sliced
6 okra pods
2 cups canola oil

For the shrimp, process the basil, peanuts, cilantro, sesame oil, lime juice, garlic, mint, red pepper flakes, fish sauce, salt and black pepper in a food processor until puréed. Lightly season the shrimp with salt and black pepper and coat with the basil pesto. Grill the shrimp on a gas grill for 1 1/2 minutes per side or until the shrimp turn pink.

For the green tomatoes and okra, mix the flour, garlic powder, onion powder, salt and white pepper in a shallow dish. Add the pecans and stir to mix well. Whisk the half-and-half and egg in a bowl until blended.

Dip the tomatoes and okra in the egg mixture and then coat with the pecan mixture. Fry in the canola oil in a deep skillet over medium-high gas heat until golden brown; drain. Serve with the shrimp.—Serves 2—**Jim Shirley, Fish House, 2002**

TIP The life cycle of a shrimp in the wild is only about thirteen months. They reproduce rapidly.

Portobello Shrimp

1 tablespoon unsalted butter
1 tablespoon chopped garlic
1 cup artichoke heart quarters
1/2 cup julienned sun-dried tomatoes
1/2 cup white wine
3 cups heavy whipping cream

1/4 teaspoon salt
1/4 teaspoon pepper
6 portobello mushrooms, trimmed
Olive oil
30 shrimp, peeled and deveined

Sauté the butter and garlic in a hot sauté pan until light brown. Stir in the artichokes and tomatoes and sauté until tender. Deglaze the pan with the wine. Cook until most of the liquid evaporates and then stir in the cream, salt and pepper. Cook until the mixture is reduced by half and of a sauce consistency, stirring frequently. Remove from the heat and cover to keep warm.

Coat the mushrooms with olive oil and arrange in a single layer on a baking sheet. Roast in a gas oven until tender. Grill the shrimp on a gas grill until the shrimp turn pink. Arrange each mushroom on a serving plate and top each with five shrimp. Drizzle with the sauce.—Serves 6—**Erika Thomas and Mark Murphy, Portabello Market, 2005**

Beach-Style Shrimp

24 (16- to 20-count) shrimp, peeled and deveined
12 slices bacon
24 (1/2-inch) chunks smoked Gouda cheese
Barbecue sauce to taste

Butterfly the shrimp slightly deeper than usual. Parcook the bacon in a sauté pan. Cut each bacon slice into halves and drain on paper towels. Place one chunk of the cheese in the center of each shrimp and wrap with bacon. Thread six shrimp on each of six metal skewers.

Sauté the shrimp in batches in a hot sauté pan until caramelized on both sides, turning once. Arrange the skewers in a single layer on a baking pan and drizzle with barbecue sauce. Bake at 350 degrees in a gas oven until cooked through. Serve with dirty rice and wilted spinach.—Serves 4—**Dan Dunn, H$_2$O, 2007**

Grilled Shrimp with Pineapple Chutney

Pineapple Chutney
1 red bell pepper, finely chopped
1 red onion, finely chopped
1 or 2 chiles of choice, finely chopped (such as jalapeño chile or serrano chile)
1 tablespoon chili powder
1 tablespoon ground cumin
2 cups chopped pineapple
1/4 cup packed brown sugar
2 tablespoons apple cider vinegar
2 tablespoons lime juice
Fresh mint to taste
Fresh cilantro to taste

Grilled Shrimp
8 ounces shrimp, peeled and deveined
Salt and pepper to taste
Canola oil

For the chutney, sauté the bell pepper, onion and chile in a nonstick skillet until the onion is tender. Stir in the chili powder and cumin; mix in the pineapple. Add the brown sugar, vinegar and lime juice and mix well. Cook until the brown sugar dissolves and the mixture thickens, stirring frequently. Stir in the lime juice, mint and cilantro.

For the shrimp, thread the shrimp through the spine on water-soaked 6-inch bamboo skewers. Season the shrimp with salt and pepper and lightly coat with canola oil. Grill on a gas grill until the shrimp turn pink. Serve with the chutney.—Serves 2—**Brian Culleton, Dharma Blue, 2008**

TIP Shrimp fishing is only done at night. In Florida, there are four shrimp species of commercial value in the Gulf of Mexico and South Atlantic waters. They are categorized by four major colors—brown, pink, white, and royal red. The majority of shrimp harvested in Florida are the pink species.

Glazed Spicy Shrimp

1/4 cup (1/2 stick) butter
3 cups shredded carrots
11/2 teaspoons chopped garlic
1/8 teaspoon nutmeg
1/8 teaspoon oregano
1/8 teaspoon cayenne pepper
Salt and black pepper to taste

3 tablespoons Grand Marnier
2 cups fresh orange juice
2 pounds shrimp with tails,
   peeled and deveined
2 cups all-purpose flour
1/4 cup (1/2 stick) butter
Grated zest of 1 orange

Melt 1/4 cup butter in a skillet and then add the carrots and garlic. Sauté until the carrots are tender. Stir in the nutmeg, oregano, cayenne pepper, salt and black pepper and sauté. Mix in the liqueur and orange juice and cook until the flavors blend.

Mix the flour, salt and black pepper in a shallow dish. Lightly coat the shrimp with the flour mixture. Melt 1/4 cup butter in a skillet and add the shrimp. Sauté until the shrimp turn pink. Add the shrimp to the orange glaze mixture and mix well. Spoon the shrimp mixture equally on serving plates and sprinkle with the orange zest.—Serves 2 to 4—**Kevin Quirk, Ramada Conference Center, 1995**

Grecian Island Shrimp

1/4 cup olive oil
10 medium shrimp, peeled and deveined
1/4 green bell pepper, chopped
1/2 fresh tomato, cut into chunks
8 ounces feta cheese, crumbled

1 garlic clove, minced
Salt and pepper to taste
1 cup hot cooked rice
1 teaspoon chopped parsley

Heat a sauté pan over gas heat and add the olive oil. Sauté the shrimp and bell pepper in the olive oil until the shrimp turn pink. Stir in the tomato, cheese and garlic and season with salt and pepper. Heat until warm. Spoon the shrimp mixture over the rice on one or two serving plates and sprinkle with the parsley.—Serves 1 to 2—**Gus Silivos, Gus's Shuck Shack, 2003**

Sautéed Shrimp with Vermouth Beurre Blanc

1/4 cup dry vermouth
1 teaspoon chopped shallot
1/2 teaspoon peppercorns
2 tablespoons heavy cream
1/2 cup (1 stick) unsalted
  butter, softened

1/4 cup olive oil
6 jumbo shrimp, peeled and deveined
Salt and pepper to taste

Mix the vermouth, shallot and peppercorns in a sauté pan. Cook over medium gas heat until the liquid evaporates. Stir in the cream and cook until almost dry. Remove from the heat and gradually add the butter, whisking constantly until well combined. Strain through a fine sieve into a bowl, discarding the solids. Cover the sauce to keep warm.

Heat a sauté pan and add the olive oil and shrimp. Cook until the shrimp turn pink and are firm. Season with salt and pepper. Ladle the sauce onto a serving plate and top with the shrimp. Garnish with chopped parsley or chervil.—Serves 1—**Gus Silivos, Skopelos on the Bay, 1999**

Shrimp Nasi Goreng Indonesian Rice Bowl

4 ounces (50- to 60-count)
  shrimp, peeled
1/2 cup blanched broccoli
1/3 cup blanched sugar snap peas
1/4 cup julienned yellow onion
1/4 cup mushrooms
1 tablespoon sesame seeds
1 tablespoon corn oil

2 teaspoons granulated garlic
1 cup cooked brown rice
1/4 cup stir-fry sauce
1/2 cup shredded cabbage
1/4 cup julienned carrots
1/4 cup almonds
2 tablespoons Asian herbs (such as
  cilantro, basil and green onion)

Combine the shrimp, broccoli, peas, onion, mushrooms, sesame seeds, corn oil and garlic in a sauté pan and cook until the shrimp turn pink, stirring frequently. Add the rice and cook until heated through. Stir in the stir-fry sauce; do not let the sauce reduce. Spoon the shrimp mixture onto a serving plate and sprinkle with the cabbage, carrots, almonds and herbs.—Serves 1—**Hans Limburg and Alan Turner, Zea Restaurant, 2005**

Shrimp and Grits

Creamy Cheddar Grits
1 quart (4 cups) heavy whipping cream
1 quart (4 cups) milk
1 teaspoon salt
1/2 teaspoon granulated garlic
2 cups grits
3 cups (12 ounces) shredded sharp
   Cheddar cheese
8 ounces cream cheese, cut into cubes
1/2 cup (1 stick) unsalted butter
1/2 teaspoon pepper

Shrimp
2 to 3 tablespoons olive oil
1 tablespoon chopped garlic
24 (16- to 20-count) shrimp
Salt and pepper to taste
1 cup chopped tomato
1/2 cup white wine
1/2 cup chopped fresh parsley
2 tablespoons unsalted butter

For the grits, bring the cream, milk, salt and garlic to a boil in a large saucepan. Add the grits gradually, stirring constantly. Reduce the heat to low and simmer for 5 to 7 minutes or until thickened, stirring occasionally. Add the Cheddar cheese, cream cheese, butter and pepper. Cook until the cheese melts, stirring frequently. Remove from the heat and cover to keep warm.

For the shrimp, heat a sauté pan and add the olive oil. Cook the garlic in the hot oil until fragrant. Season the shrimp with salt and pepper and add to the sauté pan. Sauté for 1 to 2 minutes, turning the shrimp occasionally. Stir in the tomato and cook for 30 seconds. Deglaze the pan with the wine.

Cook until the liquid is reduced by half; add 1/4 cup of the parsley and the butter. Cook until the butter melts, stirring frequently. Mound equal portions of the grits on each of four serving plates and top each serving with six shrimp and an equal portion of the sauce. Sprinkle with the remaining 1/4 cup parsley and garnish with lemon wedges.—Serves 4—**John Huggins, McGuire's Irish Pub, 2004**

 TIP When purchasing shrimp, look for tightly adhering shells, legs intact, meat that is firm to the touch, and a fresh sea breeze smell.

Shrimp and Alabama Goat Cheese Grits

Goat Cheese Grits
3 cups chicken stock
1 cup grits
1 cup heavy cream
1/2 cup (1 stick) butter
5 ounces Belle Chèvre goat cheese, crumbled
2 tablespoons chopped parsley
2 tablespoons chopped basil
1/2 teaspoon kosher salt
7 twists on a pepper mill

Shrimp
16 (21- to 25-count) shrimp, peeled and deveined
1/4 cup extra-virgin olive oil
2 tablespoons minced garlic
2 tablespoons lemon zest
1 teaspoon red pepper flakes
Salt and black pepper to taste

For the grits, bring the stock to a boil in a saucepan. Add the grits gradually to the hot stock and cook for 4 minutes, stirring constantly. Reduce the gas heat to low and stir in the cream. Simmer for 20 minutes and then mix in the butter, cheese, parsley and basil. Stir in the salt and pepper. Remove from the heat and cover to keep warm.

For the shrimp, toss the shrimp with the olive oil, garlic, lemon zest, red pepper flakes, salt and black pepper in a bowl until coated. Chill in the refrigerator. Heat a sauté pan over medium-high gas heat until hot and add the shrimp mixture. Sauté for 5 minutes or until the shrimp curl and turn pink. Spoon equal portions of the grits on each of four serving plates. Top each serving with four shrimp and drizzle equally with the pan juices.—Serves 4—**Jim Shirley, Fish House, 2008**

TIP In Florida, shrimp are harvested with trawls (cone-shaped nets) which are towed along the sea bottom in waters near the shore. The nets have doors to allow the turtles to exit.

Grits a Ya-Ya

Smoked Gouda Cheese Grits
4 cups chicken stock
2 cups grits
1 cup heavy cream
1/2 cup (1 stick) butter
1 (14- to 16-ounce) can
　cream-style corn
8 ounces smoked Gouda
　cheese, shredded

Shrimp
8 slices applewood-smoked
　bacon, chopped

1 tablespoon minced garlic
1 tablespoon minced shallot
3 tablespoons butter
Splash of white wine
1 pound deveined peeled jumbo shrimp
1 portobello mushroom cap, sliced
2 cups chopped fresh spinach
1/4 cup chopped scallions
2 cups heavy cream
Salt and pepper to taste
Hot red pepper sauce to taste

For the grits, bring the stock to a boil in a saucepan and gradually add the grits, stirring constantly. Reduce the gas heat to low and simmer for 40 minutes, stirring occasionally and adding some of the cream if needed. Stir in the remaining cream, butter and corn. Mix in the cheese. Simmer until the cheese melts and the grits are heated through. Remove from the heat and cover to keep warm.

For the shrimp, heat a large saucepan over medium gas heat and add the bacon. Cook for about 3 minutes. Stir in the garlic and shallot and sauté. Add the butter and wine. Cook until the butter partially melts and then add the shrimp.

Cook until the sides of the shrimp turn white; turn the shrimp. Stir in the mushroom, spinach and scallions. Sauté for 2 minutes. Remove the shrimp to a bowl using a slotted spoon, reserving the pan juices. Add the cream to the reserved pan juices and mix well.

Simmer until the mixture is reduced by one-third, stirring constantly. Season with salt, pepper and hot sauce. Return the shrimp to the sauce and simmer just until heated through. Spoon the shrimp mixture over equal portions of the grits on serving plates.—Serves 6 to 8—**Jim Shirley, Fish House, 2000**

 TIP Pink shrimp (*Penaeus duorarum*) are very important to the Florida fish industry in both yield and value and have been referred to as "Pink Gold."

Pasta Aglio e Olio

Olive oil
1 cup sliced mushrooms
Coarsely chopped fresh vegetables
   of choice
1¹/₂ teaspoons minced garlic
¹/₂ teaspoon oregano

Garlic salt to taste
Pepper to taste
Shrimp, peeled and deveined, or
   your favorite seafood
1 cup cooked pasta

Cover the bottom of a sauté pan with olive oil and heat over gas heat until hot. Add the mushrooms, chopped vegetables, garlic, oregano, garlic salt and pepper and sauté until the vegetables are tender. Add the shrimp and cook on one side. Turn the shrimp and cook until the shrimp turn pink. Add the pasta and toss to mix. Cook just until heated through.—Serves 1—**Steve Lillo, Lillo's Trattoria, 2004**

Jerry's Shrimp Scampi

18 (31- to 35-count) shrimp, peeled
   and deveined
2 tablespoons butter
2 tablespoons finely chopped
   green onions
1 tablespoon white wine
2 teaspoons lemon juice
1 teaspoon minced garlic
Dash of salt

Dash of pepper
Dash of Jerry's hot sauce*
Dash of basil
Dash of chopped parsley
2 tablespoons finely chopped
   green onions
1 tablespoon cornstarch
1 cup hot water
4 cups hot cooked angel hair pasta

Combine the shrimp, butter, 2 tablespoons green onions, the wine, lemon juice, garlic, salt, pepper, hot sauce, basil and parsley in a sauté pan. Cook over high gas heat for 4 to 5 minutes. Reduce the heat and stir in 2 tablespoons green onions.

Mix the cornstarch and hot water in a bowl until blended. Gradually add to the shrimp mixture, stirring constantly. Cook until thickened, stirring frequently. Spoon the shrimp scampi over the pasta on two serving plates. Garnish with lemon and parsley.—Serves 2—**Jerry Mistretta, Jerry's Cajun Cafe, 2002**

TIP *Available at www.jerryscajun.com

Shrimp and Andouille Fettuccini

2 tablespoons butter
8 ounces andouille, cut into bite-size pieces
12 ounces (31- to 35-count) deveined peeled shrimp
1 teaspoon minced garlic
1 cup chopped green onions
Juice of 1/4 lemon
2 tablespoons Jerry's Own ZydeCajun seasoning*
1 teaspoon basil
1 teaspoon thyme
1/2 teaspoon Jerry's habanero sauce* (optional)
4 cups drained cooked fettuccini
1 cup half-and-half
1 cup (4 ounces) shredded provolone cheese
1/2 cup (2 ounces) grated Parmesan cheese
Dash of Jerry's Own ZydeCajun seasoning*

Heat the butter in a large skillet over medium gas heat for about 5 minutes. Add the sausage, shrimp, garlic and some of the green onions to the hot butter and sauté until the shrimp are almost cooked through. Stir in the lemon juice, 2 tablespoons ZydeCajun seasoning, the basil, thyme and habanero sauce. Reduce the heat and mix in the pasta. Add the half-and-half and toss to coat. Cook until the mixture is heated through.

Sprinkle the shrimp mixture with the provolone cheese and Parmesan cheese and stir until combined. Add the remaining green onions and a dash of ZydeCajun seasoning. Continue cooking until the shrimp mixture is hot and the sauce is the desired consistency. Add additional half-and-half if the sauce is too thick and additional cheese if the sauce is too thin. Spoon into pasta bowls and garnish with additional shredded provolone cheese, chopped green onions and a dash of ZydeCajun seasoning.—Serves 2—**Jerry Mistretta, Jerry's Cajun Cafe, 1999**

TIP *Available at www.jerryscajun.com

Prosciutto-Wrapped Shrimp with Tortellini

6 jumbo shrimp, peeled and deveined
Salt and pepper to taste
6 (1x8-inch) pieces prosciutto
2 tablespoons olive oil
4 to 6 tablespoons heavy cream
1/2 cup tortellini, cooked al dente
1 ounce Romano cheese or Parmesan cheese, grated
1 teaspoon chopped parsley

Season the shrimp with salt and pepper. Wrap each shrimp with one piece of the prosciutto and secure with a wooden pick. Coat with the olive oil. Grill the shrimp on a gas grill for 2 to 3 minutes. Turn the shrimp and grill for 3 to 4 minutes longer or until the shrimp turn pink.

Bring the cream to a boil in a sauté pan and boil until reduced by one-third. Add the pasta and cook until the cream is reduced by half. Spoon the pasta mixture onto a serving plate and top with the shrimp. Sprinkle with the cheese and parsley.—Serves 1—**Gus Silivos, Skopelos on the Bay, 1998**

TIP To boil shrimp, drop the shrimp in boiling water in a stockpot and cook for three to four minutes per pound of shrimp. Drain and rinse immediately under cold water to stop the cooking process. Be careful not to overcook the shrimp. You may use a commercially prepared shrimp boil seasoning or season to personal taste with one or more of the following: salt, lemon slices, beer, pickling spices, whole peppercorns, and/or bay leaves.

Shrimp Pastacola

Basil Pesto
2 cups fresh basil leaves
1/4 cup pine nuts, toasted
3 garlic cloves
1/2 cup olive oil
1/4 cup (1/2 stick) butter
1/2 cup (2 ounces) grated
   Parmesan cheese
Salt and pepper to taste

Alfredo Sauce
1/4 cup (1/2 stick) butter
2 tablespoons minced garlic

1 quart (4 cups) heavy cream
Salt and pepper to taste

Shrimp
1 cup mushrooms, cut into quarters
4 ounces peeled shrimp
1 teaspoon minced garlic
1 tablespoon extra-virgin olive oil
10 ounces bow tie pasta, cooked
   and drained

For the pesto, combine the basil, pine nuts and garlic in a food processor. Pulse until the basil is coarsely chopped. Add the olive oil and butter and process until combined. Spoon the basil mixture into a bowl and fold in the cheese. Season with salt and pepper.

For the sauce, combine the butter and garlic in a saucepan. Cook just until the garlic becomes fragrant. Add the cream and cook until the sauce is reduced by one-half and heavily coats the back of a spoon. Season with salt and pepper.

For the shrimp, sauté the mushrooms, shrimp and garlic in the olive oil in a large sauté pan until the shrimp curl and are ninety percent cooked through. Add 1/2 cup of the sauce and bring to a boil, stirring frequently. Remove from the heat and stir in the 1/4 cup of the pesto.

Add the pasta to the shrimp mixture and toss to coat. Spoon the shrimp mixture into two pasta bowls. Garnish with grated Parmesan cheese and fresh basil ribbons. Reserve any remaining pesto and sauce for another use.—Serves 2—**Hans Limburg, Semolina Original International Pastas, 1997**

Jerry's Shrimp Étouffée

1 cup (2 sticks) butter or margarine
2 cups all-purpose flour
1 cup chopped onion
1 cup chopped bell pepper
1 cup chopped celery
1 tablespoon minced garlic
1/2 cup chopped green onions
4 cups shrimp stock or warm water
1 pound (21- to 26-count) deveined peeled shrimp
1 (10-ounce) can tomatoes with green chiles (optional)
1/2 cup chopped green onions
1 tablespoon dried thyme
2 tablespoons Jerry's Own ZydeCajun seasoning*
1 tablespoon dried basil
1 teaspoon sugar
1 teaspoon salt
2 bay leaves
8 dashes Tabasco sauce, or to taste
8 dashes Louisiana hot sauce, or to taste
Dash of crushed red pepper
Dash of Jerry's hot sauce*
Hot steamed rice

Melt the butter in a medium saucepan; gradually add the flour, whisking constantly until blended. Cook until smooth and creamy, stirring constantly. Stir in the onion, bell pepper, celery, garlic and 1/2 cup green onions. Sauté for about 20 minutes or until the vegetables caramelize, stirring constantly. Mix in the stock and reduce the gas heat to low.

Simmer for 15 to 20 minutes, stirring occasionally. Add the shrimp, tomatoes with green chiles, 1/2 cup green onions, the thyme, ZydeCajun seasoning, basil, sugar, salt, bay leaves, Tabasco sauce, Louisiana hot sauce, red pepper and hot sauce. Simmer for 20 minutes or until of a creamy consistency, stirring occasionally. Discard the bay leaves and ladle the étouffée over hot cooked rice in bowls. Garnish with additional chopped green onions and chopped parsley.—Serves 4 to 6—**Jerry Mistretta, Jerry's Cajun Cafe, 2008**

TIP *Available at www.jerryscajun.com

Mixed
Seafood

Gumbo. No word says seafood to the diners, cooks, and chefs of the Gulf Coast like "gumbo," a flavorful, spicy stew, often of mixed seafood including crab, oysters, shrimp, and fish, thickened with roux, and served over rice. The word "gumbo" comes to us from West Africa, where it means "okra," a vegetable that some use to thicken the stew. A form of the French seafood-based soup, bouillabaisse, gumbo was invented in Louisiana and is the perfect example of how the diverse cultures of the Gulf Coast—Spanish, African, Caribbean, Native American, French—melded together in the great melting pot of the Gulf Coast.

But with all the seafood bounty available to chefs along the coast, was there ever any doubt they would begin to combine various delicacies to form different dishes—fish stuffed with crab meat or oysters and shrimp sautéed together, combined in a sauce, and served over pasta? There is crab meat or shrimp to be used to garnish fish fillets or a perfectly seared scallop to nestle beside a well-turned fillet of beef.

On the Gulf Coast there is no shortage of seafood or chef-driven creativity. These recipes, whether traditional or nouvelle, are a great way for any cook to re-create the best our coast has to offer.

Crusted Flounder with Shrimp Dumplings

Brioche Dough
2 1/2 cups dry brioche crumbs
1 cup (2 sticks) butter, softened

Flounder
3 tablespoons butter, softened
Salt and white pepper to taste
4 (6-ounce) flounder fillets

Shrimp Dumplings and Assembly
1 1/2 pounds shrimp, peeled
   and deveined

1/3 cup heavy cream
3 tablespoons finely chopped chives
1 tablespoon lemon zest, blanched in
   simple syrup
Salt to taste
3 cups sliced leeks
Chicken stock
1 tablespoon butter
Pepper to taste
4 cups water

For the crust, mix the brioche crumbs and butter in a bowl until combined. Place the brioche mixture between two sheets of baking parchment and roll 1/4 inch thick using a rolling pin. Chill, covered, in the refrigerator. Cut the dough into strips large enough to cover each fillet. Chill in the refrigerator.

For the flounder, cut six 6-inch squares of baking parchment. Brush one side of the squares with the butter and sprinkle with salt and white pepper. Arrange the fillets on the butter-coated side of the parchment squares and roll. Roll in a tight bundle using plastic wrap and tie each end. The bundles should resemble sausages. Chill in the refrigerator.

For the dumplings, place the shrimp in a food processor fitted with a metal blade. Process until the shrimp are finely chopped and sticky. Add the cream and process until puréed. Spoon the purée into a bowl and fold in the chives and lemon zest. Season with salt.

Bring a stockpot of salted water to a simmer. Shape the shrimp mixture into dumplings between two spoons; the dumplings should be about 1/2 inch in diameter and about 2 inches long. Drop the dumplings into the simmering water and poach for 3 to 5 minutes or until cooked through. Remove to a platter and cover. Blanch the leeks in chicken stock in a saucepan; drain.

Heat the butter in a sauté pan and add the leeks and dumplings. Season with salt and pepper and cook until heated through. Remove from the heat and cover to keep warm. Poach the flounder bundles in 4 cups water in a saucepan to the desired degree of doneness. Discard the plastic wrap and arrange the fillets on a baking sheet. Top each fillet with one strip of the brioche dough and broil in a gas oven until golden brown. Arrange one fillet on each of four serving plates. Spoon the leek and dumpling mixture evenly over the fillets.—Serves 4—**Travis Herr, Bill Hamilton and Culinary Students, Pensacola Junior College, 2004**

Grouper Daniels

1/2 cup white wine
2 tablespoons cornstarch
1 quart (4 cups) heavy cream
16 ounces Gouda cheese, shredded
1 tablespoon Creole mustard
1 pound crawfish tails
8 ounces okra, sliced
8 ounces andouille, thinly sliced and seared
2 large tomatoes, chopped
4 (6-ounce) grouper fillets
1/4 cup plus 1 tablespoon blackening seasoning
4 pieces cornbread

Mix the wine and cornstarch in a bowl until blended. Bring the cream to a simmer in a saucepan and whisk in the cornstarch mixture. Stir in the cheese and Creole mustard. Cook until smooth, thickened and of a sauce consistency, stirring frequently. Sauté the crawfish, okra, sausage and tomatoes in a sauté pan. Stir the crawfish mixture into the cheese sauce and mix in 1 tablespoon of the blackening seasoning. Simmer just until heated through. Remove from the heat and cover to keep warm.

Coat the fillets with the remaining 1/4 cup blackening seasoning. Blacken the fillets on a gas grill until the fillets flake easily. Arrange one piece of the cornbread on each of four serving plates and soak with some of the crawfish sauce. Top each serving with one fillet and drizzle with the remaining crawfish sauce.—Serves 4—**Jim Shirley, Fish House, 2008**

TIP Prior to starting your grill, pour a small amount of vegetable oil on a paper towel and lightly coat the grill rack to prevent the fish from sticking.

Mixed Seafood

Grouper New Iberia

2 cups milk

1 egg

1 teaspoon Jerry's Own
   ZydeCajun seasoning*

1 large eggplant, peeled and cut into
   1/2-inch slices

2 cups Jerry's Own CajunDust fry mix*

Canola oil

4 (6- to 8-ounce) grouper fillets

1/4 cup (1/2 stick) butter, melted

1/4 cup blackening seasoning

4 cups prepared crawfish étouffée

Whisk the milk and egg in a bowl until blended; stir in the ZydeCajun seasoning. Soak the eggplant in the egg mixture for 5 to 10 minutes. Drain the eggplant, allowing any excess egg mixture to drip off the slices. Coat with the fry mix. Fry the eggplant in canola oil in a deep skillet for 5 to 8 minutes or until golden brown. Drain on paper towels.

Heat a cast-iron skillet until as hot as possible or until the bottom glows red in the center on a gas grill. Coat the fillets with the butter and sprinkle both sides with the blackening seasoning. Arrange the fillets in the hot skillet and sear on one side for about 2 minutes. Turn and sear for 2 minutes on the remaining side. It is recommended that blackening the grouper be an outdoor project.

Arrange the eggplant slices evenly on each of four serving plates and top each serving with one of the fillets. Top each with 1 cup of the étouffée.—Serves 4—**Jerry Mistretta, Jerry's Cajun Cafe, 2006**

Pesce Picante Mare (Spicy Fish)

2 (6-inch) sprigs of rosemary,
   stems removed

1 1/2 teaspoons minced garlic

2 to 3 tablespoons butter

12 large shrimp, peeled and deveined

Blackening seasoning to taste

1 grouper fillet, grilled

Sauté the rosemary and garlic in the butter in a sauté pan. Stir in the shrimp. Add blackening seasoning until the shrimp turn orange, not red. Sauté until the shrimp are cooked through. Spoon the shrimp mixture over the grilled grouper on a serving plate. For variety, substitute scallops for the shrimp.—Serves 1—**Steve Lillo's, Lillo's Trattoria, 2004**

TIP *Available at www.jerryscajun.com

Panéed Grouper Stack with Potato Crab Cakes and Leek-Pepper Beurre Blanc

Leek-Pepper Beurre Blanc
1 shallot, chopped
6 sprigs of parsley, chopped
1/4 cup white wine
1 tablespoon chopped leek
1 tablespoon chopped red bell pepper
1/4 cup heavy cream
1/2 cup (1 stick) butter, cubed

Crab Cakes
1 potato, peeled and shredded
3 tablespoons mayonnaise
2 tablespoons all-purpose flour
1/4 green bell pepper, finely chopped

1 tablespoon chopped parsley
1 egg, beaten
1 egg white, beaten
Salt and pepper to taste
4 ounces lump crab meat,
    shells removed
Vegetable oil or clarified butter

Grouper and Assembly
2 (6- to 8-ounce) grouper fillets
All-purpose flour
2 sprigs of thyme
2 tablespoons chopped leek
1 tablespoon chopped red bell pepper

For the beurre blanc, mix the shallot, parsley, wine, leek and bell pepper in a saucepan. Cook over high gas heat until almost dry. Add the cream and cook until the liquid is reduced by half. Strain into a bowl, discarding the solids. Whisk in the butter until blended. Reserve in a warm environment.

For the crab cakes, combine the potato, mayonnaise, flour, green bell pepper, parsley, egg, egg white, salt and pepper in a bowl and mix well. Fold in the crab meat. Shape the crab meat mixture into two cakes and chill. Sauté the chilled cakes in oil in a sauté pan over medium gas heat until light brown on both sides. Remove to a platter and cover to keep warm.

For the grouper, coat the fillets with flour. Sauté in a nonstick skillet until the fillets flake easily. Pool equal portions of the warm beurre blanc in the center of each of two serving plates. Arrange one crab cake on each prepared plate and top each serving with one fillet. Skewer with the sprigs of thyme and top with the leek and red bell pepper.—Serves 2— **Brad Parker, The Grille at Osceola, 2002**

Potato-Crusted Grouper with Curry Seafood Vegetables and Mornay Sauce

Mornay Sauce
2 tablespoons butter
1/4 cup all-purpose flour
2 cups milk
1/2 cup (2 ounces) grated Gruyère
  cheese
1/4 cup (1 ounce) grated
  Parmesan cheese

Potato-Crusted Grouper
4 (6-ounce) grouper fillets
All-purpose flour
4 eggs

1/4 cup cream
2 potatoes, shredded
2 yams, shredded
Vegetable oil

Stir-Fried Vegetables and Assembly
12 ounces snow peas, blanched
8 ounces pearl onions, blanched
Sesame oil
1 pound assorted seafood (crab meat,
  shrimp, scallops and/or flaked
  white fish)
1 tablespoon red curry paste

For the sauce, heat the butter in a saucepan until melted and stir in the flour. Cook until smooth and bubbly; stir in the milk. Cook for 2 to 3 minutes or until thickened, stirring frequently. Add the Gruyère cheese and Parmesan cheese and cook until blended. Remove from the heat and cover to keep warm.

For the grouper, coat the fillets in flour and dip in a mixture of the eggs and cream. Press the shredded potatoes and shredded yams on both sides of the fillets. Fry in oil in a skillet until brown and crisp on both sides; drain. Remove to a platter and cover to keep warm.

For the vegetables, stir-fry the snow peas and onions in sesame oil in a skillet to the desired degree of crispness. Add the seafood and curry paste and stir-fry just until the seafood is cooked through. Arrange the stir-fry mixture evenly on four serving plates. Top each serving with one fillet and drizzle each with 1/2 cup of the sauce.—Serves 4—**Travis Herr, Bill Hamilton and Culinary Students, Pensacola Junior College, 2003**

Cajun Surf and Turf

Crawfish Étouffée
1 yellow onion, coarsely chopped
1 green bell pepper, coarsely chopped
1/2 cup minced garlic
1/2 cup (1 stick) butter
1/2 cup all-purpose flour
4 cups seafood stock, heated
1/4 cup blackening seasoning
1/4 teaspoon cayenne pepper
8 ounces crawfish tails with fat

Corn and Red Potatoes
16 cups (4 quarts) seafood stock
1/2 yellow onion, chopped
4 ounces celery sticks
8 red potatoes

2 fresh ears of corn
Canola oil
1 teaspoon garlic salt
1 teaspoon parsley

Grouper, Beef Fillets and Assembly
2 (4-ounce) grouper fillets
1 1/2 cups all-purpose flour
1/4 cup blackening seasoning
1 tablespoon onion powder
1 tablespoon garlic powder
1 teaspoon pepper
2 tablespoons butter or margarine
2 (4-ounce) beef fillets
Salt and pepper to taste

For the étouffée, sauté the onion, bell pepper and garlic in 1/4 cup of the butter in a skillet until the onion is tender. Stir in the flour and cook until a light brown roux forms. Add the warm stock gradually, whisking constantly until combined. Cook until a smooth sauce forms. Stir in the blackening seasoning and cayenne pepper and whisk until the seasonings are well combined. Add the remaining 1/4 cup butter and cook until melted, whisking constantly. Stir in the crawfish. Cover to keep warm.

For the corn and potatoes, bring the stock, onion and celery to a boil in a stockpot. Add the potatoes and cook until the potatoes are partially cooked. Add the corn and cook until the potatoes and corn are tender. Remove the corn to a bowl. Flash-fry the potatoes in canola oil in a deep skillet; drain. Remove the potatoes to a bowl and toss with the garlic salt and parsley.

For the grouper and beef, dust the grouper lightly with a mixture of the flour, blackening seasoning, onion powder, garlic powder and 1 teaspoon pepper. Sauté the grouper in the butter in a skillet until the grouper flakes easily. Season the beef fillets with salt and pepper to taste and grill on a gas grill to the desired degree of doneness. Spoon equal portions of the étouffée into two large bowls. Layer each serving with one beef fillet, one grouper fillet and equal portions of the corn and potatoes. Garnish with chopped green onions and parsley.—Serves 2—**Tim Peck and Chris Gerlits, The Oar House, 2007**

Hoisin Mahi Mahi

Grilled Pineapple Salsa
$1/2$ cup chopped grilled pineapple
$1/4$ cup chopped papaya
2 tablespoons chopped red bell pepper
2 tablespoons chopped green
  bell pepper
2 tablespoons chopped cilantro
2 tablespoons chopped jalapeño chiles
2 tablespoons chopped red onion
$1/4$ cup rice wine vinegar
2 tablespoons lime juice
2 tablespoons lemon juice
2 tablespoons pineapple juice

Tempura Batter
1 cup all-purpose flour
$1/2$ cup cornstarch
1 cup cold water
1 egg yolk, beaten
2 tablespoons sesame oil

Mahi Mahi and Assembly
2 tablespoons hoisin sauce
2 teaspoons chili paste
$1/4$ teaspoon five-spice powder
2 (8-ounce) mahi mahi fillets
8 cups canola oil or peanut oil
1 mango, peeled and cut lengthwise into
  $1/2$-inch slices
6 ounces smoked shrimp (optional)

For the salsa, mix the pineapple, papaya, bell peppers, cilantro, jalapeño chiles and onion in a bowl. Add the vinegar, lime juice, lemon juice and pineapple juice and toss to coat. Chill, covered, for 2 hours.

For the tempura batter, whisk together the flour and cornstarch in a bowl. Add the cold water, egg yolk and sesame oil and whisk until smooth. Chill, covered, in the refrigerator.

For the mahi mahi, mix the hoisin sauce, chili paste and five-spice powder in a bowl. Rub the fillets generously with the hoisin sauce mixture. Marinate, covered, in the refrigerator for 2 to 4 hours. Grill the fillets on a gas grill over medium heat for 3 to 4 minutes per side. Watch closely and do not allow the rub to burn. Remove the fillets to a platter and cover to keep warm.

Heat the canola oil in a deep-fat fryer to 350 degrees. Dip the mango slices in the batter and remove carefully. Immediately plunge the slices into the hot oil and fry until golden brown and puffy; drain. Arrange equal portions of the fillets on two to four serving plates. Top each serving with fried mango slices and salsa. Top with the smoked shrimp.—Serves 2 to 4—**Buzz Valadao, Outrigger, 2002**

Bahamian Seafood Pasta

Creole Sauce
8 ounces tomato purée
1 large tomato, chopped
6 ounces okra
1 red bell pepper, chopped
1 yellow bell pepper, chopped
1 green bell pepper, chopped
1 small red onion, chopped
1 teaspoon minced garlic

Seafood Pasta and Assembly
1/2 cup (1 stick) unsalted butter
1/4 cup white wine
1 teaspoon salt
1 teaspoon black pepper
1 teaspoon ground cumin
1 teaspoon sage
1 ounce lemon pepper
10 ounces mahi mahi, cut into 8 portions
8 jumbo (16- to 20-count) shrimp, peeled and deveined
6 jumbo sea scallops
6 mussels, scrubbed
16 ounces penne, cooked and drained

For the sauce, combine the tomato purée, tomato, okra, bell peppers, onion and garlic in a saucepan. Cook until the bell peppers are tender and the sauce is slightly thickened, stirring occasionally.

For the pasta, heat the butter, wine, salt, black pepper, cumin, sage and lemon pepper in a skillet until hot. Add the mahi mahi, shrimp, scallops and mussels and cook for 6 to 8 minutes or until the mahi mahi flakes easily, the shrimp turn pink, the scallops are opaque and slightly firm and the mussels open. Mix the sauce and pasta in a large sauté pan and cook until heated through. Pour the pasta mixture into a large serving bowl and top with the seafood mixture.—Serves 2—
John Smith, Calypso!, 2002

Yukon-Crusted Redfish

Stone-Ground Yellow Grits
5 cups chicken stock
2 cups stone-ground yellow grits
1/2 cup chopped tasso
2 ounces goat cheese, crumbled
Salt and pepper to taste

Tabasco Butter Sauce
1/2 cup wine
3 tablespoons heavy cream
2 tablespoons minced garlic
Juice of 1 lemon
1 tablespoon minced shallot
1 tablespoon Tabasco sauce
2 cups (4 sticks) butter, chopped
Salt and pepper to taste

Redfish
4 large Yukon gold potatoes, peeled
2 tablespoons olive oil
4 redfish fillets
12 baby carrots
3 bunches baby bok choy

Pan-Fried Oysters and Assembly
3 cups canola oil
1/2 cup milk
1 egg
16 oysters
1 cup cornmeal

For the grits, bring the stock to a simmer in a saucepan and add the grits. Cook for 15 to 20 minutes or until the grits are tender, adding additional stock as needed. Stir in the tasso and cheese and season with salt and pepper. Cover to keep warm.

For the sauce, mix the wine, cream, garlic, lemon juice, shallot and Tabasco sauce in a saucepan and cook over low gas heat until reduced. Add the butter gradually and cook until the butter is incorporated, whisking constantly. Season with salt and pepper and cover to keep warm.

For the redfish, julienne the potatoes into thin strips using a mandoline. Place in a bowl of cold water. Heat a nonstick sauté pan until hot and add the olive oil. Drain the potatoes and shape into four nests. Sauté the potato nests in the hot oil on both sides. Place one fillet in the middle of each nest and fold the crust over the fillets. Arrange on a baking sheet and bake at 350 degrees in a gas oven for 8 to 10 minutes. Sauté the carrots and bok choy in a sauté pan until tender.

For the oysters, heat the canola oil in a skillet to 375 degrees. Whisk the milk and egg in a bowl until blended. Coat the oysters with the egg wash and dust with the cornmeal. Fry the oysters in the hot oil until golden brown on all sides; drain. Arrange one redfish fillet on each of four serving plates. Top each fillet with four oysters and drizzle with the desired amount of the sauce. Surround with the bok choy and carrots and a scoop of grits.—Serves 4—**Dan Dunn, H$_2$O, 2007**

Barbecued Salmon with Roasted Garlic and Mussels

1 or 2 heads garlic
Olive oil to taste
4 (4-ounce) salmon fillets, skinned
1 tablespoon olive oil
Salt and cracked black pepper to taste

Crushed red pepper flakes to taste
2 ounces mussels in shells, scrubbed
6 tablespoons white wine
1/2 cup (1 stick) butter, softened

Place the garlic heads in a baking pan and drizzle with olive oil to taste. Roast at 350 degrees in a gas oven until the garlic is soft and light brown. Cut off the tops of the garlic cloves with a sharp knife and squeeze the pulp into a bowl. Coat the fillets with 1 tablespoon olive oil. Season both sides with salt, black pepper and red pepper flakes. Grill on a gas grill until the fillets are slightly pink internally. Lightly spread the fillets with 2 tablespoons of the roasted garlic pulp. Arrange the fillets on a serving platter and cover to keep warm.

Steam the mussels in the wine in a saucepan until the shells open. Arrange the mussels over and around the fillets, reserving the pan juices. Swirl the butter into the reserved juices until blended and season with salt and pepper. Drizzle over the fillets and mussels. Garnish with fresh chives.—Serves 4—**Jim O'Brien, The Yacht Restaurant, 1997**

Grilled Salmon with Crab Fingers and Angel Hair Pasta

1 1/2 teaspoons Cajun seasoning
1 (6-ounce) salmon fillet
Clarified butter to taste
1 1/2 teaspoons chopped green onion
3/4 teaspoon minced garlic
1/2 teaspoon chopped parsley
2 tablespoons salted butter

2 ounces crab claws
1 tablespoon lemon butter sauce
1 tablespoon Italian salad dressing
1 tablespoon whipped garlic butter
10 ounces angel hair pasta, cooked
  and drained

Sprinkle 1/2 teaspoon of the Cajun seasoning on each side of the fillet and brush with clarified butter. Grill the fillet on a gas grill until grill marks appear on both sides and the edges of the fillet begin to turn opaque, turning once. Remove to platter and cover to keep warm. Mix the green onion, garlic and parsley in a small bowl. Combine half the green onion mixture, the salted butter and the remaining 1/2 teaspoon Cajun seasoning in a skillet and cook until the butter melts. Add the crab claws, lemon butter sauce and salad dressing and cook until the claws are heated through. Bring to a boil; do not reduce the sauce. Add the garlic butter and cook until the butter melts, swirling the skillet constantly; do not allow the sauce to boil. Arrange the fillet over the pasta on a serving plate and top with the crab claw mixture. Sprinkle with the remaining green onion mixture.—Serves 1—**Robbie Catton, Copeland's, 2004**

Seafood Diablo

1 pound salmon, cut into chunks
1 pound fresh shrimp
1 pound fresh scallops
3 cups sliced mushrooms
1 tablespoon minced garlic
1/2 cup olive oil
1/2 cup capers
1 teaspoon crushed red pepper
4 cups marinara sauce
3 pounds penne, cooked and drained
6 tablespoons grated Parmesan cheese
6 tablespoons chopped fresh basil
2 teaspoons crushed red pepper

Sauté the salmon, shrimp, scallops, mushrooms and garlic in the olive oil in a large deep skillet until the salmon flakes easily, the shrimp turn pink and the scallops are opaque and slightly firm. Stir in the capers and 1 teaspoon red pepper. Add the marinara sauce and bring to a boil. Mix in the pasta.

Simmer until the pasta is heated through, stirring occasionally. Spoon the pasta mixture evenly onto six serving plates and sprinkle with the cheese, basil and 2 teaspoons red pepper.—Serves 6— **Hans Limburg, Semolina Original International Pastas, 1997**

Scamp Creole

1/2 cup all-purpose flour
1 ounce blackening seasoning
1 (6-ounce) scamp fillet
Butter
4 ounces rice, cooked
2 tablespoons cream
1 tablespoon coarse-grain mustard
3 ounces crawfish tails

Mix the flour and blackening seasoning in a shallow dish. Coat the fillet with the flour mixture. Sauté the fillet in butter in a skillet until the fillet flakes easily. Arrange the fillet over the rice on a serving plate. Heat the cream, mustard and crawfish tails in a saucepan until warm and pour over the fillet.—Serves 1—**Kevin Faoutas, The Veranda at Henderson Park Inn, 1996**

Snapper Bienville

1 cup crumbled corn bread
1/4 cup chopped celery
2 tablespoons finely chopped green onion
2 tablespoons chopped parsley
2 garlic cloves, minced
Pinch of salt
Pinch of white pepper
1/4 cup (1/2 stick) butter, melted
Juice of 1 lemon
1/4 to 1/2 cup white wine
8 ounces lump crab meat, shells removed
6 (6- to 8-ounce) snapper fillets
2 tablespoons dried basil
2 tablespoons Creole seasoning
1 1/2 teaspoons salt
1 1/2 teaspoons white pepper

Combine the corn bread, celery, green onion, parsley, garlic, pinch of salt and pinch of white pepper in a bowl and mix well with your hands. Stir in the butter and lemon juice. Add the wine gradually, stirring constantly until a moist but not wet mixture forms. Fold in the crab meat. Divide the mixture into six equal portions and shape each portion into a ball.

Arrange the fillets on a hard surface with the long sides going left to right. Make slits starting in the centers and going one-third deep and halfway to the ends in each fillet. Make the same slits going in the opposite direction. Fold back the flaps creating a pocket. Place one ball of the stuffing in each pocket. Fold the flaps over the stuffing and pat the sides down with your hands. Arrange on a baking sheet.

Mix the basil, Creole seasoning, 1 1/2 teaspoons salt and 1 1/2 teaspoons white pepper in a bowl and sprinkle over the fillets. Bake at 350 degrees in a gas oven for 18 to 21 minutes or until the fillets flake easily. Broil for 2 to 3 minutes or until brown if needed.—Serves 6—**David Penniman and Katie Batchelor, Classic City Catering, 2006**

57 Snapper

2 (8-ounce) snapper fillets with skin
1 tablespoon olive oil
2 tablespoons seafood seasoning
2 large bananas, cut lengthwise into halves
2 tablespoons blackening seasoning
8 cups canola oil or peanut oil
2 eggs
1/2 cup milk
11/2 cups all-purpose flour
1 teaspoon salt
1 teaspoon baking powder
1/4 cup chopped green onions
2 ounces crab meat, shells removed
1/4 cup Heinz 57 steak sauce
2 tablespoons mango purée
2 tablespoons honey
1 tablespoon lemon juice
2 tablespoons unsalted butter

Coat the fillets with the olive oil and sprinkle with the seafood seasoning. Grill the fillets skin side up on a gas grill for 2 to 4 minutes and turn carefully. Grill for 2 to 4 minutes longer or until the fillets flake easily. Remove to a platter and cover to keep warm.

Heat a cast-iron skillet until smoking. Sprinkle the bananas with the blackening seasoning and place in the hot skillet. Cook until seared and heated through. Cover to keep warm.

Heat the canola oil in a deep-fat fryer to 375 degrees. Whisk the eggs in a bowl until frothy and stir in the milk. Whisk the flour, salt and baking powder in a bowl and mix in the egg mixture. Stir in the green onions and crab meat. Drop the crab meat mixture by spoonfuls into the hot oil. Fry until golden brown on all sides, turning if needed for even color. Remove the beignets to a platter using a slotted spoon.

Bring the steak sauce, mango purée, honey and lemon juice to a boil in a saucepan. Reduce the gas heat to low and add the butter gradually. Cook until the butter is melted and well combined, swirling the pan constantly. Arrange equal portions of the fillets on two to four serving plates and surround with the blackened bananas. Drizzle with the mango sauce and top with the crab meat beignets.—Serves 2 to 4—**Buzz Valadao, Outrigger, 2002**

Stufato of Swordfish and Shellfish

5 tablespoons extra-virgin olive oil
5 garlic cloves, crushed
5 pounds assorted shellfish (mussels, clams, oysters, shrimp and/or crab meat)
1½ tablespoons extra-virgin olive oil
1½ pounds (center-cut) swordfish steaks, skinned
Salt and freshly ground pepper to taste

4½ tablespoons extra-virgin olive oil
½ large white onion, chopped
15 to 16 pitted black olives
1 pound plum tomatoes, peeled, seeded and chopped
1 sprig of rosemary
½ cup chopped fresh Italian parsley
Hot cooked pasta or rice

Combine 5 tablespoons olive oil, the garlic and assorted shellfish, except the shrimp, in a stockpot. Cook, covered, over medium-high gas heat for 4 to 5 minutes; discard any shellfish that do not open. Remove the shellfish to a bowl using a slotted spoon and cover to keep warm, reserving the pan juices. Strain the reserved juices through a fine sieve, cheesecloth or a coffee filter into a bowl and reserve.

Heat 1½ tablespoons olive oil in a large skillet over high gas heat. Season the swordfish with salt and pepper and add to the hot oil. Cook for 2 minutes on each side or until golden brown. Remove to a platter, reserving the pan drippings. Heat 4½ tablespoons olive oil with the reserved pan drippings and add the onion. Cook over medium gas heat for 3 to 4 minutes. Stir in the olives, tomatoes, rosemary, swordfish and strained shellfish juices. Cook, covered, for 7 minutes. Add the cooked shellfish and shrimp and cook for 2 to 5 minutes or until the shrimp turn pink. Stir in the parsley and season with pepper. Ladle over hot cooked pasta or rice and serve with Crema crusty bread.—Serves 6 to 8—**David Guardanapo, Crema Coffee and Baking Company, 2008**

Jerry's Gulfuletta

2 (6- to 8-ounce) tilapia fillets, or your favorite fish
10 (22- to 26-count) shrimp, peeled and deveined
10 oysters, shucked

2 cups Jerry's Own CajunDust fry mix*
Canola oil
1 Gambino's (9-inch) muffuletta bun
1 cup Central Grocery's Italian olive salad*
Shredded Swiss cheese (optional)

Drain the tilapia, shrimp and oysters. Dust the seafood with the fry mix, shaking off any excess. Heat canola oil in a deep-fat fryer to 350 degrees. Add the tilapia, shrimp and oysters in batches to the hot oil and fry until golden brown; drain.

Cut the bun horizontally into halves and arrange cut sides up on a baking sheet. Toast in a gas oven until brown but not crisp. Spread the olive salad on the bottom half of the bun and layer evenly with the tilapia, shrimp and oysters. Sprinkle with cheese and top with the remaining bun half. Cut the sandwich into quarters.—Serves 2 to 4—**Jerry Mistretta, Jerry's Cajun Cafe, 2008**

TIP *Available at www.jerryscajun.com

Sautéed Triggerfish with Oysters and Cream Sauce

1 cup seafood stock
1 cup white wine
1 cup whipping cream
3 tablespoons chopped fresh basil
4 triggerfish fillets
16 select oysters
Seasoned flour
Olive oil

Combine the stock and wine in a saucepan. Cook until large bubbles form and the liquid is reduced. Stir in the cream and basil and cook until thickened and of a sauce consistency, stirring frequently.

Coat the fillets and oysters in seasoned flour, shaking off any excess. Sauté the fillets in olive oil in a skillet until golden brown on one side. Turn and sauté until golden brown on the remaining sides.

Sauté the oysters in olive oil in a skillet until brown on all sides. Arrange one fillet on each of four serving plates and top each serving with four oysters. Drizzle each with 2 tablespoons of the cream sauce.—Serves 4—**Chris Tingle, Gauthier's, 1998**

TIP **Seafood Portions**
Whole fish—fish just as it comes from the water; **dressed fish**—ready-to-cook whole fish with scales, head, tail, and fins removed; **fillets**—the fleshy side meat cut lengthwise along the backbone; generally boneless meat but may contain small bones and may have skin on one side

Mr. Slu's Triggerfish

2 cups water
3 tablespoons lemon pepper
1/4 cup angel hair pasta
3/4 cup panko (Japanese bread crumbs)
1 tablespoon seafood seasoning
1 (8-ounce) triggerfish fillet
1/2 cup self-rising flour
1 cup milk
2 eggs
11/2 cups peanut oil
1 tablespoon unsalted butter
1 tablespoon chopped shallot
1/3 cup honey-roasted pecans
1/4 cup Champagne or chardonnay
2 tablespoons reduced shrimp stock
1/3 cup artichoke quarters
6 tablespoons heavy cream
1 tablespoon tarragon
2 ounces fresh lump crab meat, shells removed
3 to 4 tablespoons unsalted butter
Salt and black pepper to taste

Bring the water and lemon pepper to a boil in a saucepan and add the pasta. Cook using the package directions until tender. Drain the pasta and pat dry; do not rinse. Let stand until cool. Mix the pasta, bread crumbs and seafood seasoning in a shallow dish. Coat the fillet with the self-rising flour; dip in a mixture of the milk and eggs. Shake off any excess egg wash and coat evenly with the pasta mixture. Heat the peanut oil in a deep skillet to 325 degrees. Add the fillet to the hot oil and cook for 2 minutes on each side or until golden brown; drain. Remove to a platter and cover to keep warm.

Heat 1 tablespoon butter in a skillet over medium-high gas heat until melted and add the shallot and pecans. Sauté for 30 seconds and then deglaze the skillet with the Champagne. Stir in the stock, artichokes, cream and tarragon and bring to a boil. Reduce the gas heat and cook until the sauce coats the back of a spoon. Add the crab meat gradually along with 3 to 4 tablespoons butter. Cook until the butter is well combined, swirling the pan constantly. Season with salt and black pepper. Arrange the fillet on a serving plate and drizzle with the artichoke sauce. Garnish with chopped parsley.—Serves 1—**Buzz Valadao, Ryan's Catch, 1999**

Seafood and Avocado Tostada

6 (6-inch) corn or flour tortillas
3 tablespoons olive oil
1 teaspoon southwestern seasoning
12 ounces fresh prime tuna, finely chopped
1 ripe Haas avocado, finely chopped
1 (15-ounce) can black beans, drained and rinsed
1 bunch fresh chives or scallions, chopped
3 tablespoons finely chopped cilantro
3 tablespoons fresh lime juice
2 teaspoons finely chopped red onion
Kosher salt and pepper to taste
12 (21- to 25-count) Gulf shrimp, peeled and deveined
2 teaspoons olive oil
4 ounces lump crab meat, shells removed
1 cup sour cream

Cut 2- to 3-inch rounds from each tortilla. Panfry the tortilla rounds in 3 tablespoons olive oil in a skillet or deep-fry until the rounds are crisp. Drain on paper towels and sprinkle with the southwestern seasoning.

Combine the tuna, avocado, beans, chives, cilantro, lime juice, onion, salt and pepper in a chilled bowl and mix gently. Sauté the shrimp in 2 teaspoons olive oil in a skillet until the shrimp turn pink, or grill if desired. Remove the shrimp to a platter, reserving the pan drippings. Heat the crab meat in the reserved pan drippings.

Arrange the seasoned tortilla rounds on serving plates. Layer each round with equal portions of the tuna mixture, shrimp and crab meat. Top with a dollop of the sour cream.—Serves 6—
Irv Miller, Jackson's 2007

TIP The lean meat of yellowfin tuna is widely used in sashimi, raw fish dishes popular in Japan and a connoisseur's delicacy in the United States. Yellowfin tuna steak has a firm, dense beef-like texture which makes it excellent for grilling and is traditionally cooked rare to medium-rare in the centers as beef steak.

Tuna Lagasse

Corn Salsa

Kernels of 1 ear roasted corn
2 Roma tomatoes, seeded
  and chopped
Chopped zest and juice of 1/2 lime
Chopped zest and juice of 1/2 orange
Chopped zest and juice of 1/2 lemon
2 tablespoons chopped red onion
1 tablespoon chopped parsley
1 teaspoon chopped green bell pepper
1 teaspoon chopped red bell pepper
1 tablespoon sun-dried tomato oil
1 tablespoon balsamic vinegar
Salt and pepper to taste
Sugar to taste

Tuna and Assembly

1 (8-ounce) yellowfin tuna fillet
Olive oil for coating
Southwestern seasoning to taste
1/4 cup chopped yellow onion
1 tablespoon chopped garlic
1 teaspoon chopped jalapeño chile
1 tablespoon olive oil
2 cups chicken stock
1 teaspoon southwestern seasoning
2 tablespoons heavy cream
4 (6-inch) corn tortillas, cut into
  quarters, fried and crumbled
1/2 cup (2 ounces) shredded Cheddar
  Jack cheese
1/4 cup lump crab meat, shells removed

For the salsa, combine the corn, tomatoes, lime zest, lime juice, orange zest, orange juice, lemon zest, lemon juice, red onion, parsley and bell peppers in a bowl and mix gently. Drizzle with the sun-dried tomato oil and vinegar and season with salt, pepper and sugar.

For the tuna, coat the fillet with olive oil and season with southwestern seasoning to taste. Grill the fillet on a gas grill for 2 to 3 minutes per side for medium-rare or to the desired degree of doneness. Remove to a platter.

Sauté the onion, garlic and jalapeño chile in 1 tablespoon olive oil in a small saucepan over high gas heat. Stir in the stock and 1 teaspoon southwestern seasoning. Bring to a boil. Stir in the cream and cook for 5 minutes, stirring occasionally. Whisk in the crumbled tortillas and cheese. Process the tortilla mixture in a food processor until puréed and of a sauce consistency.

Spoon the tortilla sauce over the bottom of one serving plate. Arrange the fillet over the sauce and top with the salsa. Top with the crab meat and garnish with sprigs of parsley.—Serves 1—**Buzz Valadao, Outrigger, 2001**

Grilled Wahoo and Shrimp with Field Pea Sauté

4 cups water
1 pound fresh field peas
1 pound (21- to 25-count) shrimp, peeled and deveined
1 pound fresh wahoo or swordfish, cut into 1-inch chunks
Kosher salt and cracked pepper to taste
1/4 cup olive oil

1/4 cup (1/2 stick) unsalted butter
Kernels of 4 ears sweet corn
1 large zucchini, chopped and blanched
1 red onion, finely chopped
1 green bell pepper, finely chopped
1 teaspoon stemmed fresh thyme
21/2 cups grape tomatoes
1/4 cup roasted garlic cloves

Bring the water to a boil in a large saucepan and add the field peas. Reduce the gas heat to low and simmer for 20 minutes or until tender. Drain, reserving the cooking liquid. Thread the shrimp and wahoo on metal skewers. Sprinkle with salt and pepper and brush with the olive oil. Grill on a gas grill until the shrimp turn pink and the wahoo flakes easily.

Combine the butter, field peas, corn, zucchini, onion, bell pepper and thyme in a skillet and sauté until the vegetables are tender. Add the tomatoes, garlic and just enough of the reserved cooking liquid to moisten the vegetables. Simmer just until heated through. Spoon the field pea mixture evenly on each of four serving plates. Top each serving with equal portions of the shrimp and wahoo.—Serves 4—**Irv Miller, Jackson's, 2006**

Fish Dill-ish

1 (8-ounce) grouper, snapper or triggerfish fillet
Salt and pepper to taste
1 cup all-purpose flour
1/4 cup clarified butter

2 ounces jumbo lump crab meat, shells removed
1 garlic clove, minced
1 sprig of dill weed, chopped
Juice of 1 lemon wedge

Season the fillet with salt and pepper and coat with the flour. Heat a medium skillet over low to medium gas heat and add 2 tablespoons of the butter. Add the fillet skin side down to the hot butter. Cook until the fillet is opaque around the edges. Turn and cook until the fillet flakes easily. Remove the fillet to a platter. Drain the skillet.

Heat the remaining 2 tablespoons butter in the skillet and add the crab meat and garlic, tossing to coat. Stir in the dill weed and lemon juice. Arrange the fillet on a serving plate and top with the crab meat mixture. Garnish with sprigs of dill weed.—Serves 1—**John Flaningam, Angus, 2006**

Seafood Piccata

1 (8-ounce) fish fillet
8 jumbo shrimp, peeled, deveined
  and butterflied
3 scallops or oysters
All-purpose flour
Olive oil

1/2 cup (1 stick) plus
  2 tablespoons butter
3/4 ounce beef demi-glace
1 tablespoon lemon juice
1 tablespoon capers
2 pinches of parsley flakes

Coat the fillet, shrimp and scallops lightly with flour, shaking off any excess. Add enough olive oil to a sauté pan to measure half the thickness of the seafood and heat until hot. Add the fillet to the hot oil and fry until light brown on one side. Turn the fillet and add the shrimp and scallops to the hot oil.

Fry until the seafood is cooked through, turning once. Remove the seafood to a serving plate using a slotted spoon. Drain the oil from the skillet, reserving the browned bits. Add the butter, demi-glace, lemon juice and capers to the reserved drippings and simmer just until heated through. Remove from the heat and stir in the parsley flakes. Spoon the warm sauce over the fillet, shrimp and scallops.—Serves 1—**Keith Barber, The Big Easy, 2001**

Seafood Santa Rosa

2 tablespoons brandy
1 teaspoon clarified butter
1 1/2 ounces fresh fish, cut into chunks
1 1/2 ounces (36- to 40-count) shrimp,
  peeled and deveined
1 1/2 ounces sea scallops
Pinch of minced garlic
1 1/2 ounces lobster meat, cut into chunks
1 ounce jumbo lump crab meat,
  shells removed

1/4 cup heavy cream
1 ounce Parmesan cheese, grated
1 green onion, chopped
Salt and pepper to taste
1 tablespoon water (optional)
1 tablespoon cornstarch (optional)
6 ounces fettuccini, cooked
  and drained

Heat the brandy and clarified butter in a 10-inch skillet over medium-low gas heat. Add the fish, shrimp, scallops and garlic and mix well. Cook until the seafood is almost cooked through and stir in the lobster meat, crab meat, cream, cheese, green onion, salt and pepper. Cook until the mixture is heated through. Stir in a mixture of the water and cornstarch for a thicker consistency, if desired. Spoon over hot cooked pasta on a serving plate.—Serves 1—**John Flaningam, Angus, 2003**

Louisiana Seafood Gumbo

1 cup vegetable oil
1 cup all-purpose flour
2 cups chopped onions
1 cup chopped celery
1 cup chopped bell pepper
1/4 cup chopped garlic
8 ounces andouille, sliced
1 pound claw crab meat
12 cups shellfish stock, heated
2 cups sliced green onions
1/2 cup chopped parsley
Salt and cayenne pepper to taste
Louisiana Gold pepper sauce to taste
1 pound (35-count) shrimp, peeled and deveined
1 pound jumbo lump crab meat, shells removed
2 dozen shucked oysters with liquor
Hot cooked rice

Heat the oil in a 2-gallon stockpot over medium-high gas heat until hot. Add the flour gradually, whisking constantly until blended. Cook until the roux is golden brown in color, whisking constantly. If black specks appear in the roux, discard and start over. Stir in the onions, celery, bell pepper and garlic and sauté for 3 to 5 minutes or until the vegetables are tender. Add the sausage and sauté for 2 to 3 minutes. Stir in the claw crab meat; this will begin to add seafood flavor to the mixture. Add the hot stock one ladle at a time, stirring constantly until well combined.

Bring to a low boil and reduce the gas heat. Simmer for about 30 minutes, adding additional stock if needed to retain the volume. Stir in the green onions and parsley and season with salt, cayenne pepper and pepper sauce. Fold in the shrimp, lump crab meat, oysters and oyster liquor.

Bring to a low boil and cook for about 5 minutes, stirring occasionally. Taste and adjust the seasonings. Ladle the gumbo over hot cooked rice in bowls.—Serves 12—**John Folse, Lafitte's Landing Restaurant, 1996**

TIP Store fresh-shucked oysters on ice or in the coldest part of the refrigerator for up to five days from the date of purchase.

Seafood Jambalaya

1/4 cup (1/2 stick) butter or vegetable oil
1 tablespoon all-purpose flour
2 cups chopped onions
1 cup chopped celery
1 cup chopped bell pepper
2 teaspoons minced garlic
1 (10-ounce) can tomatoes with green chiles
1 bay leaf
1 1/2 teaspoons thyme
1 1/2 teaspoons basil
2 tablespoons Jerry's Own ZydeCajun seasoning*
1 tablespoon Zatarain's crab boil powder
1 teaspoon Tabasco sauce
1 teaspoon Louisiana hot sauce
1 teaspoon pepper
2 dashes of Jerry's habanero sauce*
1 pound crawfish tail meat
1 pound (31- to 35-count or 71- to 90-count) shrimp, peeled
1 pint claw crab meat or lump crab meat, shells removed
1 cup chopped green onions
4 cups seafood stock or water
2 cups long grain rice

Heat the butter in a 5-quart cast-iron Dutch oven over medium-high gas heat until melted. Add the flour gradually, whisking constantly until blended. Cook until the roux is light brown, whisking constantly. Add the onions, celery, bell pepper and garlic and sauté for 3 to 5 minutes or until the vegetables are tender. Add the tomatoes, bay leaf, thyme and basil and sauté for 5 minutes or until the ingredients are well combined. Stir in the ZydeCajun seasoning, crab boil powder, Tabasco sauce, Louisiana hot sauce, pepper and habanero sauce.

Simmer for about 30 minutes, stirring occasionally. Add the crawfish, shrimp and crab meat and bring to a rolling boil. Reduce the gas heat and simmer for 5 minutes. Stir in the green onions. Add the stock and rice and bring to a boil. Reduce the gas heat and simmer, covered, for about 30 minutes or until the rice is tender and the jambalaya is the desired consistency. Discard the bay leaf and ladle the jambalaya into bowls.—Serves 4—**Jerry Mistretta, Jerry's Cajun Cafe, 2004**

TIP *Available at www.jerryscajun.com

Mixed Seafood

Shellfish Étouffée

6 ounces wild rice
2 tablespoons butter
Salt and pepper to taste
2 cups heavy whipping cream
1 cup sour cream
16 shucked oysters with liquor
16 (21- to 25-count) shrimp, peeled and deveined
1/4 cup (1/2 stick) butter
16 crawfish tails
1 cup chopped tomato
Cajun spice mix to taste
1/2 cup thinly sliced scallions
16 scallops, cut into halves

Cook the rice using the package directions. Stir in 2 tablespoons butter and season with salt and pepper. Cover to keep warm. Cook the whipping cream in a saucepan until reduced by one-third; stir in the sour cream. Cover to keep warm. Plump the oysters in the liquor and drain.

Sauté the shrimp in 1/4 cup butter in a skillet. Add the crawfish tails, tomato and Cajun spice and cook for 2 minutes. Stir in the cream mixture, scallions, scallops and oysters. Simmer for 2 minutes. Taste and adjust the seasonings. Ladle over the rice in bowls or in the center of a rice mold.—Serves 4—**Klaus Bertram, Executive Club, 1998**

TIP Oysters become plump and opaque and the edges begin to curl when thoroughly cooked.

Crab and Crawfish Cakes

1/4 cup (1/2 stick) butter
2 tablespoons chopped red bell pepper
2 tablespoons chopped yellow bell pepper
2 tablespoons chopped celery
2 tablespoons whole kernel corn
2 teaspoons blackening seasoning
1/2 teaspoon Old Bay seasoning
1/4 cup shrimp stock
2 ounces crawfish tails, coarsely chopped
2 ounces crab meat
1 cup panko (Japanese bread crumbs)
1 egg, lightly beaten
2 ounces (1/2 stick or 4 tbsps) clarified butter

Heat 1/4 cup butter in a skillet until melted and stir in the bell peppers, celery and corn. Sauté until the vegetables are tender. Stir in the blackening seasoning and Old Bay seasoning and deglaze the skillet with the stock. Stir in the crawfish and crab meat.

Simmer for 1 minute. Fold in the bread crumbs and cool slightly. Add the egg and mix well. Shape the crawfish mixture into three cakes. Heat the clarified butter in a skillet and add the cakes. Sauté until golden brown on both sides.—Makes 3 cakes—**Anthony Wilson, Bayside Grill, 2000**

TIP The blue crab is aptly described by its Latin name, *Callinectes sapidus*, meaning "tasty beautiful swimmer." It is common throughout Florida's estuaries, coastal bays, and sounds.

Soft-Shell Crabs Zachary

1 cup cracker meal
2 tablespoons seafood seasoning
2 jumbo soft-shell crabs, cleaned
1 cup all-purpose flour
2 cups egg wash
1 cup peanut oil
1 tablespoon olive oil
2 tablespoons chopped yellow onion
1 tablespoon chopped red bell pepper
1 tablespoon chopped green bell pepper
1 tablespoon chopped garlic
2 tablespoons chardonnay
1/2 cup strong shrimp stock
1 teaspoon Worcestershire sauce
1/2 teaspoon Tabasco sauce
Creole seasoning to taste
3/4 cup heavy cream
4 ounces bay shrimp, peeled and deveined
4 ounces crawfish tail meat
2 tablespoons chopped green onion
Salt and pepper to taste

Mix the cracker meal and seafood seasoning in a shallow dish. Coat the crabs with the flour, dip in the egg wash and then coat with the cracker meal mixture. Heat the peanut oil in a deep skillet over high gas heat. Fry the crabs in the hot oil for 1 to 2 minutes on each side; drain. Remove to a platter.

Heat the olive oil in a skillet and add the yellow onion. Sauté for 30 seconds. Stir in the bell peppers and garlic and sauté for 1 minute. Deglaze the skillet with the wine. Add the stock, Worcestershire sauce, Tabasco sauce and Creole seasoning and mix well.

Cook until the mixture is reduced by half. Stir in the cream and bring to a boil. Cook until the mixture is reduced by one-fourth and mix in the shrimp and crawfish.

Simmer for 1 minute. Stir in the green onion, salt and pepper. Remove from the heat and spoon over the crabs.—Serves 1 or 2—**Buzz Valadao, Outrigger, 2001**

Grilled Soft-Shell Crabs with Shrimp and Tasso Cream Sauce

4 large soft-shell crabs, cleaned
1 pound large shrimp, peeled and deveined
1 tablespoon butter, melted
Creole seasoning to taste
Seasoned flour
1 cup white wine
1 cup seafood stock
2 cups heavy cream
4 ounces tasso, chopped

Brush the crabs and shrimp with the butter and sprinkle with Creole seasoning. Dust lightly with seasoned flour. Arrange the crabs and shrimp on a grill rack on a gas grill. Grill until the shrimp turn pink and the crabs are slightly crisp.

Combine the wine and stock in a skillet. Cook over medium gas heat until reduced. Stir in the cream and tasso and cook until reduced again. Mix in the shrimp. Arrange one crab on each of four serving plates and top equally with the shrimp and tasso sauce.—Serves 4—**Chris Tingle, Gauthier's, 1999**

TIP How do you tell a male blue crab from a female blue crab? The tips of the female's claws are bright red. Blue crabs are found along Florida's Atlantic and Gulf coasts. As a shallow-water crab, they can live in salt, fresh, and brackish waters of bays, sounds, channels, and river mouths. They are omnivorous, feeding on plants and animals. During the winter months, blue crabs move into deeper water and enter a state of semi-hibernation.

Seafood en Brochette

Ancho Rémoulade Sauce
1 cup mayonnaise
1 ounce pickles, chopped
1 ounce red onion, chopped
1 ounce red bell pepper, chopped
20 capers with juice
Juice of 1/2 lemon
1 ounce ancho dust
1 or 2 drops of Tabasco sauce, or
  to taste
Salt and pepper to taste
Pinch of Old Bay seasoning

Seafood
1 lobster
6 scallops
6 slices bacon
1 (5-ounce) swordfish fillet,
  cut into chunks
6 (10- to 15-count) shrimp, peeled
  and deveined
1 red bell pepper, cut into chunks
5 Roma tomatoes, cut into chunks
1 purple onion, cut into chunks
6 white mushrooms, trimmed
Juice of 1 lime
1 tablespoon vegetable oil
Salt and pepper to taste

For the sauce, combine the mayonnaise, pickles, onion, bell pepper, capers with juice, lemon juice, ancho dust, Tabasco sauce, salt, pepper and Old Bay seasoning in a bowl and mix well. Store in the refrigerator.

For the seafood, soak wooden skewers in a bowl of water. Place the lobster in enough simmering water to cover in a stockpot and partially cook. Remove the meat from the tail and cut into chunks. Reserve the claws for the garnish. Reserve the shells for lobster stock for soups and sauces. Wrap each scallop with one slice of the bacon.

Thread the lobster, bacon-wrapped scallops, swordfish and shrimp alternately with the bell pepper, tomatoes, onion and mushrooms on skewers in the desired order. Rub with the lime juice and oil and sprinkle with salt and pepper.

Arrange the skewers on a grill rack on a gas grill. Sear on all sides; remove the skewers to a baking pan. Bake at 375 degrees in a gas oven until the seafood is cooked through and the vegetables are the desired degree of crispness. Arrange the skewers on a platter and garnish with the lobster claws. Serve with the rémoulade sauce or the sauce of your choice.—Serves 6—**Dan Dunn, Lou Michael's Downtown, 2001**

Sea Pearls with Marinara Sauce

Marinara Sauce
2 tablespoons olive oil
3 tablespoons chopped onion
1 tablespoon chopped garlic
2 or 3 bay leaves
2 teaspoons dried oregano
6 cups canned chopped Italian plum tomatoes
3 tablespoons chopped parsley
Salt and pepper to taste

Sea Pearls
20 ounces spinach fettuccini
6 to 8 tablespoons olive oil
8 mussels, scrubbed
16 sea scallops
1/2 teaspoon chopped fresh basil
16 select oysters with liquor
2 ounces Parmesan cheese, grated

For the sauce, heat the olive oil in a large saucepan and add the onion. Cook until the onion is tender. Stir in the garlic, bay leaves and oregano. Add the tomatoes and parsley and mix well.

Simmer until reduced by half, stirring occasionally. Discard the bay leaves and process the tomato mixture in a food processor until puréed. Season with salt and pepper. You may prepare 2 to 3 days in advance and store, covered, in the refrigerator. Reheat before serving.

For the sea pearls, cook the pasta using the package directions 1 to 2 hours in advance; drain. Heat the olive oil in a skillet and add the mussels. Sauté until the shells open and the mussels are heated through. Add the scallops and cook just until the scallops are cooked through. Add the pasta, 12 to 14 ounces of the marinara sauce and the basil and mix well. Mix in the oysters with liquor and cook just until heated through; do not overcook. Spoon the pasta mixture evenly onto each of four serving plates. Sprinkle with the cheese and garnish with sprigs of basil.—Serves 4—
Gus Silivos, Skopelos on the Bay, 1995

Pan-Fried Prawns with Scallop Mousse

Scallop Mousse
8 large scallops
2 tablespoons heavy cream
2 tablespoons white wine
1 sprig of fresh dill weed
Salt and pepper to taste

Pan-Fried Prawns
8 (16- to 20-count) prawns, peeled and deveined
1 cup seasoned flour
1 cup seasoned coarse bread crumbs
1/2 cup heavy cream
11/2 teaspoons coarsely cracked pepper
1/2 teaspoon chopped parsley
1/4 teaspoon grated fresh ginger
1/4 teaspoon sesame oil
1 cup olive oil

For the mousse, process the scallops, cream, wine, dill weed, salt and pepper in a food processor until a smooth paste forms.

For the prawns, dip the prawns in the seasoned flour, rub with the mousse and then roll in the bread crumbs. Heat the cream in a saucepan and stir in the pepper, parsley, ginger and sesame oil. Cook until thickened and of a sauce consistency, stirring frequently. Remove from the heat and cover to keep warm.

Heat the olive oil in a sauté pan until hot. Add the prawns to the hot oil and panfry for about 2 minutes per side or until light brown. Arrange four prawns on each of two serving plates and pour equal portions of the cream sauce in the middle of the plates. Garnish as desired.—Serves 2—
Jim O'Brien, O'Brien's Bistro, 1999

TIP   Choose scallop meat that has a creamy color, firm texture, and a mild sweet odor. There should be very little liquid in the package.

Grilled Scallops and Tuna en Husk

4 ears of corn in husks
10 ounces (20- to 30-count) scallops
10 ounces fresh tuna, cut into 1-inch chunks
4 mushrooms, sliced
1 bunch chives, chopped
1 cup heavy cream
Olive oil
Salt and pepper to taste

Peel back the corn husks and remove the silk. Snap off the ears of corn. Remove the kernels from ears of corn with a sharp knife and place in a bowl. Arrange equal portions of the scallops, tuna, mushrooms, chives and corn kernels in the pocket of the corn husks, reserving some of the chives and corn kernels for the sauce. Reposition the husks and secure the tops closed with a piece of husk. Spray with nonstick cooking spray.

Grill on a gas grill for about 15 minutes, turning as needed for even cooking. Your may wrap the corn husks in foil and place on the upper grill rack for grilling, if desired.

Heat olive oil in a sauté pan until hot and add the reserved corn kernels and reserved chives. Sauté until the corn is tender and stir in the cream. Season with salt and pepper. Cook until thickened and of a sauce consistency, stirring frequently. To serve, cut a slit in the corn husks and open. Place on serving plates. Pour the desired amount of the sauce over each and garnish with additional chives.—Serves 4—**Jim O'Brien, The Yacht Restaurant, 1997**

TIP When selecting whole fresh fish, look for clear eyes, bright gills, firm flesh that springs back when lightly touched, fresh sea breeze odor, and no discoloration.

Bacon-Wrapped Crab-Stuffed Shrimp

Crab Stuffing
1/4 cup chopped onion
1/4 cup chopped red bell pepper
1/4 cup chopped celery
2 shallots, minced
1 garlic clove, minced
1 pound crab meat, shells removed
1 cup bread crumbs
3 tablespoons grated Romano cheese
1 tablespoon Louisiana hot sauce
1 egg, beaten
Salt and pepper to taste

Stuffed Shrimp
1 dozen jumbo shrimp, peeled
1 pound applewood-smoked bacon slices, partially cooked

For the stuffing, sauté the onion, bell pepper, celery and shallots in a nonstick skillet for 3 minutes. Stir in the garlic. Cook for 1 minute and then mix in the crab meat. Sauté for 1 minute and remove from the heat. Let stand until cool. Mix in the bread crumbs, cheese, hot sauce and egg. Season with salt and pepper.

For the shrimp, devein and butterfly the shrimp. Place 1 tablespoon of the stuffing in the center of the butterflied area of each shrimp and wrap each with one slice of the bacon. Thread three stuffed shrimp on each of four metal skewers. Grill on a gas grill for 2 minutes per side or until the shrimp turn pink and the bacon is crisp.—Serves 4—**Jim Shirley, Atlas Oyster House, 2003**

TIP Shrimp and scallops become opaque and firm when fully cooked. One pound of medium shrimp added to boiling water should be simmered for three to five minutes. Scallops should be broiled for three to five minutes. Do not overcook.

Crab Meat-Coated Jumbo Shrimp with Cilantro Tomato Aïoli

Cilantro Tomato Aïoli
1 small tomato, chopped
2 egg yolks
2 tablespoons ketchup
1 tablespoon coarsely chopped cilantro
Pinch of sugar
Pinch of salt
Canola oil

Crab Meat-Coated Shrimp
1 pound (16- to 20-count) jumbo shrimp
4 ounces lump crab meat,
    shells removed

1 tablespoon chopped bell pepper
1 tablespoon chopped onion
1 1/2 teaspoons chopped garlic
1/4 cup mayonnaise
1 egg, beaten
1 tablespoon mustard
8 saltine crackers, crushed
1 teaspoon Old Bay seasoning
Salt and pepper to taste
Tabasco sauce to taste
1/2 cup fine panko
    (Japanese bread crumbs)

For the aïoli, combine the tomato, egg yolks, ketchup and cilantro in a food processor or blender and process until homogenous. Add the sugar and salt. Add canola oil gradually, processing constantly until the sauce is the consistency of mayonnaise. Taste and adjust the seasonings. Store in the refrigerator. If you are concerned about using raw egg yolks, use egg yolks from eggs pasteurized in their shells, which are sold at some specialty food stores, or use an equivalent amount of pasteurized egg substitute.

For the shrimp, peel and devein the shrimp, leaving the tails intact. Thread the shrimp from head to tail on 6-inch metal skewers. Combine the crab meat, bell pepper, onion and garlic in a bowl and mix gently. Mix the mayonnaise, egg and mustard in a bowl and mix into the crab meat mixture. Gently stir in the crackers, Old Bay seasoning, salt, pepper and Tabasco sauce; do not break up the crab meat. Press the crab meat mixture liberally around the skewered shrimp and then lightly dust with the bread crumbs. Arrange the skewers in a single layer on a baking sheet and chill until firm.

Sauté the shrimp in a sauté pan over medium gas heat for about 3 minutes or until golden brown on both sides. Remove the shrimp from the skewers and arrange equal portions of the shrimp and aïoli on each of two serving plates. Garnish with blanched snow peas, chopped cilantro and grape tomatoes. Serve with wheat risotto.—Serves 2—**Brad Parker, Pensacola Country Club, 2001**

Samos Shrimp

1 (8-ounce) snapper, grouper or triggerfish fillet
Vegetable oil
Salt and pepper to taste
2 ounces (36- to 40-count) shrimp, peeled and deveined
2 mushrooms, sliced
1 teaspoon minced garlic
2 tablespoons extra-virgin olive oil
1 Roma tomato, cut into quarters
1 pepperoncini, sliced
1 teaspoon sliced black olives
1/2 teaspoon capers
Pinch of Italian seasoning
1 ounce feta cheese, crumbled
1 green onion, chopped

Coat the fillet with vegetable oil and season with salt and pepper. Grill on a gas grill until the fillet is white and flaky. Remove to a serving plate and cover to keep warm.

Sauté the shrimp, mushrooms and garlic in the olive oil in a sauté pan until the shrimp turn pink. Stir in the tomato, pepperoncini, olives, capers and Italian seasoning and cook just until heated through. Spoon over the fillet and sprinkle with the cheese and green onion. Garnish with a lemon slice.—Serves 1—**John Flaningam, Angus, 2003**

TIP   There are seventeen types of snapper off Florida's Gulf and Atlantic coasts. Red and yellowtail snapper are two of the most common found in seafood markets and restaurants. Red snapper are the best known and are easily distinguished by their rosy-red skin and bright red irises. Yellowtail snapper have a distinguishing yellow stripe running from nose to tail and are found in the warm waters of south Florida.

Shrimp Isabela with Cilantro and Caper Rémoulade Sauce

Cilantro and Caper Rémoulade Sauce
4 egg yolks
3 tablespoons vinegar
1 tablespoon lemon juice
1 teaspoon dry mustard
1 cup canola oil
2 tablespoons chopped cilantro
1 jalapeño chile, chopped
4 gherkins, chopped
2 ounces capers
Salt and pepper to taste

Shrimp
1 pound (16- to 20-count)
   shrimp, peeled
8 ounces Gouda cheese, cut into
   small chunks
8 bacon slices, cut into halves
Olive oil
1 1/2 pounds sushi-grade tuna, cut into
   2-inch chunks
Salt and pepper to taste
1/4 cup canola oil
Black sesame seeds to taste
2 packages fresh spinach, stemmed

For the sauce, combine the egg yolks, vinegar, lemon juice and dry mustard in a bowl and whisk until blended. Add the canola oil gradually, whisking constantly until an emulsion forms. Stir in the cilantro, jalapeño chile, gherkins and capers. Season with salt and pepper. Store, covered, in the refrigerator. If you are concerned about using raw egg yolks, use egg yolks from eggs pasteurized in their shells, which are sold at some specialty food stores, or use an equivalent amount of pasteurized egg substitute.

For the shrimp, devein and butterfly the shrimp. Place one chunk of the cheese in the butterflied area of each shrimp and wrap each with a piece of bacon. Thread five shrimp on each of four metal skewers. Arrange the skewers in a single layer on a baking sheet and chill for 45 minutes.

Heat a sauté pan with a splash of olive oil until hot and sauté the shrimp until brown on all sides. Arrange the skewers in a baking pan and bake at 350 degrees in a gas oven for 4 to 5 minutes or until the shrimp turn pink and the bacon is cooked through.

Season the tuna with salt and pepper, coat lightly with the canola oil and then sprinkle with sesame seeds. Heat a sauté pan until very hot and add the tuna. Sear the tuna on all sides without scorching the sesame seeds. Sauté the spinach in a skillet just until wilted. Mound the spinach evenly on each of four serving plates. Layer the spinach with the tuna and then the shrimp. Top with a dollop of the sauce.—Serves 4—**Dan Dunn, Jubilee, 2003**

Sautéed Shrimp and Scallops with Roasted Garlic and Madeira Cream

Roasted Garlic and Madeira Cream
2 heads garlic
Olive oil for coating
2 tablespoons olive oil
5 shallots, minced
2 cups heavy cream
6 tablespoons madeira
Salt and pepper to taste
1 teaspoon sherry vinegar

Shrimp and Scallops
16 large shrimp, peeled and deveined
16 large scallops
Salt and pepper to taste
1 cup all-purpose flour
1/2 cup vegetable oil
1 tablespoon chopped parsley

For the cream, coat the garlic heads with olive oil and wrap in foil. Roast at 350 degrees in a gas oven for 30 minutes. Let stand until cool; peel. Press the garlic pulp into a bowl. The pulp should be soft and have a sweet smell. Heat 2 tablespoons olive oil in a sauté pan and add the shallots. Sauté until the shallots are tender and then stir in the cream and wine. Cook until reduced by half and strain into a bowl, discarding the solids. Season with salt and pepper and stir in the roasted garlic pulp and vinegar.

For the shrimp and scallops, season the shrimp and scallops with salt and pepper and coat with the flour. Heat the oil in a skillet until hot and add the shrimp and scallops. Cook for 4 to 7 minutes or until brown on all sides. Spread the cream sauce over the bottom of four serving plates and top evenly with the shrimp and scallops. Sprinkle with the parsley.—Serves 4—**Gus Silivos, Skopelos on the Bay, 1996**

TIP Store fresh shrimp at 32 degrees in the coldest part of your refrigerator for up to 2 days.

Shrimp and Scallop-Stuffed Poblano Chiles with Red Pepper Sauce

Red Pepper Sauce
2 large red bell peppers
1 tablespoon olive oil
1/4 cup chopped shallots
2 garlic cloves, minced
1 jalapeño chile, seeded and minced
1/2 cup low-salt chicken broth
Salt and pepper to taste

Stuffed Poblano Chiles and Assembly
8 large poblano chiles
1 tablespoon olive oil

1/4 cup chopped red bell pepper
2 tablespoons chopped shallots
4 ounces deveined peeled shrimp,
   coarsely chopped
4 ounces fresh scallops,
   coarsely chopped
2/3 cup soft fresh goat cheese
1/2 cup packed shredded Pepper
   Jack cheese
3 tablespoons chopped fresh cilantro
2 tablespoons chopped fresh basil
Salt and pepper to taste

For the sauce, char the bell peppers over a gas flame until blackened on all sides. Steam the bell peppers in a brown paper bag for 10 minutes. Peel, seed and coarsely chop the bell peppers. Heat the olive oil in a medium skillet over medium gas heat. Add the shallots, garlic and jalapeño chile to the hot oil. Sauté for 5 minutes or until the shallots are tender. Cool slightly and then pour into a blender. Add the bell peppers and broth and process until puréed. Season with salt and pepper.

For the chiles, char the poblano chiles over a gas flame for 10 minutes or until blackened on all sides. Steam the poblano chiles in a brown paper bag for 10 minutes; peel. Make a slit along one side of each of the poblano chiles with a sharp knife and remove the seeds, leaving the stems intact.

Heat the olive oil in a skillet and add the bell pepper and shallots. Sauté until tender; add the shrimp and scallops. Cook for 1 minute or just until the shrimp turn pink. Remove the shrimp mixture to a bowl and stir in the goat cheese, Pepper Jack cheese, cilantro and basil. Season with salt and pepper.

Arrange the poblano chiles slit side up on a baking sheet and stuff evenly with the shrimp mixture. Pull up the sides of the chiles to enclose the filling. Bake at 350 degrees in a gas oven for 15 minutes or until the cheese melts and the poblano chiles are heated through. Spoon 3 tablespoons of the sauce onto each of eight serving plates and arrange one stuffed poblano chile on each prepared plate.—Serves 8—**Angela Miller, Distinctive Kitchens Culinary Arts Center, 2007**

Cherrystone-Stuffed Squid with Tomato Tarragon Vinaigrette

Tomato Tarragon Vinaigrette
1/2 cup canned diced tomatoes
1/4 cup rice wine vinegar
1 teaspoon fresh minced garlic
1 teaspoon chopped fresh tarragon
1/2 cup grapeseed oil
1 teaspoon salt
1 teaspoon pepper

Stuffed Squid
2 tablespoons butter
1 tablespoon minced fresh garlic

24 small cherrystone clams, shucked
6 large shiitake mushrooms,
  finely chopped
1/4 cup (1 ounce) grated
  Parmesan cheese
2 tablespoons crumbled goat cheese
1/4 cup panko (Japanese bread crumbs)
1 tablespoon fresh lemon juice
1 teaspoon kosher salt
1 teaspoon freshly cracked pepper
4 squid tubes, cleaned
1/4 cup vegetable oil

For the vinaigrette, combine the tomatoes, vinegar, garlic and tarragon in a blender and process until smooth. Add the grapeseed oil gradually, processing constantly until the oil is emulsified. Stir in the salt and pepper.

For the squid, heat the butter in a saucepan over medium gas heat. Sauté the garlic in the butter until tender, but not brown. Add the clams and sauté for 1 to 2 minutes. Stir in the mushrooms and cook for 3 to 4 minutes or until the mushrooms are tender. Spoon the clam mixture into a bowl. Add the Parmesan cheese and goat cheese to the warm clam mixture and stir until well combined. Fold in the bread crumbs, lemon juice, salt and pepper.

Spoon the clam mixture into a pastry bag or a sealable plastic bag with one corner cut out. The corner should be large enough to allow the clams to fit through. Pipe the clam mixture into the squid tubes and seal the ends with wooden picks.

Heat the oil in a large sauté pan over medium-high gas heat. Sauté the squid in the hot oil until golden brown. Remove to a baking pan and bake at 350 degrees in a gas oven for 15 minutes. Remove the squid to a platter and discard any excess fat from the baking pan. Add the vinaigrette to the hot baking pan and swirl to heat the vinaigrette. Serve the squid with the warm vinaigrette and your choice of side dishes.—Serves 4—**Andrew Selz, Chef Selz Collection, 2004**

TIP Store live clams in a container with the lid slightly ajar in the refrigerator at 41 degrees. They will remain alive for up to seven days. Drain any excess liquid daily.

Creole Pasta Primavera

3 tablespoons olive oil
1 pound andouille, chopped or sliced
1/4 cup white wine
1 pound crawfish tails
1 pound scallops
1 pound shrimp, peeled and deveined
3 portobello mushrooms, sliced
1 pound asparagus spears, trimmed and chopped
3 large ripe tomatoes, chopped
3 to 4 cups heavy cream
Creole seasoning to taste
1 bunch scallions, chopped
Hot cooked pasta
1 cup (4 ounces) grated Parmesan cheese

Heat the olive oil in a skillet and add the sausage. Fry until crisp on all sides. Remove the sausage to a platter, reserving the pan drippings. Deglaze the skillet with the wine. Stir in the crawfish, scallops and shrimp.

Cook until the seafood is partially cooked. Add the mushrooms, asparagus, tomatoes and sausage and mix well. Stir in the cream and Creole seasoning and cook until the sauce is thickened and the seafood is cooked through, stirring frequently. Mix in the scallions. Spoon the seafood mixture over hot cooked pasta on serving plates and sprinkle with the cheese.—Serves 6—
Chris Tingle, Gauthier's, 1999

TIP To freeze shrimp, store in sealable plastic freezer bags to prevent freezer burn and write the date on the bag. Freeze at 0 degrees for up to 6 months. Thaw in the refrigerator or under cold running water.

Fettuccini Nantua

1 cup cooked fettuccini, drained and patted dry
2 ounces cooked crawfish meat with fat
1/3 cup shredded Parmesan cheese
2 pinches of Creole seasoning
1 egg, beaten
Self-rising flour
1 1/2 cups peanut oil
2 ounces steamed medium shrimp, peeled and deveined
1/2 cup Zatarain's Creole mustard
1/4 cup mayonnaise
1 tablespoon chopped red bell pepper
1 tablespoon chopped green bell pepper
Pinch of Creole seasoning
1 tablespoon chopped green onions
Pinch of Ritz cracker crumbs
Creole seasoning to taste

Combine the pasta, crawfish, cheese, 2 pinches of Creole seasoning and 1/2 of the egg in a bowl. Mix until combined, adding the remaining egg as needed. Add enough self-rising flour to bind the mixture. Divide the pasta mixture into two equal portions and mix each portion with your hands in a swirling motion as if you were making meatballs; be careful not to overwork the mixture or it will become dense and doughy.

Heat the peanut oil in a skillet to 325 degrees. Add the pasta balls to the hot oil and fry for about 2 minutes or until crisp and golden brown, turning as needed. Drain and remove to a platter.

Mix the shrimp, Creole mustard, mayonnaise, bell peppers and a pinch of Creole seasoning in a bowl. Arrange each pasta ball on a serving plate and spoon the desired amount of the shrimp sauce over the top. Sprinkle with the green onions and a mixture of the cracker crumbs and Creole seasoning to taste.—Serves 2 as an appetizer—**Buzz Valadao, Triggers, 2007**

TIP The King mackerel is noted for its remarkable leaps, often clearing the water by 10 feet or more. This species are schooling fish that migrate from south Florida waters in the winter to more northerly waters in the spring.

Fettuccini Seafood Pasta

1 pound fettuccini
Kosher salt to taste
Olive oil for coating
1 pound scallops
1/4 cup Old Bay seasoning
All-purpose flour
1/4 cup (1/2 stick) unsalted butter
1 pound grouper, cleaned
Freshly cracked pepper to taste
1/4 cup extra-virgin olive oil for sautéing
5 tablespoons finely chopped shallots
5 tablespoons finely chopped garlic

1 pound (21- to 25-count) shrimp,
  peeled and deveined
1 cup chardonnay
4 cups seafood broth or clam juice
1/4 cup extra-virgin olive oil
1 pound mussels, scrubbed and rinsed
1/4 cup (1/2 stick) unsalted
  butter, chilled
1 tablespoon fresh thyme leaves
2 tablespoons pine nuts, toasted
2 tablespoons chopped roasted
  bell pepper

Cook the pasta in boiling salted water in a saucepan for 5 to 7 minutes. Drain the pasta, reserving the hot cooking liquid. Plunge the pasta into a bowl of ice water and let stand until chilled; drain. Toss the pasta with olive oil to coat in a bowl.

Pat the scallops dry with paper towels. Lightly dust one side of each scallop with the Old Bay seasoning and then dip the same side in flour. Heat 1/4 cup butter in a nonstick skillet over medium-high gas heat until brown. Add the scallops floured sides down to the hot butter and sear until brown. Turn the scallops and cook for 2 minutes. Remove the scallops to a platter. Coat the grouper with olive oil to coat and season with salt and pepper. Grill on a gas grill over medium-high gas heat for 3 to 4 minutes per side or until the grouper flakes easily. Remove the grouper to a platter and cover to keep warm.

Heat 1/4 cup olive oil in a large sauté pan over medium gas heat and add the shallots and garlic. Cook for 1 minute, stirring constantly. Add the shrimp and cook for about 1 minute, swirling the pan constantly. Deglaze the pan with the wine and cook until the shrimp turn pink. Remove the shrimp to a platter using a slotted spoon, reserving the pan juices. Stir the broth and 1/4 cup olive oil into the reserved pan juices. Simmer for 10 minutes or until reduced; add the mussels. Steam, covered, for 2 minutes. Remove the mussels to a platter using a slotted spoon, discarding any mussels that do not open and reserving the pan juices. Add 1/4 cup butter to the reserved pan juices. Cook until the butter is melted and well combined, swirling the pan frequently.

Reheat the pasta in the reserved hot cooking liquid; drain. Add the pasta, shrimp and mussels to the sauce and cook until heated through. Stir in the thyme, pine nuts and bell pepper. Mound the pasta mixture equally on each of eight to ten serving plates. Top with equal portions of the grouper and scallops.—Serves 8 to 10—**Irv Miller, Jackson's, 2004**

Thailand Tiger Prawns with Montrachet-Crab Meat Stuffing

2 cups bread crumbs
1/4 cup minced green bell pepper
1/4 cup minced red bell pepper
2 ounces Montrachet cheese
2 tablespoons chopped fresh basil
1 tablespoon minced garlic
2 eggs, beaten
1/4 cup mayonnaise
1 tablespoon white wine
Salt and pepper to taste
4 ounces lump crab meat, shells removed
12 (10- to 15-count) Thailand tiger prawns
12 paper-thin slices prosciutto
Melted butter
Hot cooked spinach fettuccini

Mix the bread crumbs, bell peppers, cheese, basil and garlic in a bowl. Add the eggs, mayonnaise, wine, salt and pepper and mix until combined. Fold in the crab meat and chill, covered, in the refrigerator.

Peel, devein and butterfly the prawns. Stuff the prawns with the crab meat mixture and wrap each stuffed prawn with a slice of the prosciutto. Brush with melted butter. Grill the prawns on a gas grill over medium gas heat until the prawns turn pink. Serve over hot cooked spinach fettuccini.— Serves 4—**Chuck Morgan, Scotto's Ristorante Italiano, 1995**

TIP The stone crab can generate its claws three to four times. Florida law forbids the taking of whole stone crabs. Fishermen are allowed to remove claws at least 2 3/4 inches long and are required to return stone crabs safely to the water after removing the claws. Of course, they really do have to be careful when removing the claws, as a stone crab's claw is strong enough to crush a finger.

Seafood Penne Primavera

1/4 cup (1/2 stick) unsalted butter or margarine
1 pound (21- to 26-count) shrimp, peeled and deveined
1 pound crawfish tail meat
1 tablespoon minced garlic
2 cups chopped green onions
2 tablespoons plus 1 teaspoon Jerry's Own ZydeCajun seasoning*
1 tablespoon dried basil
1 tablespoon dried thyme
1 teaspoon Jerry's habanero hot sauce*
3 cups chopped zucchini
2 cups chopped broccoli
2 cups chopped green beans
1 cup chopped green bell pepper
1 cup chopped red bell pepper
1 cup chopped yellow bell pepper
4 cups half-and-half
1/2 cup (2 ounces) shredded Parmesan cheese
2 cups (8 ounces) shredded provolone cheese
1 pound lump crab meat, shells removed
4 cups hot cooked penne

Heat a large skillet over medium gas heat and add the butter. Cook until the butter is melted and sizzling. Stir in the shrimp, crawfish and garlic and sauté for 5 minutes or until the shrimp and crawfish are three-fourths cooked through. Reduce the gas heat and add the green onions, ZydeCajun seasoning, basil, thyme and hot sauce to the shrimp mixture.

Simmer until combined, stirring frequently. Increase the gas heat to medium and stir in the zucchini, broccoli, green beans and bell peppers. Sauté for 5 minutes; do not overcook. Reduce the gas heat and stir in the half-and-half. Simmer until hot, but not scalding. Add the Parmesan cheese and cook until the cheese melts. Add the provolone cheese and cook until the mixture is creamy. Fold in the crab meat until combined; do not break up the lumps. Add the pasta and toss gently to combine.

Cook until heated through. Add additional half-and-half if the sauce is too thick or additional provolone cheese for a thicker consistency. Spoon the pasta mixture evenly onto each of four serving plates. Garnish with lemon slices.—Serves 4—**Jerry Mistretta, Jerry's Cajun Cafe, 2006**

TIP   *Available at www.jerryscajun.com

Lou Michael's Seafood Platter
Seafood Soup

1 pound fish bones
1/2 cup chopped celery
1/2 cup chopped onion
1/2 cup chopped carrots
Salt and pepper to taste
4 clams
4 ounces grouper, coarsely chopped
2 mussels
2 shrimp, peeled and deveined
1 squid, chopped
2 teaspoons roasted garlic pulp
Fresh basil leaves to taste

Sweat the fish bones, celery, onion and carrots in a large saucepan. Add enough cool water to fill the saucepan and simmer for 2 hours; do not allow to boil. Strain, discarding the solids and reserving the stock.

Pour the reserved stock into a sauté pan and season with salt and pepper. Add the clams, grouper, mussels, shrimp and squid. Steam, covered, for about 8 minutes or until the seafood is cooked through. Stir in the garlic pulp and basil. Ladle into soup bowls and serve with baguette slices. Lou Michael's Seafood Platter is continued on the following pages.—Serves 6—**Dan Dunn, Lou Michael's Downtown, 2000**

TIP Lean fish such as flounder, grouper, mahi mahi, catfish, tilapia, and shellfish are excellent sources of protein and are low in fat. Fish that have more fat, such as mackerel, swordfish, bluefish, and trout, are recommended for their high levels of Omega-3 fatty acids.

Lou Michael's Seafood Platter
Salmon Seared with Sesame and Coriander and Ginger Sake Vinaigrette

Ginger Sake Vinaigrette
2 tablespoons canola oil
2 tablespoons sake
2 tablespoons mirin
1 tablespoon fish sauce
Chopped fresh ginger to taste

Salmon
1 pound salmon fillet, skin removed
1 teaspoon coriander
Salt and pepper to taste
1 teaspoon sesame seeds
1 tablespoon canola oil
Stalks of lemon grass
Mixed salad greens

For the vinaigrette, pour the canola oil into a bowl. Whisk in the sake, mirin and fish sauce until blended. Stir in ginger.

For the salmon, cut the salmon into 1-inch chunks. Dust with the coriander, salt, pepper and sesame seeds. Heat the canola oil in a sauté pan until hot. Add the salmon to the hot oil and sear until rare. Spear the salmon with lemon grass like skewers and continue searing until the salmon is medium-rare or well-done. Mound salad greens on six serving plates and top with equal portions of the salmon. Serve with the vinaigrette.—Serves 6—**Dan Dunn, Lou Michael's Downtown, 2000**

TIP Generally, you should cook fish at 400 to 450 degrees for 10 minutes per inch of thickness, turning halfway through the cooking time. Fish less than one-half inch thick does not require turning.

Lou Michael's Seafood Platter
Tuna and Soft-Shell Crab Rolls with
Peanut Sauce

Peanut Sauce
1/2 cup peanuts
1 tablespoon peanut oil
1 teaspoon curry powder
1/2 cup coconut milk
1 tablespoon sugar
2 tablespoons soy sauce
1 tablespoon lime juice

Tuna and Soft-Shell Crab Rolls
1 soft-shell crab
All-purpose flour
1 tablespoon vegetable oil
1 package spring roll wrappers
1 package rice noodles
6 ounces sushi-grade tuna, sliced into 12 pieces
1 1/2 cups mixed salad greens
1 mango, cut into long slices
8 mint leaves
8 basil leaves

For the sauce, process the peanuts in a food processor until crushed. Heat the peanut oil in a sauté pan over low gas heat and mix in the curry powder. Add the coconut milk and sugar and whisk until blended. Cook until heated through; do not boil. Stir in the peanuts. Remove from the heat and stir in the soy sauce and lime juice. Cover to keep warm.

For the rolls, dust the crab with flour and panfry in the oil in a skillet until crisp and brown. Let stand until cool; slice into twelve pieces. Soak the spring roll wrappers in cool water in a bowl until soft. Cook the noodles in boiling water in a saucepan for 5 minutes or until tender; drain. Let stand until cool.

Remove the wrappers from the water and arrange on paper towels to drain. Place two slices of the crab and two slices of the tuna in the middle of each wrapper. Layer with equal portions of the mixed greens, mango, mint, basil and noodles. Fold the sides of the wrappers toward the centers and roll tightly to enclose the filling. Serve with the warm sauce.—Serves 6—**Dan Dunn, Lou Michael's Downtown, 2000**

Coastal Seafood Trio

Plum Madeira Reduction
4 dried plums, chopped
3/4 cup madeira

Caramelized Onions
2 Vidalia onions, chopped
1 tablespoon butter

Choron Sauce
1/2 cup red wine vinegar
2 tablespoons chopped shallots
3 tablespoons chopped tarragon
1 tablespoon chopped parsley
1/2 teaspoon crushed peppercorns
3 egg yolks, warmed
11/4 cups (21/2 sticks) butter, clarified
1 ounce tomato purée
1 tablespoon heavy cream

Shrimp Spinach Rolls
7 large shrimp, peeled and deveined
1 tablespoon cream
1 tablespoon chili soybean sauce
1/2 teaspoon egg white
Fresh spinach leaves, slightly wilted

Scallop Crab Terrine
7 ounces lump crab meat,
    shells removed
4 ounces sea scallops
3 threads saffron
1 egg white
3 tablespoons cream
1 teaspoon lemon juice
Salt and pepper to taste
1 sheet seaweed

Flounder Paupiette
2 tablespoons butter
1/2 ounce red pepper paste
4 flounder fillets with skin

Soft-Shell Crabs and Assembly
1/2 cup all-purpose flour
3 tablespoons whole wheat flour
Salt and pepper to taste
2 soft-shell crabs, cleaned and
    cut into halves
2 tablespoons almond oil

For the madeira reduction, simmer the plums and wine in a saucepan until the mixture is of a syrupy consistency, stirring occasionally. Remove from the heat and cover to keep warm.

For the onions, sauté the onions in the butter in a skillet until caramelized, stirring occasionally.

For the choron sauce, combine the vinegar, shallots, tarragon, parsley and peppercorns in a saucepan and cook until the liquid is reduced to 2 tablespoons. Strain, discarding the solids. Combine the warm egg yolks and reduced vinegar mixture in a blender. Add the clarified butter gradually, processing constantly at high speed until blended. Add the tomato purée and cream and process to a sauce consistency.

For the rolls, process the shrimp, cream, soybean sauce and egg white in a blender or food processor until blended. Lay spinach leaves on a sheet of plastic wrap and add the shrimp mixture. Roll to enclose the filling in cigar-style portions.

For the terrine, combine the crab meat, scallops and saffron in a bowl and stir several times to infuse the saffron. Process the crab meat mixture, egg white and cream in a blender until combined. Mix in the lemon juice, salt and pepper. Spread half the crab mixture in a loaf pan or V mold lined with the seaweed. Layer with the shrimp spinach rolls and the remaining crab mixture. Bake in a water bath at 375 degrees in a gas oven until an oven thermometer registers 135 degrees. Cool slightly, but serve warm.

For the flounder, mix the butter and red pepper paste in a bowl until blended. Coat muffin tins or a timbale mold with the butter mixture. Roll the fillets lengthwise skin side out and then slice the rolls to fit the muffin tins. Arrange the rolls in the prepared muffin tins. You may spread some of the butter mixture on the fillets, if desired. Bake at 350 degrees in a gas oven for about 5 minutes or until the fillet rolls are translucent.

For the crabs, mix the all-purpose flour, whole wheat flour, salt and pepper in a shallow dish. Coat the crabs with the flour mixture. Sauté the crabs in the almond oil in a skillet until brown and crisp; drain.

Serve the terrine with the choron sauce, the flounder with the remaining red pepper butter sauce and the soft-shell crabs with the madeira reduction on a bed of the caramelized onions.— Serves 12 as an appetizer—**Travis Herr, Bill Hamilton and Culinary Students, Pensacola Junior College, 2006**

Index

Accompaniments/Seasonings.
See also Salsa, Sauces
Dill Nage, 42
Garlic Mayonnaise, 51
Garlic Mayonnaise Sauce, 57
Herbed Mayonnaise, 87
Homemade Pickles, 74
Lime Pistachio Butter, 10
Pineapple and Cranberry
    Compote, 44
Pineapple Chutney, 126
Rub Seasoning, 16
Sesame Red Chile Dust, 66
Sonoran Seasoning, 39
Spicy Mango Tomato Relish, 24

Appetizers. *See also* Salsa
Asian Guacamole, 107
Bacon and Scallop-Stuffed Mushrooms
    with Roasted Roma Cream, 77
Blackened Shrimp in Beer Butter
    Sauce, 108
Cajun Spring Rolls, 96
Chocolate Shrimp, 109
Coastal Seafood Trio, 184
Crab and Corn Beignets with
    Herbed Mayonnaise, 87
Crawfish Beignets with Sun-Dried
    Tomatoes and Roasted Corn
    Tartar Sauce, 95
Crawfish Cheesecake, 94
Fettuccini Nantua, 177
Garlic and Sherry Shrimp on
    Grilled French Bread, 108
Grilled Bacon-Wrapped Scallop Kabobs
    with Pineapple and Sweet Potato, 79
Gulf Crab and Chorizo Fritters with
    Chipotle Cream Sauce, 91
Hoisin-Smoked Salmon, 38
Lobster and Mango Summer Rolls, 101
Shrimp Lettuce Wraps, 110
Shrimp Tortellini Maria, 110
Tempura-Crusted Spicy Tuna Roll with
    Ginger Coconut Sauce, 55
Tuna Ceviche, 54

Artichokes
Basil-Tomato Stewed Mahi Mahi, 23
Mr. Slu's Triggerfish, 154
Portobello Shrimp, 125
Wasabi-Crusted Grouper, 22

Asparagus
Creole Pasta Primavera, 176
Tempura-Crusted Spicy Tuna Roll with
    Ginger Coconut Sauce, 55
Tuna Confit Salad with Fried
    Zucchini, 63

Avocado
Asian Guacamole, 107
Avocado Corn Salsa, 52
Citrus Salsa-Poached Salmon, 39
Grilled Avocado with Shrimp and
    Fire-Roasted Tomato Salad, 112
Jumbo Lump Crab Tostadas with
    Goat Cheese, 92
Seafood and Avocado Tostada, 155
Sun-Ripened Tomatoes and
    Asian-Style Lobster Salad, 105

Bacon/Pancetta
Applewood Barbecued Shrimp, 115
Bacon and Scallop-Stuffed
    Mushrooms with Roasted
    Roma Cream, 77
Bacon-Braised Salmon with
    Molasses Sauce, 34
Bacon-Wrapped Crab-Stuffed
    Shrimp, 169
Barbecued Shrimp over Grits, 117
Beach-Style Shrimp, 125
Fennel-Green Apple Hash, 42
Grilled Bacon-Wrapped Scallop
    Kabobs with Pineapple and
    Sweet Potato, 79
Grits a Ya-Ya, 131
Redfish with Figs, Bacon and
    Pecans, 28
Seafood en Brochette, 165
Shrimp Isabela with Cilantro and
    Caper Rémoulade Sauce, 172
Stuffed Redfish in Banana Leaves, 29

Banana/Plantain
Banana-Crusted Yellowfin Tuna, 65
Citrus-Crusted Swordfish Steak with
    Mango Sauce, 50
57 Snapper, 151
Plantain Planks, 75

Beans
Black Bean and Mango Salsa, 64
Black Bean Cakes, 122
Black Bean Salsa, 33
Calypso Black Beans, 92
Pole Bean and Red Onion Salad, 72
Seafood and Avocado Tostada, 155
Seafood Penne Primavera, 180

Beef
Blackened New York Strip Steak with
    Crawfish Succotash, 97
Cajun Surf and Turf, 144
Grilled Ginger Garlic
    Lobster Tails, 107
Ragin' Cajun Combo, 98

Bok Choy
Asian Slaw, 65
Grilled Grouper with Bok Choy and
    Asian Barbecue Sauce, 13
Yukon-Crusted Redfish, 147

Broccoli
Seafood Penne Primavera, 180
Shrimp Nasi Goreng Indonesian
    Rice Bowl, 128

Cabbage
Asian Cabbage and Radish Slaw, 31
Asian Slaw, 65
Chargrilled Grouper with
    Wild Mushroom Ragout, 13
Fennel-Green Apple Hash, 42
Vegetable Salad, 59

Carrots
Asian Slaw, 65
Cajun Spring Rolls, 96
Glazed Spicy Shrimp, 127
Grilled Thai Leaf-Wrapped Mahi Mahi
    with Lilikoi Reduction, 27
Poached Sea Bass Chinoise, 45
Vegetable Salad, 59
Wasabi-Crusted Grouper, 22
Yukon-Crusted Redfish, 147

Catfish
Grilled Blackened Catfish with Creamy
    Scallion Sauce, 11
Panéed Catfish, 11

Chicken
Blackened Bayou Chicken with
    Crawfish Tasso Sauce, 99
Dove's Nest, 76

Clams
Cherrystone-Stuffed Squid with
    Tomato Tarragon Vinaigrette, 175
Lou Michael's Seafood Platter
    Seafood Soup, 181
Mahogany Clams with Chorizo
    and Chiles, 71
Steamed Mahogany Clams over
    Pole Bean and Red Onion Salad, 72

Coatings/Batters
Sesame Batter, 25
Tempura Batter, 145

Corn
Avocado Corn Salsa, 52
Corn and Red Potatoes, 144
Corn Salsa, 156

Crab and Corn Beignets with
    Herbed Mayonnaise, 87
Grilled Scallops and Tuna en Husk, 168
Grilled Wahoo and Shrimp with
    Field Pea Sauté, 157
Lobster and Sweet Corn Chowder, 103
Lobster Corn Stock, 103
Pan-Sautéed Grouper with Tasso,
    Parsnip and Roasted Corn Hash, 20
Roasted Corn and Teriyaki Shrimp
    Salad, 114
Roasted Corn Tartar Sauce, 95
Smoked Gouda Cheese Grits, 131
Summer Salmon, 34

Crab Cakes
Big Sexy Risotto Crab Cakes with
    Roasted Red Pepper Aïoli, 90
Crab and Crawfish Cakes, 162
Crab Cakes, 88, 142
McGuire's Crab Cakes, 89
Miller's Crab Cakes, 88
Panéed Crab Cakes, 89

Crab Meat
Bacon-Wrapped Crab-Stuffed
    Shrimp, 169
Big Sexy Risotto Crab Cakes with
    Roasted Red Pepper Aïoli, 90
Crab and Corn Beignets with
    Herbed Mayonnaise, 87
Crab and Crawfish Cakes, 162
Crab Cakes, 88, 142
Crab Meat-Coated Jumbo Shrimp
    with Cilantro Tomato Aïoli, 170
Dungeness Crab, 93
57 Snapper, 151
Fish Dill-ish, 157
Grilled Salmon with Crab Fingers
    and Angel Hair Pasta, 148
Gulf Crab and Chorizo Fritters
    with Chipotle Cream Sauce, 91
Jumbo Lump Crab Tostadas with
    Goat Cheese, 92
Louisiana Seafood Gumbo, 159
McGuire's Crab Cakes, 89
Miller's Crab Cakes, 88
Mr. Slu's Triggerfish, 154
Panéed Crab Cakes, 89
Seafood and Avocado Tostada, 155
Seafood Jambalaya, 160
Seafood Penne Primavera, 180
Seafood Santa Rosa, 158
Snapper Bienville, 150
Thailand Tiger Prawns with
    Montrachet-Crab Meat
    Stuffing, 179
Tuna Lagasse, 156

Crabs, Soft-Shell
Andouille-Crusted Soft-Shell
    Crabs, 93
Grilled Soft-Shell Crabs
    with Shrimp and Tasso
    Cream Sauce, 164
Lou Michael's Seafood Platter
    Tuna and Soft-Shell Crab Rolls
    with Peanut Sauce, 183
Soft-Shell Crabs Zachary, 163

Crawfish
Blackened Bayou Chicken with
    Crawfish Tasso Sauce, 99
Cajun Spring Rolls, 96
Crab and Crawfish Cakes, 162
Crawfish and Sausage Frittata, 98
Crawfish Beignets with Sun-Dried
    Tomatoes and Roasted Corn
    Tartar Sauce, 95
Crawfish Cheesecake, 94
Crawfish Étouffée, 144
Crawfish Fettuccini, 99
Crawfish Hebert, 100
Crawfish Succotash, 97
Creole Pasta Primavera, 176
Fettuccini Nantua, 177
Grouper Daniels, 140
Grouper New Iberia, 141
Ragin' Cajun Combo, 98
Scamp Creole, 149
Seafood Jambalaya, 160
Seafood Penne Primavera, 180
Shellfish Étouffée, 161
Soft-Shell Crabs Zachary, 163

Dressings/Vinaigrettes
Asian Dressing, 41
Black Olive Vinaigrette, 60
Blood Orange Vinaigrette, 106
Creole Vinaigrette, 59
Fused Herb Oil, 63
Ginger Sake Vinaigrette, 182
Infused Oil, 109
Pink Peppercorn Vinaigrette, 58
Spicy Key Lime Dressing, 104
Thai Dressing, 46
Tomato Tarragon Vinaigrette, 175

Eggplant
Grilled Grouper with Bok Choy and
    Asian Barbecue Sauce, 13
Grouper New Iberia, 141
Ratatouille, 60

Fennel
Fennel-Green Apple Hash, 42
Orange Fennel Salsa, 47

Fish. *See also* individual kinds
Coastal Seafood Trio, 184
Crusted Flounder with Shrimp
    Dumplings, 139
Grilled Sheepshead with Orange
    Fennel Salsa, 47
Hoisin-Marinated Sesame Amberjack
    with Onion and Pineapple Salsa, 9
Jazz on the Grill, 67
Jerry's Gulfuletta, 152
Local Fish in Foil with Grilled
    Pineapple Salsa, 68
Scamp Creole, 149
Seafood Piccata, 158
Seafood Santa Rosa, 158
Stir-Fried Vegetables, 143
Tarragon-Crusted Striped
    Bass, 10

Fruit. *See* individual kinds

Grains. *See* Grits; Rice

Greens
Cornmeal-Crusted Oysters with
    Turnip Greens and Vidalia Onion
    Sauce, 73
Crab Cakes, 88

Grits
Barbecued Shrimp over Grits, 117
Creamy Cheddar Grits, 129
Goat Cheese Grits, 130
Smoked Gouda Cheese Grits, 131
Stone-Ground Yellow Grits, 147

Grouper
Bamboo-Wrapped Grouper, 17
Cajun Surf and Turf, 144
Chargrilled Grouper Plaki, 12
Chargrilled Grouper with
    Red Onion Confit, 12
Chargrilled Grouper with
    Wild Mushroom Ragout, 13
Fettuccini Seafood Pasta, 178
Fish Dill-ish, 157
Garden Street Grouper, 15
Greek-Style Grouper, 19
Grilled Grouper Greek Style, 14
Grilled Grouper with Bok Choy and
    Asian Barbecue Sauce, 13
Grilled Marinated Grouper, 15
Grouper Bayou with Sweet Hot
    Pecan Sauce, 18
Grouper Daniels, 140
Grouper New Iberia, 141
Grouper Pecan, 16
Grouper Pinot Noir, 21

Grouper with Pesto Sauce over
    Angel Hair Pasta, 18
Herb-Seared Grouper with Roasted
    Pepper and Tomato Compote, 20
Jerry's Blackened Grouper, 19
Lou Michael's Seafood Platter
    Seafood Soup, 181
Panéed Grouper Stack with
    Potato Crab Cakes and Leek-
    Pepper Beurre Blanc, 142
Pan-Sautéed Grouper with
    Tasso, Parsnip and Roasted
    Corn Hash, 20
Pecan-Crusted Grouper with
    Frangelico Sauce, 21
Pesce Picante Mare
    (Spicy Fish), 141
Potato-Crusted Grouper with
    Curry Seafood Vegetables and
    Mornay Sauce, 143
Provençal Grouper, 22
Roasted Grouper Cilantro, 17
Rosemary Grilled Grouper with
    Grapes and Blue Cheese, 14
Wasabi-Crusted Grouper, 22

Lime
Cashew and Lime
    Butter Sauce, 123
Chargrilled Grouper with
    Red Onion Confit, 12
Chilled Gazpacho with Ginger-Lime
    Marinated Shrimp, 111
Citrus Cilantro Salsa, 39
Lime Pistachio Butter, 10
Poached Salmon with
    Mustard Lime Sauce, 40
Spicy Key Lime Dressing, 104

Lobster
Grilled Ginger Garlic
    Lobster Tails, 107
Grilled Lobster Salad with
    Blood Orange Vinaigrette and
    Mango Saffron Coulis, 106
Lobster and Mango
    Summer Rolls, 101
Lobster and Sweet Corn Chowder, 103
Lobster Corn Stock, 103
Lobster Salad with Spicy Key Lime
    Dressing, 104
Portobello Mushroom Timbale with
    Lobster and Fresh Herb Cream
    Reduction, 102
Seafood en Brochette, 165
Seafood Santa Rosa, 158
Sun-Ripened Tomatoes and
    Asian-Style Lobster Salad, 105

Mahi Mahi
Bahamian Seafood Pasta, 146
Basil-Tomato Stewed Mahi Mahi, 23
Curry of Mahi Mahi, 25
Dorado Aguadilla, 24
Grilled Caribbean Mojo Mahi Mahi, 26
Grilled Thai Leaf-Wrapped Mahi Mahi
    with Lilikoi Reduction, 27
Hoisin Mahi Mahi, 145
Mahi Mahi Island Kabobs with
    Mango Beurre Blanc, 28

Mango
Black Bean and Mango Salsa, 64
Hoisin Mahi Mahi, 145
Lobster and Mango Summer Rolls, 101
Lou Michael's Seafood Platter Tuna
    and Soft-Shell Crab Rolls with
    Peanut Sauce, 183
Mahi Mahi Island Kabobs with
    Mango Beurre Blanc, 28
Mango Jalapeño Salsa, 56
Mango Saffron Coulis, 106
Mango Sauce, 50
Spicy Mango Tomato Relish, 24
Tropical Scallop Ceviche with
    Plantain Planks, 75

Mushrooms, 84
Bacon and Scallop-Stuffed
    Mushrooms with Roasted
    Roma Cream, 77
Chargrilled Grouper with
    Wild Mushroom Ragout, 13
Cherrystone-Stuffed Squid with
    Tomato Tarragon Vinaigrette, 175
Creole Pasta Primavera, 176
Grilled Scallops with Portobello
    Mushroom, 78
Grits a Ya-Ya, 131
Grouper Pinot Noir, 21
Lobster Salad with Spicy Key Lime
    Dressing, 104
Marinated Mushrooms, 102
Pasta Aglio e Olio, 132
Portobello Shrimp, 125
Seafood Diablo, 149
Seafood en Brochette, 165
Seared Sea Scallops with
    Mushrooms and Roasted
    Garlic Beurre Blanc, 84
Shrimp Pastacola, 135

Mussels
Bahamian Seafood Pasta, 146
Barbecued Salmon with Roasted
    Garlic and Mussels, 148
Fettuccini Seafood Pasta, 178

Lou Michael's Seafood Platter
    Seafood Soup, 181
Sea Pearls with Marinara
    Sauce, 166

Okra
Creole Sauce, 146
Green Tomatoes and Okra, 124
Grouper Daniels, 140
Stuffed Redfish in Banana
    Leaves, 29

Onions
Caramelized Onions, 184
Chargrilled Grouper with
    Red Onion Confit, 12
Cornmeal-Crusted Oysters with
    Turnip Greens and Vidalia
    Onion Sauce, 73
Onion and Pineapple Salsa, 9
Pole Bean and Red Onion Salad, 72
Ratatouille, 60
Stir-Fried Vegetables, 143

Orange
Blood Orange Vinaigrette, 106
Chargrilled Grouper with
    Red Onion Confit, 12
Citrus Cilantro Salsa, 39
Glazed Spicy Shrimp, 127
Grilled Sea Scallops with
    Mixed Greens and Orange
    Balsamic Vinaigrette, 81
Orange Chocolate Sauce, 109
Orange Fennel Salsa, 47
Orange Sauce, 120
Salt-Packed Red Snapper with
    Citrus Herb Rub, 30
Soy Orange Sauce, 65

Oysters
Cornmeal-Crusted Oysters with
    Turnip Greens and Vidalia
    Onion Sauce, 73
Jerry's Gulfuletta, 152
Louisiana Seafood Gumbo, 159
Oysters Eros, 73
Pan-Fried Oysters, 147
Sautéed Triggerfish with Oysters
    and Cream Sauce, 153
Sea Pearls with Marinara Sauce, 166
Semolina-Fried Oyster Po-Boy with
    Homemade Pickles, 74
Shellfish Étouffée, 161

Papaya
Grilled Pineapple Salsa, 145
Pineapple Papaya Salsa, 35

Pasta

Bahamian Seafood Pasta, 146
Black Pepper and Sesame-Crusted
  Tuna with Fried Southwest Ravioli, 56
Crawfish Fettuccini, 99
Creole Pasta Primavera, 176
Fettuccini Nantua, 177
Fettuccini Seafood Pasta, 178
Grilled Salmon with Crab Fingers and
  Angel Hair Pasta, 148
Grouper with Pesto Sauce over
  Angel Hair Pasta, 18
Jerry's Shrimp Scampi, 132
Lou Michael's Seafood Platter Tuna
  and Soft-Shell Crab Rolls with
  Peanut Sauce, 183
Mr. Slu's Triggerfish, 154
Pasta Aglio e Olio, 132
Prosciutto-Wrapped Shrimp with
  Tortellini, 134
Salmon-Cracked Pepper Linguini, 48
Seafood Diablo, 149
Seafood Penne Primavera, 180
Seafood Santa Rosa, 158
Sea Pearls with Marinara Sauce, 166
Sea Scallops with Rigatoni, Sun-Dried
  Tomatoes and Prosciutto, 83
Shrimp and Andouille Fettuccini, 133
Shrimp Pastacola, 135
Shrimp Tortellini Maria, 110
Thailand Tiger Prawns with
  Montrachet-Crab Meat
  Stuffing, 179

Peas

Crab Cakes, 88
Grilled Bacon-Wrapped Scallop Kabobs
  with Pineapple and Sweet Potato, 79
Grilled Wahoo and Shrimp with Field
  Pea Sauté, 157
Shrimp and Black-Eyed Pea Salad, 113
Stir-Fried Vegetables, 143

Pineapple

Grilled Bacon-Wrapped Scallop Kabobs
  with Pineapple and Sweet Potato, 79
Grilled Pineapple Salsa, 68, 145
Jazz on the Grill, 67
Mahi Mahi Island Kabobs with
  Mango Beurre Blanc, 28
Onion and Pineapple Salsa, 9
Pineapple and Cranberry Compote, 44
Pineapple Chutney, 126
Pineapple Papaya Salsa, 35
Triggerfish Del Sol, 53

Pork. *See* Bacon/Pancetta; Prosciutto;
  Sausage

Potatoes

Cedar-Planked Salmon with
  Grilled Planked Potatoes, 37
Corn and Red Potatoes, 144
Crab Cakes, 142
Fennel-Green Apple Hash, 42
Grilled Pesto Tuna Steak with
  Balsamic Pan Sauce, 62
Lobster and Sweet Corn
  Chowder, 103
Mahogany Clams with Chorizo
  and Chiles, 71
Potato-Crusted Grouper with
  Curry Seafood Vegetables and
  Mornay Sauce, 143
Yukon-Crusted Redfish, 147

Prawns

Pan-Fried Prawns with Scallop
  Mousse, 167
Thailand Tiger Prawns with
  Montrachet-Crab Meat Stuffing, 179

Prosciutto

Oysters Eros, 73
Prosciutto-Wrapped Shrimp with
  Tortellini, 134
Sea Scallops with Rigatoni, Sun-Dried
  Tomatoes and Prosciutto, 83
Thailand Tiger Prawns with
  Montrachet-Crab Meat Stuffing, 179

Redfish

Redfish with Figs, Bacon and
  Pecans, 28
Stuffed Redfish in Banana Leaves, 29
Yukon-Crusted Redfish, 147

Rice

Barbecued Shrimp over
  White Rice, 118
Big Sexy Risotto Crab Cakes with
  Roasted Red Pepper Aïoli, 90
Grecian Island Shrimp, 127
Grilled Lobster Salad with
  Blood Orange Vinaigrette and
  Mango Saffron Coulis, 106
Jasmine Rice Cakes, 66
Mahi Mahi Island Kabobs with
  Mango Beurre Blanc, 28
Poached Sea Bass Chinoise, 45
Scamp Creole, 149
Seafood Jambalaya, 160
Shellfish Étouffée, 161
Shrimp Nasi Goreng Indonesian
  Rice Bowl, 128
Tempura-Crusted Spicy Tuna Roll
  with Ginger Coconut Sauce, 55

Salads, Seafood

Grecian Shrimp Salad, 112
Grilled Avocado with Shrimp and
  Fire-Roasted Tomato Salad, 112
Grilled Lobster Salad with
  Blood Orange Vinaigrette and
  Mango Saffron Coulis, 106
Lobster Salad with Spicy Key Lime
  Dressing, 104
Roasted Corn and Teriyaki
  Shrimp Salad, 114
Shrimp and Black-Eyed Pea Salad, 113
Sun-Ripened Tomatoes and
  Asian-Style Lobster Salad, 105
Tuna Ceviche, 54
Tuna Confit Salad with Fried Zucchini, 63

Salads, Vegetable

Asian Cabbage and Radish Slaw, 31
Asian Slaw, 65
Pole Bean and Red Onion Salad, 72
Vegetable Salad, 59

Salmon

Asian-Spiced Salmon, 41
Bacon-Braised Salmon with
  Molasses Sauce, 34
Barbecued Salmon with Roasted
  Garlic and Mussels, 148
Cedar-Planked Salmon with
  Grilled Planked Potatoes, 37
Citrus Salsa-Poached Salmon, 39
Crispy-Seared Salmon with
  Fennel-Green Apple Hash, 42
Grilled Ginger Salmon with Ginger
  Soy Butter Sauce, 36
Grilled Salmon with Balsamic
  Wilted Spinach, 37
Grilled Salmon with Crab Fingers
  and Angel Hair Pasta, 148
Grilled Stuffed Scallops, 80
Hoisin-Smoked Salmon, 38
Lou Michael's Seafood Platter
  Salmon Seared with Sesame and
  Coriander and Ginger Sake
  Vinaigrette, 182
Poached Salmon with Mustard
  Lime Sauce, 40
Pumpernickel Salmon Panade, 43
Salmon-Cracked Pepper Linguini, 48
Seafood Diablo, 149
Summer Salmon, 34
Teriyaki Salmon with Pineapple
  Papaya Salsa, 35

Salsa

Avocado Corn Salsa, 52
Black Bean and Mango Salsa, 64

Black Bean Salsa, 33
Citrus Cilantro Salsa, 39
Corn Salsa, 156
Grilled Pineapple Salsa, 68, 145
Mango Jalapeño Salsa, 56
Onion and Pineapple Salsa, 9
Orange Fennel Salsa, 47
Pineapple Papaya Salsa, 35

Sandwiches
Jerry's Gulfuletta, 152
Semolina-Fried Oyster Po-Boy with
    Homemade Pickles, 74
Shrimp Sandwiches with Tarragon
    Caper Mayonnaise, 114

Sauces
Alfredo Sauce, 135
Ancho Rémoulade Sauce, 165
Balsamic Pan Sauce, 62
Basil Pesto, 135
Caramel Sauce, 16
Cashew and Lime Butter Sauce, 123
Chipotle Cream Sauce, 91
Choron Sauce, 184
Cilantro and Caper Rémoulade Sauce, 172
Cilantro Tomato Aïoli, 170
Creole Sauce, 146
Curry Sauce, 25
Leek-Pepper Beurre Blanc, 142
Lilikoi Reduction, 27
Mango Saffron Coulis, 106
Mango Sauce, 50
Marinara Sauce, 166
Mornay Sauce, 143
Orange Chocolate Sauce, 109
Orange Sauce, 120
Peanut Sauce, 183
Plum Madeira Reduction, 184
Red Chile Sauce, 52
Red Pepper Coulis, 57
Red Pepper Sauce, 174
Roasted Corn Tartar Sauce, 95
Roasted Garlic and Madeira Cream, 173
Roasted Garlic Beurre Blanc, 84
Roasted Red Pepper Aïoli, 90
Roasted Red Pepper Coulis, 122
Roasted Roma Cream, 77
Soy Orange Sauce, 65
Sweet Hot Pecan Sauce, 18
Sweet Red Chile Sauce, 66
Tabasco Butter Sauce, 147
Tahini Sauce, 66

Sausage
Andouille-Crusted Soft-Shell Crabs, 93
Crawfish and Sausage Frittata, 98
Creole Pasta Primavera, 176

Grouper Daniels, 140
Gulf Crab and Chorizo Fritters with
    Chipotle Cream Sauce, 91
Louisiana Seafood Gumbo, 159
Mahogany Clams with Chorizo
    and Chiles, 71
Shrimp and Andouille Fettuccini, 133

Scallops
Bacon and Scallop-Stuffed Mushrooms
    with Roasted Roma Cream, 77
Bahamian Seafood Pasta, 146
Creole Pasta Primavera, 176
Dove's Nest, 76
Fettuccini Seafood Pasta, 178
Grilled Bacon-Wrapped Scallop Kabobs
    with Pineapple and Sweet Potato, 79
Grilled Scallops and Tuna en Husk, 168
Grilled Scallops with Portobello
    Mushroom, 78
Grilled Sea Scallops with Mixed Greens
    and Orange Balsamic Vinaigrette, 81
Grilled Stuffed Scallops, 80
Pan-Fried Prawns with Scallop
    Mousse, 167
Pesto-Marinated Sea Scallops, 80
Sautéed Scallops with Grape Tomatoes
    and Feta Cheese, 82
Sautéed Shrimp and Scallops with
    Roasted Garlic and Madeira
    Cream, 173
Seafood Diablo, 149
Seafood en Brochette, 165
Seafood Piccata, 158
Seafood Santa Rosa, 158
Sea Pearls with Marinara Sauce, 166
Seared Sea Scallops with Mushrooms
    and Roasted Garlic Beurre Blanc, 84
Sea Scallops en Papillote, 78
Sea Scallops with Lemon Grass
    Ginger Sauce, 81
Sea Scallops with Rigatoni, Sun-Dried
    Tomatoes and Prosciutto, 83
Shellfish Étouffée, 161
Shrimp and Scallop-Stuffed Poblano
    Chiles with Red Pepper Sauce, 174
Tropical Scallop Ceviche with
    Plantain Planks, 75

Sea Bass
Grilled Sea Bass with Pineapple and
    Cranberry Compote, 44
Poached Sea Bass Chinoise, 45
Sautéed Sea Bass over Wilted Frisée
    with Thai Dressing, 46

Seafood. See Fish; Salads, Seafood;
    Shellfish

Shellfish. See also Clams; Crab Cakes;
    Crab Meat; Crabs, Soft-Shell;
    Crawfish; Lobster; Mussels; Oysters;
    Prawns; Scallops; Shrimp; Squid
Coastal Seafood Trio, 184
Stir-Fried Vegetables, 143
Stufato of Swordfish and Shellfish, 152

Shrimp
Asian Almond Shrimp, 119
Bacon-Wrapped Crab-Stuffed
    Shrimp, 169
Bahamian Seafood Pasta, 146
Beach-Style Shrimp, 125
Blackened Shrimp in Beer Butter
    Sauce, 108
Chilled Gazpacho with Ginger-Lime
    Marinated Shrimp, 111
Chipotle Shrimp, 121
Chocolate Shrimp, 109
Crab Meat-Coated Jumbo Shrimp
    with Cilantro Tomato Aïoli, 170
Creole Pasta Primavera, 176
Crusted Flounder with Shrimp
    Dumplings, 139
Fettuccini Nantua, 177
Fettuccini Seafood Pasta, 178
Garlic and Sherry Shrimp on
    Grilled French Bread, 108
Glazed Spicy Shrimp, 127
Grecian Island Shrimp, 127
Grecian Shrimp Salad, 112
Grilled Avocado with Shrimp and
    Fire-Roasted Tomato Salad, 112
Grilled Gulf Shrimp with Black
    Bean Cakes and Roasted Red
    Pepper Coulis, 122
Grilled Gulf Shrimp with Cashew and
    Lime Butter Sauce, 123
Grilled Shrimp with Pineapple
    Chutney, 126
Grilled Soft-Shell Crabs with Shrimp
    and Tasso Cream Sauce, 164
Grilled Wahoo and Shrimp with
    Field Pea Sauté, 157
Grits a Ya-Ya, 131
Jerry's Gulfuletta, 152
Jerry's Shrimp Étouffée, 136
Jerry's Shrimp Scampi, 132
Lou Michael's Seafood Platter
    Seafood Soup, 181
Louisiana Seafood Gumbo, 159
Most Excellent Fried Shrimp, 120
Pasta Aglio e Olio, 132
Pesce Picante Mare (Spicy Fish), 141
Portobello Shrimp, 125
Prosciutto-Wrapped Shrimp
    with Tortellini, 134

Rim Pesto Shrimp, 124
Roasted Corn and Teriyaki
    Shrimp Salad, 114
Samos Shrimp, 171
Sautéed Shrimp and Scallops with
    Roasted Garlic and Madeira
    Cream, 173
Sautéed Shrimp with Vermouth
    Beurre Blanc, 128
Seafood and Avocado Tostada, 155
Seafood Diablo, 149
Seafood en Brochette, 165
Seafood Jambalaya, 160
Seafood Penne Primavera, 180
Seafood Piccata, 158
Seafood Santa Rosa, 158
Shellfish Étouffée, 161
Shrimp and Alabama Goat
    Cheese Grits, 130
Shrimp and Andouille Fettuccini, 133
Shrimp and Black-Eyed Pea Salad, 113
Shrimp and Grits, 129
Shrimp and Scallop-Stuffed Poblano
    Chiles with Red Pepper Sauce, 174
Shrimp Isabela with Cilantro and
    Caper Rémoulade Sauce, 172
Shrimp Lettuce Wraps, 110
Shrimp Nasi Goreng Indonesian
    Rice Bowl, 128
Shrimp Pastacola, 135
Shrimp Sandwiches with Tarragon
    Caper Mayonnaise, 114
Shrimp Tortellini Maria, 110
Soft-Shell Crabs Zachary, 163

Shrimp, Barbecued
Applewood Barbecued Shrimp, 115
Barbecued Shrimp, 116
Barbecued Shrimp over Grits, 117
Barbecued Shrimp over White Rice, 118
Big Sexy-Style Barbecued Shrimp, 118
Jamaican Barbecued Shrimp, 119
Marinated Barbecued Shrimp, 117

Snapper
57 Snapper, 151
Samos Shrimp, 171
Snapper Bienville, 150

Snapper, Red
Crispy Pan-Fried Red Snapper with
    Asian Cabbage and Radish Slaw, 31
Fish Veracruz, 32
Grilled Snapper with
    Mediterranean Salsa, 29
Red Snapper with Black Bean Salsa, 33
Salt-Packed Red Snapper with
    Citrus Herb Rub, 30

Soups
Chilled Gazpacho with Ginger-Lime
    Marinated Shrimp, 111
Lobster and Sweet Corn Chowder, 103
Lobster Corn Stock, 103
Louisiana Seafood Gumbo, 159
Lou Michael's Seafood Platter
    Seafood Soup, 181

Spinach
Garlic and Sherry Shrimp on Grilled
    French Bread, 108
Grilled Pesto Tuna Steak with
    Balsamic Pan Sauce, 62
Grilled Salmon with Balsamic
    Wilted Spinach, 37
Grits a Ya-Ya, 131
Shrimp Isabela with Cilantro and
    Caper Rémoulade Sauce, 172

Squash
Cajun Spring Rolls, 96
Poached Sea Bass Chinoise, 45
Ratatouille, 60

Squid
Cherrystone-Stuffed Squid with
    Tomato Tarragon Vinaigrette, 175
Lou Michael's Seafood Platter
    Seafood Soup, 181

Sweet Potatoes
Carbie Tuna Napoleon with
    Pink Peppercorn Vinaigrette, 58
Dorado Aguadilla, 24
Grilled Bacon-Wrapped Scallop
    Kabobs with Pineapple and
    Sweet Potato, 79

Swordfish
Citrus-Crusted Swordfish Steak with
    Mango Sauce, 50
Grilled Swordfish with Horseradish
    Mustard, 49
Grilled Swordfish with Smoked
    Salmon-Cracked Pepper Linguini, 48
Seafood en Brochette, 165
Stufato of Swordfish and Shellfish, 152

Tasso
Blackened Bayou Chicken with
    Crawfish Tasso Sauce, 99
Grilled Soft-Shell Crabs with Shrimp
    and Tasso Cream Sauce, 164
Pan-Sautéed Grouper with
    Tasso, Parsnip and Roasted
    Corn Hash, 20
Stone-Ground Yellow Grits, 147

Tomatoes
Basil-Tomato Stewed Mahi Mahi, 23
Cilantro Tomato Aïoli, 170
Green Tomatoes and Okra, 124
Grilled Avocado with Shrimp and
    Fire-Roasted Tomato Salad, 112
Herb-Seared Grouper with Roasted
    Pepper and Tomato Compote, 20
Roasted Roma Cream, 77
Sautéed Scallops with Grape
    Tomatoes and Feta Cheese, 82
Sea Scallops with Rigatoni, Sun-Dried
    Tomatoes and Prosciutto, 83
Spicy Mango Tomato Relish, 24
Sun-Ripened Tomatoes and
    Asian-Style Lobster Salad, 105
Tomato Tarragon Vinaigrette, 175

Triggerfish
Grilled Triggerfish with Peppers and
    Garlic Mayonnaise, 51
Grilled Triggerfish with Roasted
    Garlic Vinaigrette, 51
Mr. Slu's Triggerfish, 154
Pecan-Crusted Triggerfish, 54
Red Chile-Crusted Triggerfish with
    Avocado Corn Salsa, 52
Sautéed Triggerfish with Guajillo
    Beurre Blanc, 53
Sautéed Triggerfish with Oysters
    and Cream Sauce, 153
Triggerfish Del Sol, 53

Tuna
Banana-Crusted Yellowfin Tuna, 65
Black Pepper and Sesame-
    Crusted Tuna with Fried
    Southwest Ravioli, 56
Blushing Lady Tuna, 57
Carbie Tuna Napoleon with
    Pink Peppercorn Vinaigrette, 58
Crusted Tuna Medallions with
    Vegetable Salad, 59
Grilled Pesto Tuna Steak with
    Balsamic Pan Sauce, 62
Grilled Scallops and
    Tuna en Husk, 168
Grilled Yellowfin Tuna with
    Black Bean and Mango Salsa, 64
Lou Michael's Seafood Platter Tuna
    and Soft-Shell Crab Rolls with
    Peanut Sauce, 183
Mediterranean Tuna, 61
Red Hot Chile and Sesame-Seared
    Tuna with Jasmine Rice Cakes, 66
Seafood and Avocado Tostada, 155
Shrimp Isabela with Cilantro and
    Caper Rémoulade Sauce, 172

Tempura-Crusted Spicy Tuna Roll with
  Ginger Coconut Sauce, 55
Tuna Ceviche, 54
Tuna Confit Salad with Fried
  Zucchini, 63
Tuna Lagasse, 156
Tuna Stack, 61
Tuna with Ratatouille and
  Black Olive Vinaigrette, 60

Vegetables. *See also* individual kinds
  Crawfish Succotash, 97
  Fennel-Green Apple Hash, 42
  Stir-Fried Vegetables, 143

Wahoo
  Grilled Wahoo and Shrimp with
    Field Pea Sauté, 157
  Grilled Wahoo with Gazpacho Sauce, 67

Zucchini
  Cajun Spring Rolls, 96
  Crawfish and Sausage Frittata, 98
  Grilled Wahoo and Shrimp with
    Field Pea Sauté, 157
  Poached Sea Bass Chinoise, 45
  Ratatouille, 60
  Seafood Penne Primavera, 180
  Tuna Confit Salad with Fried Zucchini, 63

Fiesta Seafood Cookbook
A TASTE OF PENSACOLA

Energy Services of Pensacola
1625 Atwood Drive
Pensacola, Florida 32514

850-436-5050

E-mail: info@espnaturalgas.com
Web site: www.espnaturalgas.com